STILL OPEN ALL HOURS

ALL HOURS

The Story of a Classic Comedy

STILL OPEN ALL HOURS

The Story of a Classic Comedy

By Graham McCann

Foreword by Roy Clarke,
writer and creator of *Open All Hours*

3 5 7 9 10 8 6 4

BBC Books, an imprint of Ebury Publishing
20 Vauxhall Bridge Road,
London SW1V 2SA

BBC Books is part of the Penguin Random House group of companies
whose addresses can be found at global.penguinrandomhouse.com

Penguin
Random House
UK

This book is published to accompany the television series entitled
Still Open All Hours first broadcast on BBC One in 2014.

Executive producer: Gareth Edwards
Producer: Alex Walsh-Taylor
Associate Producer: Sarah Hitchcock
Director: Dewi Humphreys

First published by BBC Books in 2014
This edition published in 2019

www.penguin.co.uk

A CIP catalogue record for this book is available from the British Library

ISBN 9781785944659

Printed and bound in Great Britain by Clays Ltd, Elcograf S.p.A.

Penguin Random House is committed to a sustainable future for
our business, our readers and our planet. This book is made
from Forest Stewardship Council® certified paper.

MIX
Paper | Supporting
responsible forestry
FSC
www.fsc.org   FSC® C018179

For My Mother

FOREWORD

I am grateful to the author for his diligence and his burrowing among the archives. His unearthing of the details of the story of *Open All Hours* has been a revelation to me. Although I wrote the series, I have only ever known my own view of it and even this has been eroded over time by the termites which nibble at memory.

Graham McCann has done a historian's job on the documents and surviving testimony relating to the programme. He tells the full story in an entertaining manner entirely suitable to its subject matter. I find it fascinating as I'm sure will anyone interested in the hiccups and flukes which hide behind the apparent seamlessness of a successful series.

Graham tells a story full of surprises for me. Does it seem odd that, as the writer of the series, I knew so little of its adventures in the hands of others? Perhaps, and yet this is often the fate of the writer – certainly this writer. I work from home, far removed from that enormous, civilized but often brutal clinic where all scripts go to die or be nervously born.

The story began for me with an invitation. I was one of several writers asked to come up with an idea for a situation comedy starring Ronnie Barker. So that was it, you might think. How could anyone go wrong with a sitcom for Ronnie Barker? Well, I did with one later but that's another tale entirely. This invitation was my first chance to meet and work with one of the superstars of comedy. Luck enough, it could be said. But there was even more to come. I would also be working with one who would quickly become another superstar of comedy – Sir David – then plain David Jason.

And that's how *Open All Hours* always felt to me from its first steps. A gift – a huge bundle of luck – an enormous pleasure. The writing went well. I had great joy in the characters as they came alive for me. And so it went on. The show's production and direction was in the hands of a master, the brilliant Sydney Lotterby. The casting produced not only an uber-talented but a happy company. And finally, to top it all, the viewers loved it.

As I think back to the sitcom across the distance in time I still see it under that cosy glow. For me it was the show where everything came together smelling of roses. And so I've been amazed and fascinated by Graham McCann's disclosures of the many potholes and bumps along the way.

In the end, of course, they don't alter anything. For me it's still the show that smells of roses. I loved it then and I love it still. And once again I can hardly believe my luck in that I've been invited back to open up that corner shop again.

Roy Clarke
June 2014

CONTENTS

To found a great empire for the sole purpose of raising up a people of customers may at first sight appear a project fit only for a nation of shopkeepers. It is, however, a project altogether unfit for a nation of shopkeepers; but extremely fit for a nation whose government is influenced by shopkeepers.

(Adam Smith)

I knew what I wanted. I wanted me own business. But people were like that in them days. You know, you could go for weeks without ever s-seeing a soul who worked for the state. Nowadays, if you put all the government officials end to end I doubt if anyone would notice.

(Arkwright)

PROLOGUE

I want a w-w-word with you.

The shop on the corner. It was such an inspired context for a comedy.

Like a bar (*Cheers*) or hotel (*Fawlty Towers*), it guaranteed the two things that any sitcom requires to ensure it remains familiar and yet fresh: a fixed set of characters stuck *in situ*, and a fluid collection of new characters just passing through. Every time the door opened, a bell rang, welcoming the arrival of another bright comic idea.

Everyone knew of a shop like the one in *Open All Hours*. Everyone knew of a shopkeeper like Arkwright. Britain might have been in the process of swapping the quiet little shop on the street corner for the big, brash supermarket on the outskirts of town, but, in the mid-1970s, everyone still either frequented a place like Arkwright's, or had vivid memories of once having done so. Right from the start, the show knew how to make the viewer – and the customers – feel at home inside that increasingly quaint-looking corner shop.

Think of the start of the episode. It only took a few seconds for the context to crystallize.

There, in the early morning light, is the shop, with its shadowy windows cluttered with commodities; there is its middle-aged owner, emerging to put the crates of fruit and veg out on display, muttering about the state of the shopfront ('The swallows are leaving – and they're leaving it on our window!'); there is his slope-shouldered young nephew, summoned from deep indoors to help out ('F-F-Fetch a cloth!'); and there, across the road, is the shapely local nurse, bending down, being watched ('I know that face').

That was all you needed to see, all you needed to know. The three constant preoccupations were already on show: money, family and sex.

I

This is not, however, just a book about a little shop that survived in a world of big supermarkets. It is also about a little sitcom that survived in a world of big blockbusters.

Open All Hours was not supposed to be the massive success that it was. It was supposed to know its place, like a modest little corner shop, and look up to its more favoured competitors.

It was tucked away in humble little areas of the schedules, like quiet provincial street corners, first on BBC2 (which never attracted an audience anywhere near as big as the one enjoyed by its sister channel) and then on Sunday evenings on BBC1 (in a slot seemingly designed to catch those who had dozed through *Songs of Praise*). It was starved of any publicity. It was overlooked or ignored by most of the critics.

It overcame all of this, however, because the public loved it. Winning fans without any prior fanfare, it ended up being watched by an audience of just under 19 million people – the great ratings phenomenon of its era – and in a BBC poll of 2004 it was voted one of the top ten British sitcoms of all time.[1]

Why, against all the odds, did this corner shop sitcom succeed? What made it so special?

It was, one could argue, a 'show about nothing', some 13 years before the sitcom that assigned itself that description, the much-celebrated *Seinfeld*, reached the screen. Indeed, episodes of *Open All Hours* usually had much less of a plot than even *Seinfeld* did, long before such an unconventional aimlessness was seized on by over-excitable critics as a sign that a show was daringly 'postmodern'.

There had, of course, been the odd slice of nothing before in sitcom history. There was, most notably, Galton and Simpson's brilliant episode of *Hancock's Half Hour*, called 'Sunday Afternoon at Home', in which little happens while the characters wait for the long day to end. *Open All Hours*, however, did the same kind of thing for the whole week, the whole month, the whole year. It peeled away the plots to allow us to focus on the people.

It showed us Arkwright, Granville and Nurse Gladys Emmanuel, along with numerous regular customers, not having larks or jumping sharks but just living life. It was a sitcom that found what was funny in what was ordinary, a sitcom that crafted comedy from character rather than from convoluted capers. 'Life is what happens to you while you're busy making other plans,' wrote John Lennon,[2] and *Open All Hours*, time and again, provided ample proof of that particular sentiment: life kept happening whenever a plot threatened to develop and intrude.

It was also a very British show, filled to the brim with British humour. When a bell rang in *Open All Hours*, it was never to herald another angel winning its wings (as in Hollywood's *It's a Wonderful Life*); it was always to signal Arkwright preparing to conquer another innocent customer. Downbeat and dry-witted, this was a world in which pretentions were pricked, pomposity was mocked and flaws were embraced. It was also a world in which eccentricity was not merely tolerated but also cherished, and occasional failures were treated as inevitable rather than unbearable. It was a sitcom for people who wanted to laugh at themselves instead of others. It was, in other words, a sitcom for the best of the British.

It was also, of course, a sitcom that inspired a fond sense of nostalgia, although by no means as strongly or simply as some might now assume. Thanks to our prolonged exposure to a plethora of pop cultural histories, it is all too easy these days for younger people to assume that, for example, 'flower power', free love and psychedelia in the 1960s reached out far beyond London to captivate places like Preston, Coventry or King's Lynn, or that 'glam rock' fashions in the 1970s rapidly became de rigueur everywhere from Chichester to Carlisle. It is rather like Woody Allen's medieval court jester urging a woman to hurry up and make love to him because 'before you know it, the Renaissance will be here and we'll all be painting'.[3]

In the case of *Open All Hours*, it is true that it did first emerge at a time when the humble little corner shop was being lost in the growing shadows of the superstores and hypermarkets, but there really were still plenty of places like Arkwright's around. In the mid-1970s, after all, the market was made up of 49% independent stores, 44% retail chains and 7% cooperatives, which by the mid-1980s would change to 42% independent stores, 52% retail chains and 6% cooperatives. Admittedly not all, or even most, of these 'independent stores' were tiny little corner shops, but a fair proportion of them most certainly were, and they persisted much longer than popular memory might now suggest. It would not be until the 1990s (when the ratio changed to 13% independent stores, 82% retail chains and 5% cooperatives) that the landscape really changed dramatically to start resembling what is the norm today.[4]

The same kind of exaggeration needs to be resisted when it comes to the show's appeal as so-called 'escapism'. *Open All Hours* was fun, but it was not a fantasy. True, there were no episodes about riots or racial unrest, but this was no more a sign of 'escapism' than was *Yes Minister's* lack of interest in the humdrum lives of the inhabitants of the Home Counties. Having a focus is not in itself escapism. Before it is decided what should be consigned to the blank pages of the history books, it should be understood that there is humour to be had in many aspects of any era.

This might have been the age of the Cold War and the Irish 'Troubles', industrial squabbles and strikes, the National Front and the Militant Tendency, and, eventually, privatization and deregulation, but not everywhere in the mid-1970s and early 1980s was whirling in a violent maelstrom of class and ethnic conflict. There were still countless little quiet communities scattered around the country, very much like the one pictured in *Open All Hours*, which still looked, sounded and behaved much like the Britain from a couple of decades or more earlier – and quite a few of them still had the odd little corner shop open and ready for sales. For many people outside the big cities, the so-called present, like the so-called past, was something that they only really saw on TV.

Open All Hours was thus not just a sitcom that referred back to how things used to be. It was also a sitcom that reflected, for some, how things still were, but would probably not be for much longer.

It was also a sitcom for women just as much as it was for men. In contrast to so many other examples of the genre at the time, which tended to be dominated by male characters and male preoccupations and perspectives (with the representation of women usually being limited to a solitary battle-axe, bimbo or bride), *Open All Hours* always displayed a fascination not just for Arkwright and Granville, but also for the many female characters who inhabited the same comic space. For every cheeky innuendo from Arkwright, there was a smarter and sharper response from Nurse Gladys. There was a comic equality at the heart of this show: equality of wit, equality of vulnerability, equality of foolishness. It was not about gender, it was about individuals, all individuals, and was much the healthier, and funnier, for it.

Finally, it was about the underdog. Arkwright is a communicator who is compromised by a stutter, a small corner shop owner who struggles to survive in a world of slick, 'big box' supermarkets, an uncle who is perplexed by having to act as a parent to his nephew, and a would-be lover who is repeatedly left frustrated by his fiancée. He might well be too mean and avaricious by most people's standards, but beneath that hard exterior is another soft human being, getting knocked down, getting up again, and getting on with it. We do not see all of ourselves in Arkwright, but we see enough to make us smile and nod in rueful recognition.

It is much the same now with *Still Open All Hours*. Granville (who in the original series was not so much an underdog as a grudging underpuppy) has now assumed Arkwright's mantle, with the same entertainingly underwhelming results. Failure runs through the lineage of this family like fallen arches and male pattern baldness.

It is just as well, because, traditionally, fans of British sitcoms tend to respond coolly to the winners and only really warm to the losers. We might respect those who seem to glide swan-like through life, but we identify with those whom we know, like the rest of us, have to keep paddling frantically just to stay afloat. We can understand Arkwright, because, like us, every time he thinks that his slate is almost clean he goes and spots yet another smudge ('Granville! F-F-Fetch a cloth!')

It was therefore no real surprise when, in a 2010 *Which?* consumer poll to find the nation's favourite shopkeeper, Arkwright came out on top.[5] After enduring many years of queuing impatiently behind a line of well-stocked trolleys at the 'Baskets Only' checkout in the big supermarkets, and shouting helplessly at the frozen screens of the 'express' self-service machines, the prospect of pitting one's wits against Arkwright must have seemed a far more preferable shopping experience. He might have wanted your cash just as much as, if not more than, the average branch manager of Tesco or Sainsbury's, but at least he knew you and you knew him, and you were part of the same community.

These were the kinds of things that helped make people not only love the show at the time but also stay devoted to it in its absence. The fourth and final series of *Open All Hours*, in 1985, was the highest-rated sitcom of the decade.[6] The 'comeback' Christmas special, *Still Open All Hours*, 28 years later in 2013, was the highest-rated sitcom in five years, and the third highest in over a decade.[7] That was quite an achievement for a corner shop sitcom, and it was accomplished without even the need for a loyalty card.

There is much, then, that deserves to be celebrated about *Open All Hours*. It had, in Roy Clarke, one of Britain's best and most subtly elegant comedy writers, and, in Ronnie Barker, David Jason and the rest of the cast, some of Britain's most accomplished and admired comedy actors. It was all put together and polished by a splendidly professional team led by the now legendary Sydney Lotterby.

It made us laugh then. It still makes us laugh now.

As sitcoms go, therefore, this one really was special. This is the story of how it achieved its rare success.

PART ONE

*I'm making a little list
of everything you've got to do.*

CHAPTER ONE

One of Seven

An odd little ambition you might think.
Just a shopkeeper's quirk. So get cracking
t-till I can see me quirk in it!

The year was 1972, and Ronnie Barker was in the mood to experiment. Riding high on the success (shared with Ronnie Corbett) of *The Two Ronnies*, which had now completed its first series on BBC1 after consistently good ratings, Barker felt that the time was right to branch out on his own.

This was by no means an unexpected ambition. It was actually anticipated in his contract. The initial BBC deal that had secured the services of Barker and Corbett as a duo had also promised each of them the right to develop a separate solo sitcom (along with a one-off comedy special).[8] Corbett, at this stage, was content to wait for something suitable to come his way, but Barker was eager to press ahead and pick a project.

This had happened before. The two performers had a habit of approaching potential solo projects with a different frame of mind. In the late 1960s, for example, when the two of them were still under the wing of David Frost at London Weekend Television and playing supporting roles in *Frost on Sunday*, both were offered solo vehicles. Corbett considered the options casually on paper and then committed himself to starring in a variety-style show called *The Corbett Follies* (1969), whereas Barker immediately asked for a series of one-off pilot shows to be produced under the banner of *The Ronnie Barker Playhouse* (1968).

Of these pilots, the winner, as far as Barker was concerned, was 'Ah, There You Are', a comedy in which he appeared as a crusty old aristocrat called Lord Rustless, and which was developed initially into a 'mini sitcom' (sharing airtime each week with some sketch material) in a show called *Hark at Barker* (1969–70). Convinced that he could take the character further, Barker would go on to revive Lord Rustless for a full-blown sitcom of his own, entitled *His Lordship Entertains* (1972), which, as it was set in a stately home-turned-hotel, he later dubbed 'Fawlty Towers Mark 1'.[9]

The same basic process was followed by Barker when he moved to the BBC. While Corbett again remained patient as he pondered the occasional outlines that came his way (filling up his free time with regular summer seasons and pantomimes), Barker worked hard to prepare another set of pilots with his *Two Ronnies* producer of the time, James Gilbert (known to all who work with him as Jimmy).

There was, perhaps, an added reason on this occasion for his rapid immersion in the new solo project. Earlier on in the year he had experienced voice problems which, following tests, led to surgeons trimming a small piece off his vocal cords to test for signs of a tumour. He was subsequently given the 'all clear', but was ordered to stop smoking immediately (he was, by this stage, getting through 60 cigarettes a day), and returned to work feeling both relieved to have survived such a scare (his surgeon, bizarrely, had reassured him that he could compensate for not smoking by drinking a bottle of wine every night) and determined to make the most of every moment.

He scribbled some basic thoughts on a piece of paper. One suggestion simply said 'Prison'. Another idea was summed up as 'Shop'. Armed with this set of comic cues, he arranged to meet Jimmy Gilbert in his office at Television Centre.

Gilbert, who was already convinced that Barker's versatility as a character actor was well worth exploring, proved an exceptionally willing and supportive collaborator, resolving to hire the best writers that he could find to create a set of seven self-contained pilot episodes. Barker's original idea – which reflected a certain desire to hedge his bets – had been for the BBC to commission six scripts now and then six more for the following year, so that he could call the two series, respectively, *Six of One* and *Half a Dozen of the Other*. He was initially, therefore, somewhat resistant to Gilbert's decision to 'go for broke'[10] and commission no fewer than seven pilot scripts here and now, protesting that it would spoil the title of the sequel (or perhaps scupper his chances of getting a sequel at all), but the executive was adamant, and so the show was stuck with the awkward-sounding umbrella title of *Seven of One*.

Gilbert, in consultation with Barker, ended up rejecting several ideas (including one from the absurdist playwright N.F. Simpson[11]) before choosing two scripts by the experienced team of Dick Clement and Ian La Frenais ('Prisoner and Escort' and 'I'll Fly You for a Quid'), two by the up-and-coming Roy Clarke ('Open All Hours' and 'Spanner's Eleven'), and one each by the veteran Hugh Leonard ('Another Fine Mess'), the newcomer Gerald Frow ('My Old Man') and, under the pseudonym of 'Jack Goetz', Ronnie Barker himself ('One Man's Meat'). Barker was enthusiastic about making all of them – as someone who had served his apprenticeship in repertory companies, playing a different character in a different play every week, he relished the challenge of adapting swiftly to each new role and situation – and he began working in earnest on a range of individuals that would take him from crafty Cockney rascal to scheming Welsh gambler, and from cantankerous Yorkshireman to eccentric would-be American. It was just the kind of liberating experience that he had craved.

The overall results, however, were – inevitably – mixed in terms of both power and potential. The oddest, by a long way, was Hugh Leonard's 'Another Fine Mess', which saw Barker team up with Roy Castle to portray a pair of British-based Laurel and Hardy *doppelgängers* who sought to sneak away from their wives (in the style of *Sons of the Desert*) in order to take part in a talent contest, as Laurel and Hardy, at their local pub. Three more – Roy Clarke's 'Spanner's Eleven' (about a garrulous local football fanatic), Clement and La Frenais' 'I'll Fly You For A Quid' (about an avaricious son in search of his late father's betting slip) and Barker's own 'One Man's Meat' (about a permanently peckish husband forced into following a strict diet by his bossy wife) – were mildly amusing without ever suggesting that they had the substance and scope to sustain their own sitcom.

The remaining three pilots, on the other hand, seemed full of potential as possible series, and, indeed, would go on to spawn their own shows. Clement and La Frenais' 'Prisoner and Escort', of course, inspired the sitcom *Porridge*, with Barker displaying an immediate understanding of Norman Stanley Fletcher's distinctively roguish charm. Gerald Frow's 'My Old Man' had seen Barker score some laughs as an irascible old working-class man who finds himself having to live with his daughter and her 'posh' husband, and, although Barker himself decided against pursuing the premise any further, it was subsequently taken on by Clive Dunn, who starred in two series of the sitcom on ITV.[12]

The third success was Roy Clarke's 'Open All Hours'. Once again, as with Norman Stanley Fletcher, Ronnie Barker seemed at ease right from the start as the money-grabbing, nurse-groping grocer, Arkwright, and perfectly at home inside the context of the cluttered corner shop. With a young nephew, Granville, to control, and a local woman, Gladys Emmanuel, to court, as well as a potentially endless supply of quirky customers to con out of their cash, there was an obvious sense that this particular pilot had the right ingredients to inspire another sitcom.

Barker had been drawn to the idea for a number of reasons. First, he liked the notion of playing a shopkeeper.

'During our first lunch together,' Roy Clarke would later recall, 'Ronnie said more or less straightway, "I've always wanted to play one of those guys who runs a little shop that sells everything".'[13] Barker had always been fascinated by shopkeepers, going all the way back to his childhood, mainly because they, too, seemed like actors, emerging time and again from the darkness of their own backstage area to project a certain image upon their own little stage, and deliver a certain style of patter, to a captive audience of consumers.

He studied the various ways that they hid their desperation and irritation, and the ways that they sought to charm, intrigue, impress and excite. Every product was a possible prop, every fresh encounter part of a new plot. It was like a prosaic theatrical lesson: the better the performance, the bigger the profit.

There was even one family-run corner store, called Meecham & Son, in Crewkerne, Somerset (not far from where Barker and his family used to stay at their holiday cottage down the road in Beaminster), that used to arouse his curiosity so clearly, glancing around inside as he did while waiting for a bag of his favourite boiled sweets, that the proprietors would later jump to the (entirely erroneous) conclusion, when they first watched Arkwright in action, that the sitcom must have been modelled on their shop.[14] Selling everything from carbolic soap to homemade ice cream, and dominated by a no-nonsense owner in a light-brown warehouseman's coat, it did at least give Barker an insight into such an environment, one which he could draw upon when the time was right.

Another factor that attracted him to the concept of 'Open All Hours' was the fact that it was set in the north of England. Ever since the Bedford-born actor had spent a spell at Bramhall in Cheshire during the early 1950s, as a member of Frank H. Fortescue's Famous Players repertory company, he had felt a great sense of fondness for the north and its people. 'They're genuinely friendly, witty, and down to earth,' he would say of the northerners that he knew. 'Somehow (this will get me into trouble) there don't seem to be as many strange people up north, there are more down to earth, common-sensical folk about.'[15]

He was delighted, therefore, to not only play a northern character, but also to play one who had been created for him by a northern writer. One of the things, indeed, that would help make Roy Clarke so distinctive as a writer of sitcoms was his northern-ness, and, more specifically, his Yorkshireness: the outlook, the idioms, the disposition that informs the people of that region.

Born in 1930 in the hamlet of Austerfield in the Borough of Doncaster in South Yorkshire, Clarke (a former teacher and policeman) had not, up until this point, set any of his most substantial fictions in a context so close to home. His debut sitcom, *The Misfit* (ITV, 1970–1), was an interesting, and somewhat melancholic, comedy that had starred Ronald Fraser as Basil 'Badger' Allenby-Johnson, a very southern Edwardian gent who has returned to Britain after spending many years living on a rubber plantation in Malaya.

By 1972, however, after being drawn over to the BBC by its then-head of comedy Duncan Wood ('He is anxious to write situation comedy for us,' the executive had noted in a memo, 'and I am equally anxious that he should do so'[16]), he was working on not one but two sitcom pilots set in his native land – 'Open All Hours' in Doncaster and 'Last of the Summer Wine' in Holmfirth – and, by doing so, he was, partly unwittingly, carving out a precious new niche for himself in British comedy. The strange anomaly that he could now start to correct was the fact that, while British humour has always owed so much historically to the gritty irreverence and witty defiance of industrial northern life, and the vast majority of Britain's best stand-up comedians and double-acts have been shaped by the very same area, the genre of the sitcom, perversely, has been dominated by the south.

This is true of the writers: John Sullivan (*Citizen Smith, Only Fools and Horses*); Ray Galton and Alan Simpson (*Hancock's Half Hour, Steptoe & Son*); Frank Muir and Denis Norden (*The Glums*); Sid Colin (*The Army Game*); Richard Waring (*Marriage Lines, Not in Front of the Children*); Johnny Speight (*Till Death Us Do Part*); David Croft and Jimmy Perry (*Dad's Army, Hi-de-Hi!*); David Croft and Jeremy Lloyd (*Are You Being Served?*); John Esmonde and Bob Larbey (*The Good Life, Ever Decreasing Circles, Brush Strokes*); Ronald Chesney and Ronald Wolfe (*The Rag Trade, On the Buses*); David Nobbs (*The Fall and Rise of Reginald Perrin*); Peter Spence (*To the Manor Born*); David Renwick (*One Foot in the Grave*); Laurence Marks and Maurice Gran (*Birds of a Feather, The New Statesman, Goodnight Sweetheart*); Ben Elton (*Blackadder, The Young Ones*); Simon Nye (*Men Behaving Badly*); Simon Pegg and Jessica Stevenson (*Spaced*); Andrew Marshall (*2point4 Children*); Miranda Hart (*Miranda*); Andy Hamilton and Guy Jenkin (*Outnumbered*); Ricky Gervais and Stephen Merchant (*The Office*); John Cleese (*Fawlty Towers*) and Antony Jay and Jonathan Lynn (*Yes Minister/Yes, Prime Minister*) all hailed from places south of the Watford Gap, while even the New Zealand-born Richard Curtis (*Blackadder*) and the Americans Connie Booth (*Fawlty Towers*) and Lise Mayer (*The Young Ones*) came to base themselves in Britain well below the Midlands.

It is just as true of the locations: Peckham; Purley; Cricklewood; East Cheam; Shepherd's Bush; Wapping; Westminster; Walmington-on-Sea; Crimpton-on-Sea; Tooting; Torquay; Tufnell Park; Mole Valley; Chigwell; Chiswick; Slough and Surbiton. The list, limited to the lower half of England, goes on and on.

As far as the north is concerned, however, only the Mancunian Craig Cash (*The Royle Family*, with Caroline Aherne, and *Early Doors*, with Phil Mealey), the Liverpool and Farnworth combination of Neil Fitzmaurice,

Peter Kay and Dave Spikey (*Phoenix Nights*) and the solo Liverpudlian Carla Lane (*The Liver Birds, Bread*) have succeeded in making a truly memorable sitcom about an area to the west of the Pennines, while, from the early 1970s onwards (with the sole exception of Clement and La Frenais' *Whatever Happened to the Likely Lads?*), Roy Clarke has been left to plough a lonely furrow in the land that lies to the east.

It was a propitious time for him to begin. Just when his compatriot Alan Bennett was starting, in other areas of comedy and drama (such as the 1972 TV play *A Day Out*), to reflect on his own personal northern heritage, Roy Clarke was on the verge of becoming the one sitcom writer to convey much of what makes the Yorkshire brand of British humour so particular.

It differs markedly, for example, from the type that belongs to Lancashire. Lancastrian humour has always been much more engaging and direct – like a firm handshake for a friend or a head-butt for a foe. Yorkshire humour, traditionally, is less open and sociable, more heavy-lidded and heedful, as rough-hewn and defensive as a Dales-dressed dry-stone wall.

Even some of Yorkshire's most loyal and affectionate sons have alluded to this disparity. York's W. H. Auden admitted that his 'great good place'[17] ('Tramlines and slagheaps, pieces of machinery/That was, and still is, my ideal scenery'[18]) surrendered little to outsiders save for an intimidatingly 'bleak philosophy',[19] and Bradford's J. B. Priestley contrasted his county's downbeat style of delivery ('quieter, less sociable and less given to pleasure') with the appetite for irony, mockery and 'impish delight' typically evident in the tones of its neighbour, Lancashire.[20]

A Lancastrian put-down is designed to be seen, heard and felt by its target. Like Eric Morecambe smacking the cheeks of Ernie Wise, it is a public act that is meant to have a stingingly direct effect. A Yorkshire put-down, in contrast, is often more of a private and inexplicit affair, something to be muttered at the back of someone as, mercifully, they head off to another place.

Yorkshire folk typically tend to keep their comedy for themselves, as an internal tonic, like a furtive tot of Scotch, warming themselves on the inside as they gaze out impassively on the chilly greyness of their terrain, trying hard not to stare straight into the abyss ('Ooh, I wish I could win the pools,' Rotherham's famously saturnine stand-up Sandy Powell would mutter to himself. 'I'd pack this bloody lark up straight away!'[21]) They can laugh at their own aspirations, and find something funny in their failures, but they do so subtly, and often obliquely, so that it takes those in the know to recognize the joke. They can also use humour like a gnarled old walking stick, handy for holding out to keep nosy people at a distance, pointing out peculiarities and bringing it down hard on those with over-sized heads.

It was not, to be honest, the most amenable style of humour when it came to mainstream comedies, as it relied so much on understated irony and subtle satire, but, when given a chance, it was engagingly impressive. The good fortune that it had, at this time, was that Roy Clarke was around to show what it could achieve at its very best.

Clarke, a very modest but clever and quietly insightful man, would become a master at mining the mother lode of this darkly lugubrious humorous mood, and lend a noticeably Yorkshire inflection to the British comic voice. Always listening out for local lines that failed to notice their own natural oddity (from foolish consistencies to beguiling contradictions), he would proceed to draft his scripts with a pencil, always to a deadline ('I couldn't work without deadlines. I need the pressure'[22]), and craft comedy that seemed casually organic, as discreetly observant and critically concise as the county that had nurtured it. The critic Nancy Banks-Smith put it well when she said that his work, with its slow-burning wit and sympathy for ordinary idiosyncrasies, displayed a 'fondness for the rich pond life of small and unpromising puddles'.[23]

Ronnie Barker certainly knew, right away, that he had found the ideal writer to create not only an authentic northern character for him but also an authentic northern community. This pilot, after all, was not just going to be about Arkwright. It was also going to be about Arkwright's quirky little world.

That corner shop door was going to be open. A potentially endless number of new characters would come in and out. Roy Clarke had the eyes and the ears to ensure that they would all ring true when they entered.

There was, however, one more reason – perhaps the most important one of all – why Barker was drawn so deeply into Clarke's comic vision.

It was because this vision contained, at its heart, precisely the kind of social and emotional grit that had always delivered sitcom gold.

All great sitcoms consist, in essence, of tense trapped relationships. Captain Mainwaring and Sergeant Wilson, for instance, might be opposites in terms of class and character, but the war has thrown them together, and, so long as the war continues, neither can do without the other. Basil and Sybil Fawlty might drive each other to distraction, but she is too indolent to survive without him, and he is too erratic to survive without her, so they cling to each other while bemoaning that their union goes on. Del Boy and Rodney might be baffled and angered by their differences in terms of ambition, but are still held stubbornly together by the fact that they are brothers. Jim Hacker and Sir Humphrey Appleby might regard each other as infuriating opponents, but they also realize that they need each other to protect their own positions.

No situation comedy can be based on people who hug, love and agree. No situation comedy can be created out of happy and cosy cliques.

Situation comedies come out of conflict within a walled environment: class conflict, moral conflict, cultural conflict, political conflict, familial conflict, or various combinations of these conditions. Situation comedies take two or more needy misfits and stick them in the same jar, screw the lid on, give it a shake every now and again and settle back to watch the clashes that ensue.

The classic sitcom, in this sense, was Ray Galton and Alan Simpson's *Steptoe & Son*. Here, in the form of a pair of working-class rag-and-bone men, Albert and Harold Steptoe, were two men united by blood but divided by dreams. There was an old man, set in his ways, and a young man, desperate to break away. There was a father, too proud to admit how much he now needed his son, and a son too scared to acknowledge how much he still loved his father. Stuck together in the Stygian gloom of that cluttered junkyard in Oil Drum Lane, it is clear, to those of us on the outside looking in, that neither of them, no matter how hard they struggled, would ever escape the other.

There was even one memorable episode, entitled 'Divided We Stand,'[24] that could serve as a template for the great British sitcom, conveying with such rare wit and clarity the ways that life can cage and confine two separate human spirits. Desperate to feel that he is at least moving on aesthetically if not physically, Harold proposes redecorating their shared hovel of a home in the most bourgeois style that he can imagine ('Wedgewood blue on the ceiling... Etruscan red for the woodwork...'), only to be rebuffed, yet again, by his obstinately proletarian father ('Bleedin' awful – it'll look like a Peruvian brothel!') Unable to agree on anything except their incompatibility, they try to find freedom within their mutual prison by partitioning the house in two, but even this fails to bring any relief (each doorway is too narrow, the hot and cold taps are separated on the sink, the salt and pepper are divided on the dining table, and, perhaps most infuriatingly of all, there is no way of achieving consensus as to who watches what on the split screen of the TV set: HAROLD: 'I've got the law of *contract* on my side'; ALBERT: 'I have the *knobs* on my side!'), and they are dragged kicking and screaming back to face their familial fate.

Roy Clarke's 'Open All Hours' would feature the same kind of close-knit conflict, using adversity as the adhesive of comic animation, with Arkwright as the arch-conservative surrogate father, and Granville as the desperately idealistic surrogate son. This archetypal sitcom dynamic was further complicated, however, by the tantalizing presence, on the other side of the street, of a woman, Nurse Gladys Emmanuel, who might one day transform the duo into a trio by moving in with Arkwright, or render it more fractious than ever by staying a safe distance away, but whose existence, in the meantime, would remind both men of the liberty that they lack.

It was for this and all of the other reasons, therefore, that Ronnie Barker was so positive about the idea for 'Open All Hours' and, as a consequence, his initial meetings with its writer were exceptionally bright and productive occasions. Barker, as they chatted away, was particularly fascinated to hear about the various influences that would help Clarke to dream up the show.

Clarke explained that he had spent most of his adult life surrounded by shopkeepers. 'My wife's father had worked in a corner shop,' he recalled. 'So I was aware of that environment all the time before we were married. And then after we were married, in the early days, she used to run her own little shop, in Thorne in South Yorkshire, while I was teaching. So the idea held no fear for me. I knew exactly what it was all about. Ronnie put it straight in my lap.'[25]

A few myths would later arise concerning other so-called influences on Clarke, such as the one about the little store, called L. E. Riddiford in Thornbury, South Gloucestershire, that Clarke was supposed to have visited as an adult while travelling around southwest England, which, with its layout and owner, Len Riddiford, had made the writer think once again about the situation as a subject for a sitcom.[26] 'Not true,' he would later say. 'The only influences, as far as I'm concerned, would have been my father-in-law – who used to open his shop in the pitch dark at five in the morning and really put in hours of dogged, hard work – and the various people I grew up around in Thorne. Ronnie might have been influenced by other people, I don't know, but for me, from my angle, there was no-one else.'[27]

Another myth that would later take root was that Clarke soon decided not only to call his own shopkeeper Arkwright but also to give him the first name of 'Albert'. 'That isn't true, either,' he later confirmed. 'His first name was never used. He was only ever "Arkwright".'[28]

The writer's actual, very vivid, memories, however, were more than rich enough to convince the actor that something seemingly authentic could be created from the basic premise. It was clear that he was ready to conjure up a believable character in a believable context.

It was then Clarke's turn to be intrigued, and rather surprised, when he asked Barker for his own opinions on what they could do with this pilot. It all began fairly predictably, with the actor outlining his ideas for the look and demeanour of Arkwright, but then Barker brought up one more detail that he wanted to add – a stammer. Recalling the discussion some years later, Barker explained:

> The stammer was laid on from outside. Roy asked me what I wanted to do with this character to whom he'd just introduced me. Looking for ways to make him different from anyone I'd played before, I thought of the stammer [...]. Roy was slightly taken aback, one could see him thinking, 'Stutter? I wonder why?' but he told me to go ahead and try it.[29]

The inspiration for the Arkwright stutter came from the stage rather than the street. Barker, always an excellent student of comic technique, was drawing on a great tradition of performers who realized that there was humour in how human beings trip themselves up with words as well as deeds.

One master of the oral stumble was Jack Casey, the Stockton-on-Tees comedian who, under one or other of two stage names, Bretton Woods or Eli Woods, served for many years from the 1940s onwards as a stooge to his uncle, the brilliantly droll Jimmy James. In one of their most famous routines (about someone claiming to have two lions in a small cardboard box), James would stand between Woods and his other stooge, Hutton Conyers, and try to make sense of the stereo insanity, with Woods making things even worse with his stammer:

JAMES:	Go and get two coffees.
CONYERS:	Are you tellin' him about the lions?
JAMES:	Er, yes, he's got two lions in that box.
WOODS:	How m-m-much are they?
JAMES:	How much are – *No,* he doesn't want to *sell* 'em!
CONYERS:	Are you telling him about the giraffe?
JAMES:	Oh, yes, he's got a giraffe in there, with the lions.
WOODS:	Is it b-black o-o-or white?
JAMES:	I dunno. He wants to know what colour the giraffe is.
WOODS:	The c-c-c-coffee I mean![30]

Another accomplished practitioner of the art was Oldham-born Danny Ross, a fine comic actor in the 1950s to 1970s best known for playing a well-meaning but dim-witted character called Alfie Hall. The character appeared in several Arthur Askey stage and cinema vehicles but also, most notably, alongside Jimmy Clitheroe in the long-running radio show (devised by Jimmy James's son) called *The Clitheroe Kid*. It was in the latter show, as the bumbling young boyfriend of Jimmy's posh sister, Susan, that Alfie Hall's mouth would frequently fight a losing battle with his brain:

ALFIE: Ooh, hello, Susan, there you are! *Ooooh*, I-I say, I can see 'em! Y-Your legs. They're shorts. Y-Y-Y-You're wearing short legs.

SUSAN: What?

JIMMY: He means you're in the slips.

ALFIE: Yeah, that's ri- *shurrup will yer!*

SUSAN: Well, it's such a lovely day I thought I'd wear my new shorts. Mother doesn't think they're long enough.

ALFIE: Oooh, they're not too short for shorts. I mean, I-I-I wouldn't mind seeing a bit more of your, er, I-I-I m-mean you've g-got such nice, um, I mean b-both, er, b-b-both of, er – in't it *HOT?*[31]

A third, and more recent, exponent of the skill was Derek Nimmo, who (rather like Frankie Howerd) had managed to turn his natural tendency to stutter into a distinctive comic device, particularly when playing a succession of upper-middle-class types, from priests to people who urged you to 'p-p-p-pick up a Penguin', whose eagerness to please seemed to make even their words sound as if they were bending over backwards (and then losing their balance). In *All Gas and Gaiters* (1966–71), for example, as the Reverend Mervyn Noote, he had ample opportunities to stumble vocally for comic effect, such as when he was obliged to deal with an attractive young member of the opposite sex:

WOMAN: Oh, it's you – hello!

NOOTE: Hah-Hah-Hah-Hello, I…um…

WOMAN: Yes?

NOOTE: Uh, th-th-the Bishop, y-you see I-I'm –

WOMAN: Yes, I know, you're the Bishop's chaplain, aren't you?

NOOTE: Y-Yes. W-Well, the Dean…um…the D-Dean …u-um…w-w-well, the Dean –

WOMAN: No, I'm afraid I don't know the Dean. Is he nice?

20

NOOTE:	No. Oh, w-w-well, I-I mean, er, y-your car, ah, your car –
WOMAN:	Oh, do you like it?
NOOTE:	Oh, yes! Tell me: is it the 1922 or the 1923 model?[32]

There was even, on one memorable occasion, a sort of celebrity 'stammer-off' when Nimmo (as J. B. Ironside) joined Danny Ross (as Alfie) for an episode of *The Clitheroe Kid* in which the pair were trying to replace what they had mistakenly assumed was a stolen sum of money:

JB:	Now, Alfred, stand by for action. As soon as I open the till, I put in the money and you pop in the conscience note.
ALFIE:	The what?
JB:	The note you wrote saying you were returning the money because your conscience was troubling you.
ALFIE:	Oh, yes, er, it's here. And th-th-th-then kn-kn-kn-nock something over, Jimmy yells, and then we r-r-r-r-run for it.
JB:	Yes. N-N-N-Now, d-d-don't be nervous. Are you ready? Now! Now, there's the money in, now the note Alfred…
ALFIE:	H-H-Here you are.
JB:	Thank you. Oh! Ha-Ha-Ha-Ha-Hang on a moment! This is a blank piece of paper!
ALFIE:	I know. I-I-I-I-I haven't written it yet!
JB:	Oh *really!* Well, for goodness sake, h-h-h-hurry up!
ALFIE:	Ha-Ha-Have you got a pencil, Mr Woodentop??[33]

By far the biggest, and the only genuinely direct, influence on Ronnie Barker, regarding the stammer, was an actor named Glenn Melvyn. Acting alongside Arthur Askey in numerous sketches, stage plays and movies during the 1950s and 60s, the tall and whippet-thin Melvyn (whose moustache would also be copied by Barker for Arkwright) had played a succession of stuttering sidekicks (usually called Wally Binns) whose struggles to finish sentences always invited a suitably brusque comic intervention. In one case, for example, he appeared as a barman (this time named, for a change, Charlie) in the comedy Western *Ramsbottom Rides Again* (1956), where in one scene his boss, Bill (Askey), catches him downing a pint furtively under the bar and responds by blasting his head with ale:

BILL: In case you don't know, *that's* my beer!

CHARLIE: And in c-case you don't know, *this* is your coat! What are you p-p-playing at? That *hurt!*

BILL: *Hurt?* It were only light ale! Anyway, what do you think you were doing?

CHARLIE: Well, there was nobody b-b-buying the stuff, so I may as well s-sup it meself!

BILL: They *would* have been buying it if it hadn't have been for *your* bright idea: 'Why don't you get a t-t-t-television set?'

CHARLIE: Well, it was only so I could attract the customers.

BILL: *Customers?* There's not one of 'em had more than half a pint!

CHARLIE: Well give 'em a ch-chance – they've only been in for four hours![34]

Ronnie Barker had first met Melvyn in 1950, when they started working together in rep at Bramhall. Melvyn, at 32, was already well established as the leading man of the troupe, while Barker, at 20, was just a budding actor in the background, but Melvyn soon became a mentor to the younger man. Barker studied Melvyn intently, as he moved from one role to the next, using make-up, costumes and a dazzling range of accents and vocal mannerisms to make every character seem different, interesting and amusing.

Melvyn explained each crafty technique to his willing protégé, treating him to a masterclass in all the tricks of the trade. 'He taught me virtually everything I know about comedy,' Barker would later say.[35]

Something that particularly impressed him was the stutter that Melvyn sometimes used in his performances. Barker would later say that he had found the stutter to be 'beautifully observed' and 'a work of art', with 'terrific facial expressions blended to the sounds'.[36]

Melvyn stuttered with his whole body. While his tongue tussled with simple sounds, his head would tilt back, his brow would start to undulate, his eyelids rolled up and down, his nostrils flared, his chest tensed and stuck out and his legs froze like icicles. One could almost hear his toes curling up inside his leather boots. The muddled mouth was merely a symptom of a malfunctioning man, a distress signal straight from the soul.

Barker got the chance to witness, and hear, the stammer at close hand in 1955 when Melvyn, who had just written a new play (*Hot Water*) for himself and Arthur Askey, invited Barker to join the cast for a try-out tour of the production. It was here, from one night to the next, that Barker watched with fascination as the stutter was used not only as a simple comic conceit but also, much more interestingly, as a means of choreographing comic lines and bits of physical business, searching for where the funniest breaks in the delivery might be and then exploiting them for their full effect.

It was thus with the memory of Melvyn in mind that Barker decided to pass on the stutter to Arkwright. 'It was never in the same place twice, that stutter, but it worked,' Barker later remarked. 'And it was a marvellous comic device as a help with timing – you could hold back on a word for exactly as long as was needed.'[37]

Roy Clarke, once the idea had been suggested to him, knew exactly how to weave it into his script. 'I'd seen Glenn Melvyn myself many times. I particularly remember watching him in a film called *The Love Match*, in which he'd played a character with that stutter, and I'd ended up howling with laughter at him, he did it brilliantly. So, long before I put pen to paper, I knew just what Ronnie was after.'[38]

The impact that it went on to have on the script for the pilot episode can be gauged by imagining how it might have developed without it. In one memorable exchange, for example, the stutter-free version would have gone like this:

BREAD MAN:	All fresh.
ARKWRIGHT:	Never knew a breadman wot wasn't. If they get these loaves any whiter I shall have to wear dark glasses. That's how they third degree you nowadays, you know? Lock you in a tiny cell and flash a slice of bread at your naked eye balls.
GRANVILLE:	People like it white.
BREAD MAN:	Whitest bread in the world![39]

Once Barker had demonstrated his stutter, however, it not only altered his delivery of certain words but also inspired him and Clarke to come up with the odd new idea for an extra gag:

BREAD MAN:	All fresh.
ARKWRIGHT:	Never knew a breadman wot wasn't. If they make this bread any whiter I'll have to wear dark glasses. That's how, that's how, they third degree you now, you know? Oh yes, they lock you in a tiny cell and then they flash a slice of this bread in front of your naked eye b-b-b-
GRANVILLE:	People like it white.
ARKWRIGHT:	-balls!
BREAD MAN:	Pardon??
ARKWRIGHT:	At your naked *eye* balls! I *wish* you'd let me finish!
BREAD MAN:	Whitest bread in the world![40]

This version would end up earning one of the biggest laughs of the night. It was a sign of how the stutter could contribute so much more than just a trademark tic.

It was also there to give Arkwright some much-needed vulnerability. Barker knew that, without some kind of perceived weakness, the tough old shopkeeper, with his wily ways for relieving customers of their cash, and his domineering attitude towards his nephew, could easily strike viewers as an unsympathetic figure. The stutter, therefore, would be a regular reminder that Arkwright was fallible, and, Barker hoped, would encourage people to care about him in spite of his colder qualities.

'Arkwright,' Roy Clarke would say, 'is, in many ways, an impossibly mean old bat, so the stutter did help in that sense. He certainly needed something to allow people to like him in spite of how he behaved. And, of course, Ronnie, as an actor, had the ability to personalize him, and make him endearing. So we could draw on that.'[41]

This was the start of a great collaboration between author and actor. A situation comedy put on paper and now on the verge of being picked up and brought to life.

The BBC had commissioned the pilot. The producer Jimmy Gilbert believed in it. Ronnie Barker, like Roy Clarke, was committed to it.

The next step, therefore, was to cast it, plan it and film it. The pilot of 'Open All Hours' was about to go into production.

CHAPTER TWO

Stocking Up

Let me finish, will yer?

The journey from script to studio, for a sitcom, can be as hazardous as any adventure in Greek mythology. A key character can be miscast; a key actor can drop out; a relationship can break down; the director can misjudge the tone; real-life occurrences can outdate the theme; the situation, when brought to life, can suddenly seem horribly implausible; the comedy, when performed, can suddenly fall depressingly flat; and the audience can then reject, carelessly, callously, all that it has to offer. Anything can happen. Stout hearts and steady nerves are essential.

Jimmy Gilbert, fortunately, had proven over the course of a long career that he possessed both of these qualities. As executive producer of *Seven of One*, he had been primarily responsible for the creation of 'Open All Hours' and the other episodes, and so, in consultation with his star, he embarked on the process of taking the show from the page to the stage. Finding the supporting actors was one of his earliest and most important priorities.

The first task was to cast Granville, and, as far as Ronnie Barker was concerned, there was only one actor in contention for the part: David Jason. Even if Jimmy Gilbert had objected – which he most certainly did not – it was actually a *fait accompli*.

Jason, like Barker, had started slowly and humbly. He had worked as an electrician before making his professional debut as an actor in 1965, at the age of 25, in a production of Noël Coward's *The South Sea Bubble* at Bromley Rep. His first major break on television arrived in 1967 when he became a regular member of the new ITV children's comedy show *Do Not Adjust Your Set*, alongside the future *Monty Python* stars Eric Idle, Michael Palin and Terry Jones.

He had first worked with Barker in 1970, when he was hired to play an impossibly ancient gardener called Dithers, alongside Barker as Lord Rustless, in the second series of *Hark at Barker* (Dithers had been mentioned in the first series, but never seen). Recalling the 'thrill' that he experienced when asked to be a regular on the show, he would say: 'I had always wanted to work with Ronnie Barker, ever since I had seen him on *The Frost Report* in the sixties. He was already a legend in the business. This was a dream offer as far as I was concerned.'[42]

The two actors struck up a rapport, both on and off the set, more or less immediately, and from this point on Jason would be treated as a member of Barker's unofficial little troupe of tried and trusted performers. They next worked together later on in 1970 on *Six Dates with Barker*, in a wickedly funny episode ('The Odd Job') in which Barker played an abandoned husband contemplating suicide and Jason, quite brilliantly, a would-be hit man, and then, in 1972, they revived their respective roles as Dithers and Lord Rustless for the sitcom *His Lordship Entertains* (1972). It was already clear that, as talented character actors and comedians, and, indeed, as people, they were kindred spirits.

'I called Ronnie Barker "The Guv'nor",' Jason would say. 'It was a jokey nickname at first, but it grew to express exactly what I felt about him. The Guv'nor is what he was to me, and always will be. It wasn't just the depth of his comic gift, the abilities he had as a writer and a performer and a composer and an artist (even his handwriting was a work of art), it was the way he conducted himself, the kind of man he was. I've always tried to emulate him a bit and feel him on my shoulder.'[43]

Barker would be similarly warm in his praise of Jason, stressing his 'wonderful sense of timing',[44] as well as his professionalism and reliability, and ranking him among the rare few who have the gift to be able to 'make you laugh as soon as they appear'.[45] It came as no surprise, therefore, when one of the first names that Barker mentioned to Jimmy Gilbert, when the actor and producer started to discuss casting the various shows for *Seven of One*, was that of David Jason. The only doubt, at that stage, was which episode he should be in.

Barker decided to telephone Jason, tell him about the series and talk about some options. 'There's a part for you in practically every one of these,' he said, 'but I can't have you in all of them.'[46] Barker suggested either 'Prisoner and Escort' or 'Open All Hours' as the scripts most suited to his skills. After considering the respective merits of the supporting roles in both pilots, they agreed that Granville was the right choice, so Barker promised to send Jason the 'Open All Hours' script as soon as possible.

When it arrived, however, Jason was rather underwhelmed by what it contained. The context, at least, held some nostalgic appeal for him: 'When I lived in Finchley in north London there was a shop very similar to Arkwright's. It was called Chad's. We used to take in empty Tizer bottles claiming the tuppence refund. And the shopkeeper would go out and put them in the back yard. Then we'd nip round and lean over the wall to pick them out again. We'd go back and give them to him again and we'd get another tuppence.'[47] The character, however, failed to elicit much enthusiasm.

'When I first saw the script,' he later revealed, 'I secretly found the part a little thin and disappointing. I had no idea that this rather lost character in his Fair Isle jumper would propel my career to another level.'[48] There was no doubt, however, that he would take on the role, because he trusted Barker's judgement: '[T]he main thing was, if Ronnie thought it was worth pursuing, I felt there must be something to it. And it meant I would be working with the Guv'nor again'.[49]

The first supporting role was thus cast. Arkwright had his Granville.

Things were similarly straightforward when it came to deciding on someone to play Nurse Gladys Emmanuel. She was not written originally to be from any particular place or have any particular accent. It was clear, however, that she would have to strike Arkwright as the most alluring woman in the area.

The first person whom Gilbert thought of was Sheila Brennan, a bright, strong, strikingly attractive young Irish actor who, with her long red hair and large knowing eyes, looked as though she had just stepped out of a painting by Dante Gabriel Rossetti. A graduate of Dublin's Gate Theatre, who had also appeared in the first production of Sean O'Casey's sharply sardonic play *The Bishop's Bonfire* at the Gaiety in 1955, she had gone on to act in many other serious and challenging dramas, and had also worked occasionally in movies (such as 1955's *Captain Lightfoot* and 1961's *The Curse of the Werewolf*) and often in television (in programmes as diverse as a 1968 episode of the fashionable crime drama *Man in a Suitcase* to the 1972 satirical comedy series *Clochemerle*).

What particularly impressed Gilbert about her, when he was considering casting the role of Nurse Gladys, was her calmness and confidence as a performer. As the object of Arkwright's desire, Nurse Gladys would have to look and act like the kind of woman whose presence was powerful enough to lure the avaricious shopkeeper away – at least for a moment or two – from his passionate pursuit of pounds and pence. Brennan, Gilbert felt, would have both the composure and the craft to stand her ground opposite Ronnie Barker in their shared scenes of flirtation and frustration.

It would have been unusually quick and convenient for Gilbert to check on her availability – her husband, Gerald Savory, was the BBC's head of plays at that time and thus occupied an office nearby in the same building – but he followed the proper procedure and contacted her agent directly. She, in turn, was delighted to accept:

I already knew and liked Jimmy. The first time I'd met him was when Milo O'Shea had suggested me to him for a comedy that they were making [*Tales from the Lazy Acre*, 1972], and it was great fun. But it hadn't started well. The night I arrived, we had dinner and I was not in the best of tempers for some reason or other, and Jimmy said, 'I don't know if you realise it but tomorrow you're going up in a crane above Dun Laoghaire Harbour.' So I said, 'No I'm not!' He said, 'Yes, you are.' And sure enough the next morning I was up there, swinging in the wind, and the boat came in below, and off it came this band of Irish singers, who were looking up at me, just hanging around, wondering why I was there. It wouldn't have happened today with Health and Safety! So that wasn't a great start, but after that I got on very well with Jimmy. And then when he got in contact about 'Open All Hours' I was really very pleased and excited, especially as I already adored Ronnie Barker and couldn't wait to work with him.[50]

The show's comic triangle of key characters was thus complete. The production now had a sound foundation.

By this time Jimmy Gilbert had also appointed Sydney Lotterby to serve as the episode's producer/director. Lotterby was already one of the BBC's most experienced programme makers, having been with the Corporation since 1958 and worked on such successful shows as *Sykes and a...* (1963–4), *The Likely Lads* (1965), *Broaden Your Mind* (1968–9) and *Up Pompeii!* (1970). Few of his contemporaries had such an instinctive feel for filming sitcoms, grasping each one's distinctive tone and texture, and unobtrusively but expertly deploying the cameras to capture all of the colour and comedy.

Gilbert then moved on as swiftly as possible to cast the remainder of the minor characters, enlisting Yootha Joyce, for example, to play the seedy Mrs Scully, David Valla to portray the man who delivered the ultra-white loaves of bread, and a 15-year-old Liverpudlian actor named Keith Chegwin to play a boy in search of an ice lolly. He also hired several extras – Henry Rayner, Rex Eaton, Reg Lewis, Francis Batsoni, Alex Jones and Nicholas Kane – to give certain scenes a 'busier' look.

He then needed to attend to the matter of the music. Wanting a theme tune that would instantly draw the viewer into the fiction and foster a suitable mood, he turned to Max Harris to compose it. Harris was a familiar figure in British sitcom circles, having contributed the theme tunes to the likes of Anthony Newley's notoriously unconventional *The Strange World of Gurney Slade* (1960) and the notoriously conventional *On the Buses* movie (1971), and, much to many a producer's relief, he was particularly good at working to a tight deadline.

Once Gilbert had explained the kind of modest, wistful, 'northern' sort of sound that he wanted, Harris gave the matter some serious thought and eventually came up with the idea of a tune that he adapted from a pretty old waltz-style melody (composed in 1861) entitled 'Alice, Where Art Thou?' by the Dutch musician Joseph Ascher and the English lyricist Wellington Guernsey. Originally written for a pianist accompanying a singer (the opening lines were: 'The birds sleeping gently, sweet lyra gleameth bright/Her rays tinge the forest, and all seems glad to-night'), but usually performed over the ensuing years by a string quartet, Harris decided that it would be more apt, in these particular circumstances, to have it played by a cornet.

Recorded in half a day at Lime Grove studios in Shepherd's Bush, Jimmy Gilbert and Ronnie Barker heard it – an air for Arkwright – and judged it to be just right for the show. 'Open All Hours' had its theme tune (although, for reasons left unexplained in the archives, it would not actually be heard in the pilot episode, which used another, far less memorable, Max Harris composition instead).

Sydney Lotterby, meanwhile, had to arrange for various external shots – of both the shop itself and some of the streets that were supposed to surround it – to be filmed for later insertion into the finished studio recording. As there was neither the budget nor the time for the cast and crew to spend several days away at some distant location, the director had to find somewhere as close as possible to Television Centre in London to pass off as a suitably characterful corner of Yorkshire.

After a rushed spot of reconnaissance, Lotterby settled on a shop front on the western intersection of Drayton Avenue and Manor Road in Ealing W13, about a 20-minute drive from the BBC's base in White City, to serve as Arkwright's humble emporium. During a week of filming, from 6 to 11 February 1973, some brief shots of the exterior were staged, and several sites nearby were used for Granville's solitary bike rides. Lotterby, with the clock ticking, was relieved to have secured a site, but, in truth, he was never happy about the place: 'Wherever you go in London, whatever location you choose, it reeks of London somehow. It doesn't seem to be the north of England.'[51]

The one unexpected challenge encountered during filming, as Sheila Brennan would recall, concerned the brief scene outside the shop, when Nurse Gladys was supposed to drive up in her Morris Minor just behind Granville on his unreliable delivery bike:

There was a slight problem. No-one had asked me if I could drive. And I don't. So that only came out when we were actually filming with that car. After I'd told them, they coped with it by getting a prop man to lie at my feet inside the car while I was driving around. And, being a redhead, I'm also very short-sighted, so after the third take the cameraman said, 'If she does that *once* more I'm walking off!' Because I'd nearly killed him![52]

Sydney Lotterby faced an even more unusual problem back at Television Centre when it came to working with his designers on the studio sets. While there would be no difficulty in constructing the cosy interior of Nurse Gladys's little house (it only required the standard off-the-peg domestic sitcom scenery) or Arkwright's back room (which was supposed to seem 'clean but very non-modern'[53]), the key context of the grocer's shop itself represented rather more of a challenge.

Roy Clarke's script contained the following description of what, ideally, it should look like:

> The place is cluttered but clean. It sells groceries, confectionery, sweets, tobacco, hardware, nylons, household goods, proprietary medicines, ladies' cardigans, aprons, babywear. It has a bacon counter. An off-licence. It's all dark mahogany. The cash register is ancient and ornate and still pre-decimal. One or two ancient advertising posters have survived among the new.[54]

All of this made perfect sense to the designer, Tim Gleason, and his team, but rendering it in reality would not be without its difficulties. Arkwright's shop, of course, would have to be filled with all kinds of contemporary commodities, but, at a time when even a glimpse of a Steinway sign on a piano on a BBC programme could prompt accusations of advertising, stocking up was by no means going to be a straightforward process.

There was no question of the show getting involved in actual product placement (which was defined by the BBC as 'the inclusion of, or a reference to, a product or service in return for payment or any consideration in kind'[55]). The acceptance of any product placement for licence fee-funded services was (and remains) prohibited under the terms of the BBC's Charter. It was also deemed impractical, however, for the shop to be filled with a mass of distractingly unfamiliar fictional brands.

Ultimately, it was decided, after discussions with the relevant internal authorities, that it would be 'editorially justified' for the shop set to have actual brands on display, on the grounds that it had a right to 'reflect the real world', so long as verbal references were avoided whenever possible and close-ups of particular products were resisted.[56] It was not long before all of the newly assembled shelves were straining under the combined weight of such noticeable items as PG tips, Lyle's Golden Syrup and Princes Pork Luncheon Meat, cans of Heinz Baked Beans, colourful drums of Mackintosh's Quality Street, big bars of Terry's Chocolate and gleaming, golden bottles of Lucozade. One or two fake brands were added to placate any potential protestors.

The production team were also busy preparing a small range of props as options for Barker and Jason to use in physical comic business, and by far the most important of these was Arkwright's demon cash register. Invested with a strange mechanical malevolence worthy of the sociopathic computer HAL in the Stanley Kubrick movie *2001: A Space Odyssey*, the antiquated till was meant to contain a potentially lethal spring clip, and the tray would slide shut so quickly that amputation was a daily possibility.

Barker and Jason would have to pretend to battle with the clip (with the help of an off-camera sound effect), but the designers came up with a more devious solution to the problem of animating the terrifying tray. A piece of string was attached to the back of it, and then threaded through to the other side of the wall, where, during the recording, the assistant floor manager would be waiting for the cue to pull it violently shut.

Ronnie Barker supervised all of these telling little touches with a sharp and knowledgeable professional eye. Having worked early on in his career as an assistant stage manager, which obliged him, among other things, to ensure that all of the props were present, in their proper place and in good working order, he knew the importance of maintaining a close attention to such details, and therefore devoted plenty of time to checking that everything was just right.

His primary concern at this stage, however, was, as with the other members of the cast, to learn his lines and master his character. It was time for the production to pick up some pace.

Rehearsals began soon after the start of March 1973 (in a week marred by the first violent outbreak of the IRA's new campaign of terror in London[57]), in one of the many bland-looking and somewhat reverberant rooms in the BBC's purpose-built, multi-storey rehearsal block in Victoria Road, North Acton (a building known affectionately by those who used it as the 'Acton Hilton'). Ronnie Barker, in spite of the unsettling events elsewhere in the city, was always in good spirits on such occasions, partly because they took him back to the happy days that he had spent in rep (when every week saw the company start work on a new play), and partly because he was relishing reviving the rapport he always had with David Jason.

'I remember on the first day of rehearsal,' Sheila Brennan would recall, 'Ron said to me, "That young man is going to be a very big star." So I said, "Who? *Who?*" And of course it was David Jason. At the time, he *was* just a boy, and not very well known at all, but that comment showed the faith that Ron already had in him.'[58]

Overseen by Sydney Lotterby, the sessions were admirably balanced in terms of precision and playfulness. Barker, especially, was a great believer in mastering the nuts and bolts of a script as soon as possible: learning the lines, blocking out the action and generally settling into the situation. The more confident that he felt about these basic things, the keener he was to move on, try out some ideas and interact, eye-to-eye and toe-to-toe, with the rest of the cast. Each day, therefore, saw another layer added to the complexity of the performances as the actors relaxed and felt more secure within the skin of their respective characters.

They could all progress a little further, in this sense, when they had their individual meetings with the make-up supervisor, Penny Delamar, and the costume supervisor, Penny Lowe. To Barker and Jason, in particular, these collaborations were fascinating periods of experimentation, when they could draw on all of their instincts about a character to help summon them up from the script and bring them into vision.

Ronnie Barker had clear ideas about how he wanted Arkwright to look. As far as make-up was concerned, he wanted his face to have a cloistered pallor befitting a man who rarely ventured outside his shop. He also decided to sport a Glenn Melvyn-style moustache, but it had to suit the age and personality of the character. When Penny Delamar presented him with a tray of brand-new artificial moustaches, therefore, he studied them all, picked one up, examined it closely, expressed his satisfaction with it, but then asked her to 'put it on the floor and tread on it lightly, like you're stubbing out a cigarette'.[59] He then examined the moustache again, judged it sufficiently 'lived-in' looking, and had it put by for the performance.

Moving on to consider the costume options, there was only one thing that he really wanted: a light-brown overcoat, just like the one that all of the old-fashioned grocers seemed to wear. Once he had that, and the moustache, he felt right. He was ready.

David Jason was similarly busy rooting through all of the clothes in the wardrobe. The first item that he seized upon was a patterned Fair Isle tank top of the type much beloved by Britain's sartorially challenged youths in the early 1970s. Versatile only in the sense that it jarred with just about any other style of clothing that had been invented, it seemed to suit an inexperienced misfit like Granville, serving as a symbol, beneath his plain white pinny, of his inchoate cravings for a life of colour, rebellion and adventure. Added to that was a sober shirt and tie, to show how meekly conformist he really was, and a baggy cloth cap to confirm his deep working-class roots.

It was this kind of down-to-earth garb that would always undermine Granville's airy idealism, providing a visual pin to puncture his wordy pretensions just as surely as this kind of look had done in the past for every desperate dreamer from Oliver Hardy to Harold Steptoe. Appearing like this, David Jason knew, was the best way to convey the pathetic plight of poor Granville.

The costume needs of Sheila Brennan, in contrast, were simple and very straightforward. 'I just had the nurse's uniform,' she would recall. 'No padding or anything of that sort. Just the uniform and that was that.'[60]

The final day or two of rehearsals were, as Brennan later remembered, confident and creative occasions when everyone was polishing their performances and even coming up with the odd new comic detail. Ronnie Barker himself, she noted, was a great source of encouragement to his colleagues during these sessions: 'Ron was so lovely. He was always so kind and generous. And fun. And he was absolutely thrilled if you got a laugh. Some leading actors would react by thinking, "He's taking everything away from me." That wasn't Ron at all.'[61]

The only thing that still bothered Barker right up to the last moment (and, indeed, would continue to niggle away at him throughout all four of the subsequent series) was the short ruminative voiceover that Arkwright had to give at the end of the show. 'I never felt it worked, really,' he later explained. 'It was the one thing I didn't like much, mainly because it didn't sound like Arkwright. It was a director's thing, that it was very quiet, he was ruminating. And it felt strange after they'd been shouting all day in the shop. I think we just didn't do it right. My fault really.'[62]

The general opinion among the team, however, was that there was nothing at all 'strange' or jarring about this 'calm after the storm' – a shop, after all, *is* very quiet at that time of night, just before it closes, and a lonely obsessive like Arkwright *would* mull over all the events of the day in his mind – and neither was there any problem with how Barker delivered it. 'I thought it was one of the best things in it,' Roy Clarke would later say. 'I certainly never had a minute's qualm about how he did it. I thought he did it brilliantly.'[63]

Barker was thus persuaded to push on with the piece as planned. The preparation was now complete.

The actual show was then recorded on Sunday 11 March 1973, in the capacious Studio 8 at the BBC's Television Centre. The schedule for that day, which would remain the norm throughout the show's existence, was as follows (verbatim):

10.30am: Camera Rehearsal
12.45pm–1.45pm: Lunch
1.45pm–6.30pm: Camera Rehearsal
4.15pm–4.45pm: Tea
5pm–6pm: Final Run-Through
6.30pm–7.30pm: Dinner
7.30pm–8pm: Line-Up
7.50pm–8pm: Warm-Up
8pm–10pm: Recording[64]

The warm-up man was Felix Bowness. This Berkshire-born comedian and actor was probably the busiest 'cheerer-upper' in the business at that time, employed by countless BBC producers (including Terry Hughes, who used him for *The Two Ronnies*) to get studio audiences in the right mood to laugh all the way through a recording. Although he would later be known to the broader viewing audience at home for his performance as the permanently glum-faced former jockey Fred Quilley in the sitcom *Hi-de-Hi!* (1980–8), he was, as a warm-up, irrepressibly jolly and genial, roaming among the audience chatting, teasing and generally making them all feel a valued element of the production. Ronnie Barker, a shy man who had a natural aversion to coming out and being himself in front of an audience, had a genuine respect for professional warm-up men like Bowness, who could keep reappearing every time there was a break in the recording to ensure that the atmosphere never fell flat.

Buoyed by Bowness, therefore, those present to watch the pilot being made, even though they were unfamiliar with the situation and the characters, were in the perfect frame of mind to welcome this new fiction. It was a sitcom tradition for the cast to emerge at this point, shortly before the recording was due to commence, to greet the audience, but, on this occasion, not all of them did so: 'I said, "I can't do that,"' recalled Sheila Brennan. 'I get so frightened anyway, I thought I cannot, cannot, do it. Coming from drama and being new to that sort of thing, it just seemed a very bad system to me. You know, actors are screwed up enough anyway, and then they have to go out, do that, and then go back again and start trying to get into character. But then, thankfully, Yootha [Joyce], who felt the same, said that she wouldn't do it either, so I was saved from that.'[65]

Ronnie Barker, however, did come out, in costume, as the star of the show, to acknowledge the audience, and then the cameras began to roll and the first scene started. 'Open All Hours' was on its way.

It was evident right from the start that Barker and Jason were an inspired pairing. In every scene that they shared, the understanding that they had, the timing and the technique, was a delight to watch.

It was just as encouraging to see the on-screen rapport that existed between Barker and Brennan. Unlike many lesser sitcom actors, who, when seen close up, can look like they are merely waiting to say their next line rather than actually engaging with another character, Brennan genuinely gazed into Barker's eyes and listened to Arkwright's comments.

As Nurse Gladys she conveyed a fascinating mixture of coldness and warmth as she balanced the sense of resistance with glimpses of a mischievous spirit. It augured well for the future of this relationship.

The only moment of anxiety during an otherwise very smooth-running recording involved, of all people, that normally most unflappable of professionals Ronnie Barker himself. Sheila Brennan later recalled:

> We were in the studio, and we'd just done a take, when Ron came up to me and whispered in my ear, 'I've never been so frightened in my life!' And I said, '*You?*' He said, 'Yes!' It was very sweet, because he had his son [Adam] there, who was five at the time, doing a brief little scene, uncredited, just with him in the shop. Ron was behind the counter, and his son had to come into the shop, stand on a wooden box, and Ron had to take his order, talk to him and then watch him leave again. And although he was this wonderful actor, because he was acting with his own little son, he was so nervous about doing the scene. It was very endearing.[66]

Once that tiny trial had been negotiated safely, the rest of the show flowed on freely towards its conclusion. The audience applauded, the cast came back out to take a bow, and the studio slowly emptied.

The team had done all that it could. The show's fate was now in the hands of the viewers at home.

CHAPTER THREE

The Pilot

I can guarantee you the finest loin bacon,
and-and-and a full entertainment schedule.

'Open All Hours' was chosen to start the series of *Seven of One*. This was not, however, the fulsome stamp of approval that it might now appear to be. The truth is that the Clement and La Frenais pilot 'I'll Fly You for a Quid' had originally been favoured to go first, but, as it was set in a mining village, and a mining disaster had occurred at the Lofthouse Colliery earlier in the week,[67] 'Open All Hours' was selected as an inoffensive late replacement.

This should still have been an advantage for the episode, because there was something of a tradition for this kind of *Comedy Playhouse*-style 'selection box' format to attract its biggest and most open-minded audience at the very start of its run, after which the viewing figures tended to tail off to some degree. In this case, however, any benefit ended up being bungled.

'Open All Hours' was scheduled to be shown on Sunday 25 March, on BBC2, but the publicity for this particular episode was as shambolic as it was slight. It did not help that no-one associated with the most prominent media outlets of the time was willing to commit anything to print about the pilot (the fear then, as indeed now, being that one might be caught backing a flop, or, worse still, dismissing what would later turn out to be a classic). What made things even worse, on this occasion, was that few seemed even to know which pilot it actually was.

Several newspapers actually listed the wrong pilot, promising the Clement and La Frenais episode, 'Prisoner and Escort', for that particular night.[68] Another newspaper, the *Daily Express*, failed to update its old information and thus incorrectly listed the other Clement and La Frenais pilot, 'I'll Fly You for a Quid', in that slot.[69] Many viewers, therefore, were probably taken by surprise when, rather than seeing Ronnie Barker dressed up as a convict or sounding like a Welshman, they saw him instead as a Yorkshire-born grocer.

It was within this somewhat disorientating context, therefore, that the would-be sitcom about the corner shop made its debut on the screen. At 8.15pm, straight after a sombre documentary about an expedition in Canada, the *Seven of One* series was introduced, and the comedy began.

The show opens with a shot of the name above the shop: 'ARKWRIGHT'. Then the camera moves back to reveal the moustachioed man in the grubby-looking overalls, standing outside on the pavement with a cardboard crate in his hands, shouting out for assistance: 'Granville – f-f-fetch a cloth!' A shorter, younger man, his shoulders slumped, duly emerges, clearly resentful of having been summoned so abruptly into action: 'Why *me?*'

The third character is then introduced, as a red-haired nurse, all in blue, appears across the street and, turning her back, bends down to examine one of the headlights on her old Morris Minor. 'I know that face,' mutters Arkwright admiringly as he stares at her bottom. 'Nurse Gladys Emmanuel. P-P-Possibly the finest backside in the north of England. And it all belongs to the state.'

The next thing we see is an early-morning scene, with a milk float gliding by and Granville, yawning helplessly, pulling up the shutters and, with some reluctance, turning the sign on the door slowly over from 'CLOSED' to 'OPEN'. It is the start of another long day.

Arkwright is already up and about inside the shop, busy scribbling figures into his ledger and barking out orders to Granville. The difference in outlook and values between the two characters is evident right from the start, with the young man moaning about a lack of leisure and the old man carping about a lack of commitment:

ARKWRIGHT: I 'ope you're not abusing your health, are you?
You look to me as if you could do with a good
night's sleep.

GRANVILLE: Aye, I could, but we always have to get up in the middle of it!

ARKWRIGHT: Listen, you c-can't be lying in bed with *customers* passing the door! Have you no sense of *avarice*, lad?

GRANVILLE: I'm not a *lad* anymore!

ARKWRIGHT: Oh, been through some sort of ceremony, have you? Painfully initiated while me back was turned? Twenty-four hours of unflinching agony to prove yourself to the elders of the G-G-Grocers' Federation? Here – do they still practise that terrifying trick with the glacé cherry?

GRANVILLE: I'm *twenty-five*, you know!

ARKWRIGHT: Oh, that bang we heard was you going through puberty, was it? I thought we had a slate off!

GRANVILLE: I could be out in the world developing me full personality!

ARKWRIGHT: You *'AVE* got a slate off! Look, the world's gone *mad* out there! You don't want to go out *there!* Sanity begins at *home!*

There is no doubt that, although they may be bound together in terms of family, there is no real connection in terms of philosophy:

GRANVILLE: It's sordid asking for money.

ARKWRIGHT: Oh, listen: you may be flesh and blood, but that doesn't give you a licence to *blaspheme*, y'know!

GRANVILLE: Don't you ever think about serving the poor?

ARKWRIGHT: Who do you think comes in the shop? I spend me life serving the poor! It's easy – all you have to do is remember to n-never give them any credit.

It is a classic dialogue of the deaf:

GRANVILLE: There's more to life than possessions.

ARKWRIGHT: Ooh, been watching B-B-B-B-BBC2, have we? I told you to leave that channel alone! They don't know any better! They've not had your advantages, have they?

GRANVILLE: *What* advantages?

ARKWRIGHT: Oh, that's right – w-wound me to the quick, won't you! Wh-Who got you out of school as soon as they could, eh? Who s-struggled and sacrificed to keep you out of university, eh? And that's all the gratitude I get?

We soon get an insight into just what a creature of habit and tradition Arkwright actually is. Whatever he has inherited – be it a shop, a job, a nephew or even a troublesome till – he would clearly rather put up with it, and moan about it, and eventually bequeath it, rather than go to all of the bother of replacing it:

ARKWRIGHT: Why haven't you put the f-float in the till?

GRANVILLE: I put the silver in but I wish you'd do the notes. I don't like that spring clip.

ARKWRIGHT: Oh, give it here!

[He squeezes the notes under the clip and then leaps back as it snaps back down]

GRANVILLE: That'll have somebody yet, that. I *dread* opening that till! I just know that one of these days I'm going to find somebody's fingers in there! Mine!

ARKWRIGHT: Well, it'll all be yours, one day, lad!

Granville, in contrast, is a young man aching to immerse himself in modernity, or at least get a new van instead of his old delivery bike. It is while he is out on his bike that he finally has a precious few minutes of peace and quiet in which to fantasize about living another, better, kind of life. As he pedals slowly along each street, he allows himself to be distracted by such sights as a large pair of power station chimneys, a young woman slotting a petrol pump in the tank of her car, and another young woman sucking on a straw. All of his daydreams seem of a vaguely sexual nature, but each one tends to end prematurely with him losing his balance and falling off his bike.

'You know, van drivers have got numerous advantages over people on shop bikes,' he moans. 'I mean, as a class, they've got more panache. I mean, you can't swan up to some bird on a shop bike.' Arkwright, as usual, reacts to such 'extravagant' demands for change by leaving Granville to tire himself out with his talk. 'Have you *tried* casually dismounting and lighting up your monogrammed cigarette?' his nephew continues. 'You don't smoke,' Arkwright replies wearily. 'Well,' Granville corrects himself awkwardly, 'sucking on your monogrammed ice lolly, then, pausing only to adjust the cut of your flaming pinny!'

While Granville's hopes of romantic companionship only reside, so far, within the reveries of his solitary bike rides, Arkwright's are rather more palpable, as he keeps trying to attach them on to the shapely form of Nurse Gladys Emmanuel:

ARKWRIGHT: Listen, when are you going to chuck up this lark and come and look after *me*, eh? Yours is no profession for a handsome lass! I mean, I fancy the uniform, yes, but it's never knowing where your hands have been.

GLADYS: Look, just keep taking the tablets, Mr Arkwright. It will all go away.

ARKWRIGHT: Listen, marry me, Gladys Emmanuel, and I can guarantee you the finest loin bacon, and-and-and a f-f-full entertainment schedule.

GLADYS: You're at a funny age. That's all. You'll soon have this bit of trouble with your hormones over and then life will become much more simple.

Nothing much of note happens as these characters move from scene to scene. The ordinary is something the sitcom seeks to get into, rather than out of.

A number of customers are encountered. There is, for example, a crowd of cloth-capped men topping up their coughs with another dose of cigarettes ('That's British grit, that is,' announces Arkwright approvingly as he stuffs away their payments. 'That's the British public waving two V-shaped lungs at the experts!'), and a tiny boy too small to be seen above the counter ('Oh, it's *you*, is it? Get your mam to buy you heavy boots!'), and a woman who, having bred a succession of sociopaths, now uses the pram to bring back her empties ('You'd do better keeping the bottles and trading the kids in!').

Things are no more flashily dramatic in the room out the back, where Arkwright washes away the stains in a ceramic tea mug and Granville works to remove the creases from a cream-coloured shirt. Voices do become raised just a little when, during the course of some run-of-the-mill gossip, it is mentioned that someone in the vicinity now has a verruca ('Damn show off! He probably got it on HP!'), but most of the action is engagingly aimless.

The closest that the episode gets to telling a conventional story occurs when it transpires that Nurse Gladys might have another admirer. Even then, however, most of the action only takes place in the mind.

The problem starts when Granville is gossiping about how many trips she seems to be making to see the local church organist, Wesley Cosgrave. Arkwright tries to dismiss such talk as worthless tittle-tattle, but the more that his nephew alleges ('She has medical *relations* with him') the more unsettled he becomes ('Nobody liked Wesley Cosgrave, even at school,' he snaps. 'He had that brand of Christianity that was worse than B.O.!').

While Arkwright is falling deep into his fears and Granville is floating off into his dreams, it is noticeable how little the pair of them – two loners living under one roof – actually listen to each other, let alone try to help each other:

ARKWRIGHT: I wonder what happened to my watch?
GRANVILLE: Well, *I* haven't had it!
ARKWRIGHT: Look, we're not discussing *your* problems, we're talking about *my* watch!

GRANVILLE:	You shouldn't leave it lying about. It shows a deep-seated neurotic anxiety about time passing.
ARKWRIGHT:	Oh, it c-couldn't just be that me *strap* broke, I suppose?
GRANVILLE:	You don't go great licks on psychology, do yer?
ARKWRIGHT:	Well, I don't *need* it, do I? I'm not a criminal, am I? Bit of humpty, that's what they want. That's what *he* could have done with an' all – W-Wesley Cosgrave. A b-belt round the ear with a Methodist hymn book! Or even a pew or two! Or a small chapel, really.
GRANVILLE:	I'm disenchanted with ironing.
ARKWRIGHT:	You know, he split on me one Sunday School outing at Bridlington for toying with what can only be described as the affections of Mabel Hemsley. I'd only just got started an' all. Six months' ground work right up the Swannee! D'you know, that girl could get through bars of wholenut chocolate quicker than anything I've ever seen. It was like watching McAlpine starting a motorway.
GRANVILLE:	You know, ironing is in direct conflict with the main stream of my personality.
ARKWRIGHT:	Wasn't half a fuss about it an' all. Cost me a part in the Christmas play, that did.
GRANVILLE:	In a word, I *hate* it!
ARKWRIGHT:	Yes, I *was* going to be St Paul. But they struck me down before I got anywhere near Damascus. Well, I'd hardly got back from Bridlington!

Granville does nothing to extricate himself from the ironing. Forever confused by the fact that he is the nephew of his boss, he remains rooted to the spot, in the shop, waiting, albeit reluctantly, to be told what, and what not, he should do next.

Arkwright himself, on the other hand, is, if anything, too ready to get up, get out and get scheming when it suits him. On this particular occasion, he puts an arm in a sling and sets off across the road to seek help, and some answers, from Nurse Gladys.

After attempting to justify his visit – 'I was j-just reaching up to get me Bible and the stool slipped' – he starts sounding her out about her schedule:

ARKWRIGHT:	W-were you just going out? I mean, I mean, th-this can wait till morning. If it has to.
GLADYS:	Just one more call, that's all.
ARKWRIGHT:	Ur-urgent, was it?
GLADYS:	No, more social, really.
ARKWRIGHT:	*Social?* Oh, I-I didn't think you were supposed to get social with the patients. No, that sounds a bit rammy to me, that. I thought you were s-supposed to be above suspicion, like corset fitters and tattooists.

[She checks his temperature]

GLADYS:	Ah, the world's sorriest sight: homo sapiens – male with a string broke. Let's have it off, then.
ARKWRIGHT:	I beg your pardon?
GLADYS:	The sling, you *fool!*
ARKWRIGHT:	Oh, I see.

[She starts removing the sling in a brisk and business-like manner]

ARKWRIGHT:	Well, less of the sweet talk, then. Do you soft soap everybody like this?
GLADYS:	Typical! Men! They all come running for sympathy before efficiency.

[She grabs his arm and starts manipulating it]

ARKWRIGHT:	OW! *OOOH!* Careful!! You'll break it in half! Ooh! *Oof!* Hey, tell me, what was it like in the Waffen SS?
GLADYS:	Are your bowels all right?
ARKWRIGHT:	Me *bowels?!* Your idea of sweet talk – really!

	Hey, next time you see him, r-remember me to Jackie Pallo,[70] won't you?
GLADYS:	I want you to drink this – it's for shock.
ARKWRIGHT:	Well, I haven't got shock.
GLADYS:	You *will* have when you get that down you!
ARKWRIGHT:	*Ohhhh!* God, where did you get the recipe for that? *The Farmers' Weekly?* I should think that's been handed down from generation to generation, hasn't it? Like typhoid! Does it shift rust?
GLADYS:	You'll find out what it will shift!
ARKWRIGHT:	Look, look, you know very well I-I'd go through fire and water for you, but not in the same glass!
GLADYS:	Poetic justice. You shouldn't come here wasting my time!
ARKWRIGHT:	But have you no compassion for the sick at *heart?* I mean, do you think of *everything* in terms of medicine? Could you not just clasp me to your bosom with a motherly gesture? You've got the chest for it!
GLADYS:	Get off home!
ARKWRIGHT:	Listen, *don't* go there tonight. He's *no* good for you!
GLADYS:	Who are you talking about?
ARKWRIGHT:	Wesley Cosgrave. I know you go up there every night, 'cause your car's been seen in his yard!

The crisis is over almost as soon as it had started, because Gladys, partly irritated and partly flattered by Arkwright's possessiveness, explains that the only thing that poor Wesley Cosgrave has been doing is letting her use his parking place when she pays a visit on her sister who resides nearby.

Greatly relieved, if a little queasy from swallowing the superfluous medicine, Arkwright returns to his shop, where he finds Granville on the verge of leaving for a brief date with the girl from the garage. The grocer does his best to sound discouraging – 'Go on, go and fritter away the golden moments of your youth' – but he does at least grant his nephew's request to take a couple of choc-ices with him from stock ('Certainly. Just put your money in the till.')

Once Granville has departed, Arkwright is back outside the shop, looking cold and lonely without any customers, picking up his products as the darkness creeps up to the entrance. It is, sadly for him, the end of the sales for the evening and, as he prepares to turn the sign around to say 'CLOSED', he reflects to himself on the doings of the day:

> They think 'cause you're middle-aged you don't know what romance is. It's that magic something that enables you to survive chat like: 'What are your bowels like?' Huh, she'd be a riot if I took her to the Federation dinner with vernacular like that... She's got a right old grip. With a partner like that beside him a man would have somebody to unload his delivery wagons for him!

As he disappears inside carrying an aluminium ladder, the *Seven of One* theme tune starts to play, the credits roll, and the studio audience begins to applaud. The pilot episode is over.

Watched by an estimated audience of just over 2 million,[71] it had done what any decent pilot should do. It established its situation, it introduced its key characters, it explained why the latter were destined to remain stuck with the former, it hinted at the potential for future humour and generally suggested it possessed the 'legs' to last for at least a full series. It did, in short, a good job at encouraging further inspection.

The reaction to it, however, was muted. There were no major reviews. There were no public discussions. As far as the lay observer was concerned, the episode (in those days long before VCRs, DVRs and PVRs) simply disappeared for good up into the ether just as soon as it was screened.

The BBC, as was its standard practice,[72] did conduct a certain amount of audience research to gauge how the programme had performed. The results – which were based on questionnaires completed by a viewing panel composed of a 'representative' cross-section of the public – were actually very encouraging.

The episode, it was said, had been received 'with rare enthusiasm'. Ronnie Barker's portrayal of Arkwright 'was a joy to watch', and the 'really original and amusing script' produced 'more laughs in the first ten minutes than in the whole of some "comedy" series'. One person on the panel complained that a speech impediment was not a suitable subject for 'amusement', but the vast majority not only enjoyed the show but also regarded it as an excellent curtain-raiser for the series as a whole: 'If the rest are as good,' wrote one viewer, 'we are in for a treat.'[73]

The signs, therefore, were promising, but, trapped as it was in the mechanically transient medium of television, the show had precious little time to secure its future. The team behind it just had to hope that it would impress the people with power.

It was repeated, this time on BBC1, on 31 July, and then again the following year, on 16 July 1974, when it won a much bigger audience (more than three times the original size[74]), but, once again, it was ignored by the press and had to rely on being kept alive in the viewers' memory as television moved on restlessly to the next day's set of schedules. There was not a trace left to be treasured.

The story was much the same for the six subsequent editions of Seven of One. Attracting modest-sized audiences, they came and went without provoking any significant critical comment.

Inside the BBC, however, plenty of analysis was taking place. Ronnie Barker, Sydney Lotterby and Jimmy Gilbert were holding a post-mortem on each pilot's performance, and assessing what was best to do next. 'We had a lunch party at the Gun Room restaurant in Hammersmith,' Gilbert would recall, 'with Duncan Wood, who was head of comedy, and Ronnie Barker and myself, and we discussed our options.'[75]

'Open All Hours' and 'Prisoner and Escort' were rated collectively as the two strongest episodes for development into series, but the problem was that Barker, as fond as he was of both, would not have the time to develop the two of them more or less simultaneously. His top priority, in terms of commitment, remained The Two Ronnies, and, if he wanted to work on a sitcom during however much free time was left, he would have to make a choice between these two possibilities – or at least order them in terms of urgency.

There was instant agreement between Jimmy Gilbert and Sydney Lotterby: both were convinced that 'Prisoner and Escort' was the one to pursue first. Ronnie Barker, however, was by no means so sure. There was a third option, Gilbert would remember, that Barker still wanted to discuss:

> He was also keen on the other Clement and La Frenais script, 'I'll Fly You for a Quid'. I agreed: I thought that it was brilliant. And Ronnie Barker always wanted to do a comedy series playing a Welsh character, and he used to pull my leg that, because I came from Scotland, I was not favouring the Welsh! In fact, the only problem I had with the episode was that I felt it was almost like the perfect short story, with a beginning, middle and end. And it would have had to be very artificially twisted in order to open it out into a series. So we passed on that one.[76]

The options were back down to two. Barker was then faced with a straight choice between the prison and the shop, and he opted, after some thought, for the prison.

It was partly due to the situation (there was no more trapped a figure than a convict), and partly due to the character (Norman Stanley Fletcher had struck him as the most natural, and sharp, of all the lead roles in the series) and partly due to the impressive track record of the two writers (apart from *The Likely Lads*, and the imminent sequel *Whatever Happened to the Likely Lads?*, Clement and La Frenais had also contributed screenplays for several movies as well as numerous sketches for *The Two Ronnies*). Barker was also, by nature, a pragmatist in terms of the entertainment business, and with his two trusted advisors assuring him that this sitcom would have the best prospect of establishing a popular appeal, he decided it was right to place it in pole position. 'Open All Hours', as a consequence, was consigned to the shelf for the foreseeable future ('We didn't reject it,' Jimmy Gilbert later insisted. 'We just agreed to put it down on the list as the next one in line'[77]).

'Prisoner and Escort' thus duly became *Porridge*, and the BBC went ahead and promoted the new sitcom with great enthusiasm, ensuring that a broad audience was ready to watch BBC1 on 5 September 1974, when the first episode of the first series went out on the air. It attracted plenty of high-profile praise (*The Times*, for example, judged it 'classy' and 'extremely funny',[78] and it won the BAFTA for Best Situation Comedy) and the show went from strength to strength. A second series would follow soon after in the autumn of 1975 (winning Barker a BAFTA for Best Light Entertainment Performance, as well as a Royal Television Society award for the year's 'outstanding creative achievement in front of the camera'[79]), and, just as Gilbert, Wood and its producer Sydney Lotterby had predicted, the sitcom was well on its way to establishing itself as one of the best sitcoms in the history of British comedy.

Roy Clarke, meanwhile, was left to push on with another show, *Last of the Summer Wine*. Originating as a pilot episode in the BBC's regular potential sitcom showcase *Comedy Playhouse* in January 1973 (where it won a fair amount of critical applause[80]), it was promptly commissioned as a series and made its debut, in November, on BBC1. A second series would reach the screen two years later, with subsequent series following, on average, at a rate of one every 12 months (along with such plaudits as Alan Coren's celebration of the show as '*Winnie the Pooh* recycled through Samuel Beckett'[81]).

This was only one of several projects either being planned or polished by the hard-working Clarke, who was now considered so strong a writing prospect that the BBC (in the form of Jimmy Gilbert, as head of comedy, and Bill Cotton, as head of light entertainment) was in the process of negotiating with his agent to secure his services for the foreseeable future on a 'non-exclusive contract'.[82] Among the projects that followed as the fruits of this faith was a fascinating-sounding sitcom pilot for Morecambe and Wise (although commissioned, it was not recorded due, it seems, to the double act getting cold feet about trying their luck with the genre),[83] several scripts for such drama programmes as *Dial M for Murder* (1974), and two more pilots for a new series of *Comedy Playhouse* ('Pygmalion Smith', which starred Leonard Rossiter, and 'It's Only Me, Whoever I Am', starring David Jason), as well as his own new sitcom, inspired by his past career as a policeman, *The Growing Pains of PC Penrose* (1975).

It seemed, therefore, as though both Barker and Clarke had moved on. The line of least resistance was to leave 'Open All Hours' behind.

Ronnie Barker, however, was already growing restless after two hugely successful series of *Porridge*. Almost a year before he had even recorded the 1975 Christmas special, he informed Jimmy Gilbert that he wanted another challenge. 'Let me try something else,' he asked, explaining that he was wary of being associated for too long with one particular character.[84]

What he now wanted to do was to turn 'Open All Hours' into his next sitcom. He wanted to move from Norman Stanley Fletcher to Arkwright.

It was a telling admission. Comic actors, it has often been said, are drawn to what they dread,[85] and for Ronnie Barker that meant playing characters who are caged and confined. Fletch is stuck in a prison; Arkwright is stuck in a shop. It takes someone who can appreciate the tragedy of that condition, as well as the comedy, to bring such figures fully to life. It was therefore ironic and yet entirely apt that the ever-restless Barker now wanted to switch from one prisoner to another.

The news, however, could hardly have been greeted with less enthusiasm within the BBC. The reason for these reservations was twofold: first, because Barker was abandoning a sitcom that had proven itself to be a phenomenally popular prime-time programme (whose appeal was still in the process of getting even stronger), and second, because he was proposing to replace it with a sitcom that, in the eyes of most executives, represented a much more modest model. By this stage, however, Ronnie Barker was considered too big a star to be bullied into continuing something against his will, and so, grudgingly rather than gladly, his request was rubber-stamped.

Referred to initially, in a memo dated 21 January 1975, as a new project with the working title of 'The Shop', it would not be until 7 October of that year when it finally started to be called, officially, *Open All Hours*.[86] As the various contracts were drafted, Roy Clarke was promised, after some spirited haggling from his formidable agent Sheila Lemon (who was blessed with just the right mixture of menace and wit), £1450 per episode (the same rate that he was currently on for *Last of the Summer Wine*),[87] while Ronnie Barker, as the star, was set to receive £1200.[88] David Jason, at this stage in his career, was not yet able to command anything like such a sizeable fee, so he would have to settle for a mere £250 per episode,[89] with the supporting cast receiving even more modest sums.

If Barker was in any doubt as to how reluctant the powers-that-be were about his plans, he would soon be rudely disabused. The news came through that the first series of *Open All Hours* was going to be broadcast early in 1976 on BBC2 rather than BBC1, supposedly on the grounds that it was deemed a 'gentle comedy' and therefore better suited to the less pressurized context of a minority channel. Privately, Barker was angry and offended – 'When they say it's "gentle",' he confided to David Jason, 'they normally mean they don't think it's funny'[90] – but the perceived slight only made him, and Roy Clarke, even more determined to prove them all wrong.

Open All Hours, at long last, was going ahead. It was set to be the underdog, the 'anti-*Porridge*', the sitcom that few insiders seemed eager to sell, but at least it was going to get out on the air. Once it reached an audience, Barker felt, anything could happen.

PART TWO

Granville – let's have this door open!

CHAPTER FOUR

Series One

*It's all gone through this keen commercial
brain, which is linked through all the ingenious
circuits t-to me wallet.*

The first series began on Friday 20 February 1976, at 9pm on BBC2. Three years on from the broadcast of the pilot episode, *Open All Hours* would have to introduce itself all over again.

Most things were still the same – Barker, Jason, Sydney Lotterby and the team behind the scenes were all back as before – but one major thing had changed. In place of Sheila Brennan, Lynda Baron had been recruited to play the part of Nurse Gladys Emmanuel.

The reason why Brennan did not appear, despite giving a fine performance in the pilot episode, has never been reported. Indeed, it remains a mystery that seems, in a Sherlockian sense, a veritable 'three-pipe problem'.

No explanation for the change has been preserved in the BBC archives, and Sheila Brennan herself – who certainly wanted to return – was left in the dark as to the reasons. 'For nearly two years, whenever I saw Jimmy [Gilbert] anywhere, he'd come over and say, "It's going to happen, don't worry, it'll be made into a series,"' Brennan would say. 'But it never did happen. At least not with me in it! And I was never told I wasn't doing the series.'[91]

It was certainly not Roy Clarke's decision to make a change. 'I had no input into that,' he later explained. 'None at all. I didn't know what happened. It was a shame, she looked very good in it, I remember that.'[92]

It was also not something that Jimmy Gilbert had suggested. 'It's puzzling, but I'd handed the show over by that stage,' he said. 'I liked her very much, personally, and I thought she was very good in that episode. So I'm really not sure, quite honestly, what happened.'[93]

It was also, it seems, not a switch sanctioned by Sydney Lotterby. 'I must admit I'd always thought that Sheila didn't want to do it,' he would say. 'So I beg her pardon. All I can say is that it certainly wasn't me who decided to make the change.'[94]

It also seems unlikely that Ronnie Barker himself would have been responsible for such a change, because he had established an obvious rapport with Sheila Brennan while working on the pilot. He never referred to the matter either in interviews or print, but, as Brennan would recall, there were certainly no problems between them either personally or professionally. 'He was lovely to me, always,' she noted, 'and we got on so well. Even after he'd retired, if he and his wife were out and they saw me somewhere he'd always come over and be so friendly and nice. And I adored working with him.'[95]

The reason for the switch, therefore, remains, alas, a matter for speculation, but, given the reactions of those who were there at the time, it seems most plausible to put it down more to the cock-up, rather than the conspiracy, theory of history. As sometimes happened at the BBC, and other broadcasters, in those days, it is possible that no-one (after three years of dealing with other things) actually thought to check that Brennan was still available, and so the role was made available again for casting.

Whatever the truth of the matter ('I guess we'll have to just say "it just happened",' said Jimmy Gilbert[96]), it was, at best, a careless and clumsy way to treat someone who had shone in the previous production. 'No-one ever got back to me,' she would reflect with regret. 'It was a great pity, because I would have loved to have done it.'[97]

Her loss would be another's gain. Lynda Baron would take her place.

The Lancashire-born Baron, an accomplished singer and dancer as well as an actor, had been one of the most recognizable young women on British television during the mid-1960s, having joined the regular cast of the new BBC satirical show *BBC3* in October 1965. Frequently featured in glamorous poses on the front and inside pages of newspapers, accompanied by such captions as 'Luscious Lynda',[98] the 'shapely red-head',[99] 'the sort of body schoolboys draw on walls',[100] the woman whom 'half the men in the country lusted for'[101] and 'The BBC's new TV satire girl',[102] she quickly impressed the critics with her clever and confident performances on a show that was dominated by such sharp-tongued male wits as John Bird, Alan Bennett, Robert Robinson, John Fortune and Denis Norden.

When the 1960s ended, however, she disappeared for a while from the screen, concentrating instead on working in the theatre, where she appeared in productions ranging from such sophisticated parodies as Tom Stoppard's *The Real Inspector Hound* to a frantic farce like Anthony Lesser's *The Bedwinner*. The offer to return to television as Nurse Gladys came out of the blue.

The actor Dennis Ramsden (with whom she had recently appeared on tour in *A Bedfull of Foreigners*) had recommended her for the role. He was working on a sketch for an episode of *The Two Ronnies* when, during a tea break, Ronnie Barker suddenly announced: 'I'm doing a series and need a girl who's got to be good at comedy and have big tits.' Ramsden immediately responded: 'Lynda Baron!'[103]

Signed up on a contract that would pay her £262 for her first episode, and then £190 for each one that followed,[104] she was thus welcomed to the cast. The character of Nurse Gladys, as a result, was promptly changed from Irish to northern English.

There was no danger of Baron being influenced one way or another by Brennan's interpretation of the role, for the simple reason that she had never seen it. 'I hadn't watched the pilot episode,' she later confirmed, 'and quite deliberately I've not watched it since'.[105] She thus approached the role purely by focusing on what she saw in the script.

Baron certainly needed help from the wardrobe department to transform herself physically into the character. Her figure was shapely but slender, while Nurse Gladys, in the mind of Roy Clarke, had been somewhat 'enlarged' since the pilot, and was now described as having a bottom like 'the fenders of a Morris Minor'. Baron was obliged to wrap 60lb of padding under her nurse's uniform:

I didn't have long to prepare, but we had a wonderful woman called Mary Husband, who was one of the best ever costume designers in television, and we just knew that she had to make me twice the size. She said to me, 'I'm a dab hand with Dunlopillo,' and she went ahead and designed me this wonderful body. It went down from the elbows and down to my knees, and had a marvellous bosom and a very big bottom. After that, the costuming was easy, because a district nurse is a district nurse. But we had a lot of fun. We used to go into this place where you'd buy uniforms, and I'd go into a cubicle as a size 10, and I'd come out as a size 22 – but nobody batted an eyelid! Nobody said anything at all, which we thought was hilarious![106]

That was not quite the end of the 'embellishments': for certain scenes, when Arkwright's ogling was particularly obsessive, her already impressive *poitrine* was sometimes further enhanced by the addition of a pair of the wardrobe mistress's socks.

Once the shape was settled, Baron could concentrate on cultivating the personality of the character. She had little time to dwell on any details, as she was still working in the West End at the time, but she felt confident about growing quickly into the role.

With the core of the cast thus suitably reconstituted, the production once again could progress, and all energies were channelled towards the goal of delivering a top-class series right on time. Location filming took place, on this and all subsequent occasions, in the sitcom's proper spiritual home of South Yorkshire (18–31 January 1976), after Sydney Lotterby managed to find a suitable-looking corner shop – a hair stylist's called Beautique, owned and run by Helen Ibbotson, situated at 15 Lister Avenue in the Doncaster suburb of Balby. 'The producer rang me,' Ibbotson later recalled, 'and asked "could we borrow your shop?" and I said "you're joking aren't you?", but he said he wasn't. He came and met us at the shop and then the rest is history really.'[107]

It was not quite so straightforward, Lotterby revealed, when he ventured across the road to arrange to use the property directly opposite at number 34:

I'd got myself a sheepskin coat for the occasion, because it was very cold up there. And when I had to choose Nurse Gladys's house, I went along to the place that I'd thought, 'This is the one,' but when I knocked on the door and rang the bell I couldn't get any reply. So I thought I'd better try the next house and see if they know where their neighbour is, so I knocked on that door, and again I didn't get any reply. And I must have gone to about five or six houses in a row, until it seemed as though I was now miles away from the one opposite the shop, when one person finally answered the door. And I said to them, 'I can't get any replies,' and they said, 'No, well, they think you're the tallyman!'[108]

All six of the studio recordings then took place back in London. Meeting up at Television Centre (following the standard week of rehearsal at the 'Acton Hilton') every Sunday morning, from 15 February (five days before each episode was due to reach the screen), the cast and crew worked all through the day until, at 8pm, the actual recording commenced in a variety of studios (3, 6 or Barker's personal favourite, the capacious home of *The Two Ronnies*, Studio 8).

By the time, therefore, that Friday 20 February had arrived, and the series was due to make its debut, the team was already busy getting ready for their second weekend of recording, but the general mood, as they all anticipated the initial broadcast, was one of cautious optimism and positive thoughts. How the public would respond, however, was, as they all knew only too well, something that was very hard to predict.

The portents, this time around, seemed somewhat mixed. Friday was – and still is – a fine day for sitcoms, as they tend to be greeted by an audience ready to sit back and celebrate the end of the working week in a relaxed and happy frame of mind. On this particular Friday, however, *Open All Hours* risked arriving just at that time in the evening when the audience was feeling satiated as far as sitcoms were concerned.

BBC1 was screening two well-established and popular sitcoms back-to-back over the course of the previous hour, with a new episode of *The Liver Birds* starting at 8pm followed by a vintage repeat of *Steptoe and Son* at 8.30pm. ITV, meanwhile, had scheduled one of its own best-performing sitcoms of the time, *Yes – Honestly!*, for 7.30pm in most of its regions. The debut episode of *Open All Hours*, therefore, faced the unenviable task of wringing a fresh set of laughs from those who were close to being laughed out.

As was the norm in those days (the promotion of *Porridge* had been an exception), there was precious little help for the new show in terms of pre-publicity ('There was hardly anything at all, much to our chagrin,' Sydney Lotterby would later recall[109]). In stark contrast to all of the noisy bells and whistles that announce the imminent arrival of any sitcom in today's almost neurotically competitive multi-channel age, back in 1976, when there were still only three channels and journalists were not even invited to preview new programmes, the likes of *Open All Hours* were left to attract attention largely by word of mouth as the first series went out.

The popularity of Ronnie Barker ensured that his new show did at least receive a brief mention in a few of the newspapers that morning – *The Times*, for example, predicted that the sitcom 'should pull in customers',[110] and the *Daily Mirror* previewer rated it as a possible 'winner'[111] – but that was as close as the first outing of *Open All Hours* would get to generating anything that approximated to 'hype'. The best that even the *Radio Times* could muster was a sheepish-sounding description of the show as 'a series based on a one-off programme you may remember from 1973'.[112]

There were no promotional interviews, no ad campaigns, no posters and no on-screen trailers. There was just the hope that enough people would study the schedules, spot the new show, and remember to tune in at the right time.

Those who did so were treated to a clever opening episode that echoed many of the elements that had been presented in the pilot, but also bound them all together with greater clarity and confidence. It was more than a mere scene-setter; it was also a relationship-revealer. It captured and conveyed, with subtle charm and deft precision, the context of quiet desperation that was set to house the humour throughout the run.

The episode – which was entitled 'Full of Mysterious Promise' – began with the sound of a solitary cornet and a bird's eye exterior shot of the shop, caught between the shadows and the sunrise. Two thick-coated, sensible-hatted women walk purposefully past. A delivery bike is perched on the kerb. As the camera moves in a little closer, we see the cluttered array of fruit and vegetable crates, straw brushes, aluminium bins, plastic laundry baskets and seed packet racks. Then the freshly painted prices on the windows become clear: Sugar 21p, Butter 16p, Bacon 54p and Tea 9p.

The doorbell rings and Arkwright emerges, hands tucked inside his pockets, his eyebrows raised in readiness for a new day of hard selling. Scrutinizing the view from a customer's perspective, he squints and spots the blemishes that have been left behind by the early birds. 'Granville,' he shouts, 'f-f-fetch a cloth!'

Granville duly appears, hands on hips, his expression stuck somewhere between a grin and a grimace. In a subtle sign of his meek resistance, he has come out without his cloth, and so, with a sigh, he shuffles back inside to get on with the unwelcome job.

Nothing much happened after that. Nothing much happened except ordinary interactions. It was just a slice of life.

The odd customer came in for a gossip: 'Yes, she showed me the baby last week. I don't think it's his. It looks more like him that comes to read the meter!' Another one – a leather-clad biker with his head hidden in a helmet – came in to feed his fierce addiction to Lucozade: 'I'll have the usual!' A third one – an unenthusiastic DIY enthusiast – turned up to get an elastoplast: 'I'd better have a large.' A rogue rodent also made a brief appearance in the back room: 'I'll kill that f-flaming mouse!'

Granville was glimpsed out riding his delivery bike, and then pushing it back once the front wheel had buckled. Epitomizing the state of his obstructed life, he had ridden straight into a stationary object. The same thing then happens to Arkwright himself, distracted by the sight of Nurse Gladys ironing her underwear, when he crashes into the back of a Morris Minor. It seems, fatalistically, par for the course for this pair of sitcom characters.

There *was* a theme, lurking behind all of the froth and nonsense in the foreground. The theme concerned the gap between desire and knowledge, and it was symbolized by the presence in the shop of a large consignment of fire-damaged stock. Here were masses of cheap tins of food that had all lost their labels, offering the prospect of being sold on for a healthy profit if only their contents could be confirmed.

Everything else of any consequence, it soon becomes clear, is very much like these tins. They are all objects of desire, but no-one who covets them really knows what lies inside.

Arkwright's object of desire, aside from money, is Nurse Gladys Emmanuel ('If I don't marry her soon I will have to buy a new electric blanket'). He is drawn to the exterior – looking longingly at the shapely legs, the bulbous bottom and the bountiful breasts – but remains in doubt about the 'mysterious promise' that resides inside.

Being an earthbound and business-like man, rather than a spiritual and reflective one, his instinctive response to such ignorance is to touch rather than think. Faced with crates of label-less tins, he starts picking a couple up and shaking them near his ear: 'Mu-Mulligatawny and Leek' and 'Beefy Chunks in Gravy'. Undeterred by the hopeless inaccuracy of such wild guesses, he is keen to subject Nurse Gladys to a similar exploratory squeeze and shake.

Granville, meanwhile, is painfully aware that he has yet to land his eyes on any particular object of desire, let alone start investigating its nature. Faced with the same crates of label-less tins, he is content merely to take his can opener to any one of them and, as instructed by Arkwright, start 'j-j-jiggling it a bit' until it reveals what is hiding inside.

Everything is like a label-less tin to Granville. He is not sure what anything is, and whether or not he will like it, but he is desperate to get his hands on it and explore it.

This is the difference that emerges during the opening episode. Arkwright lusts after Nurse Gladys, and Granville lusts after life.

Arkwright, convinced that he knows what he wants, is worried that time might run out before he gets it. Spying Nurse Gladys on the other side of the road, perched on a set of wooden steps as she reaches up and washes her windows, he cannot resist one of his frequent trips over in the hope of edging a little closer to intimacy, only to find her almost as obdurately inscrutable as one of his troublesome tins:

ARKWRIGHT: You were out early this morning, Nurse
Emmanuel, fresh from your l-lonely warm bed.
GLADYS: I never said it was lonely.
ARKWRIGHT: Don't you ever make a wish that you'll wake up

one morning and find a handsome l-local shopkeeper in it?

GLADYS: No.

[She continues wiping the windows, acting as if he is not there]

ARKWRIGHT: Time is passing us by, you know. It's no longer spring time. Why don't we get engaged, before we've both got a moustache? While I can still look at your legs without thinking about orthopaedic shoes? *Come on* – let's strike while the iron's still lukewarm!

[She steps down to the pavement, and looks at him with a mixture of pity and irritation]

GLADYS: I can't get engaged right now. In half an hour I've got to go to Chartholmley Street and have a baby.

ARKWRIGHT: Listen, why don't you come over one night and-and rub me chest with Vicks, eh?

[She has turned her back and is ignoring him again]

You know, to tell you the truth, I've been thinking a lot about us two lately. It's not the same as actually doing it, though, is it?

[He stares in wonderment as Gladys bends down to rinse out her cloth in the bucket]

You know, I don't know why some folks say 'L-Let the devil take the hindmost'. As far as I'm concerned he can g-get in the queue.

[She stands up and addresses him]

GLADYS: How can I be sure you *really* fancy me? That you're not just trying to stop me order going to the supermarket round the corner?

ARKWRIGHT: I want you to *marry* me, Gladys Emmanuel!

64

There's nobody appreciates your shape more than a member of the G-Grocers' Federation!

[She bends down and gives her cloth another rinse, while Arkwright studies her bottom. He mutters to himself: 'I wonder what it would look like with a bit of parsley around it.' She gets back up and starts carrying the steps towards her door]

GLADYS: *[Sarcastically]* You'll stop at nothing, will you?!? You *shower* me with gifts. Last time it was half a pound of butter – way past its expiry date!

[He follows her round to the back of her house, where she starts hanging up some washing on the line. Peering down at her from over the wall, he continues with his pleading]

ARKWRIGHT: We were meant for each other. A man with a s-stutter needs a big target to make love to.

GLADYS: What a golden tongue he's got!

ARKWRIGHT: Who cleans the nipples on your windscreen washers for you? *I* do! *Me!* Devoted Arkwright! Have you no words of encouragement for me at all?

GLADYS: *[Sighing]* Save me a small brown loaf, unsliced, and two large tea cakes.

Granville, meanwhile, is craving information. Blind faith is no good to him, in spite of Arkwright's advice to adopt such an attitude. 'How do you know the price was right,' he asks his uncle as he studies the piles of tins, 'if you don't know what's in 'em?' Arkwright's glib insistence that they should both trust his 'r-razor sharp instinct' for such things – a 'powerful b-but primitive' compulsion to bid for dirt-cheap anonymous tins – fails to satiate the young man's hunger for education.

Just the sight of a woman passing by outside is enough to make Granville, painting new signs on the window, re-style his 'w' into a pair of pert little cheeks. Just the mention of the notorious 'woman at number 87' is enough to make his eyes go wide with wonder. He knows just enough to know that he does not know enough.

'I've never had any of the things that other young men take for granted,' he groans as he gently squeezes a couple of pleasantly pliable sliced loaves. 'You'd b-better *not* have had either!' exclaims his reluctant surrogate father. 'If I ever c-catch you ever having *have* had, you will be in trouble!'

Too much thought, he is warned, will only keep making him 'emotionally knotted'. His brain, nonetheless, refuses to stop buzzing: 'What is the point of being on the threshold of life if you've always got to wear a flaming *pinny*?'

'You don't know you're born,' sneers Arkwright dismissively. Granville, however, realises glumly that it is actually far worse than that: 'I don't know much about what *causes* it, either!'

By the end of the episode, neither character has managed to blunder his way into anything like real enlightenment. Arkwright has failed to convince Nurse Gladys that she needs to have a look at the top of his leg, and is once again reduced to watching her through binoculars as she gets on with the ironing. Granville, even though he has managed to make a delivery to the woman at number 87, has returned with the wistful admission that, 'when the time came for me to jiggle it a bit I found I hadn't had enough experience'.

All that is confirmed, as the long day comes slowly to a close, is that both of them, still loveless and label-less, are stuck with each other:

ARKWRIGHT: Listen, Granville, just remember that, as my nephew, all of these old tins will be yours, y'know, when I'm gone.

GRANVILLE: Ah, yes, but will I be able to withstand the notoriety? I mean, they'll be nudging each other as I walk down the street. And they'll be saying: 'Ey-up, there he goes! You see him? Well, you wouldn't believe it to look at him, but he's *rolling* in old tins!'

There were no fierce fights or bitter battles. No final lines were crossed. There was just more of the same old pragmatism that gets ordinary people through each day.

The solution to the problem of the mysterious tins was solved by putting up a sign that said: 'TINNED SURPRISE. THE ORIGINAL EDIBLE-BINGO. GET YOUR TICKETS HERE'. The solution to Arkwright's lust for Nurse Gladys, and Granville's lust for life, remained, predictably and appealingly, unresolved.

The opening episode ended, as all future ones would do, with a brief monologue from Arkwright, straining to make sense of life's latest lack of a lesson. Delivering his remarks from just outside his shop, reluctantly preparing to take back inside his commodities before the darkness creeps over and smothers them, he looks up grudgingly at the cosmos that he cannot control:

> It's been a long day. Th-That's a lot of sky to be a small shopkeeper under. I wonder if there's a planet up there somewhere with another Gladys Emmanuel on it, saying 'No' repeatedly in a strange tongue. *[Granville rides past on his bike, ringing his bell]* Ey up. That's that Gloria he's got in the carrier. Well, well, well! Passion on pedals. Squeals on wheels. At least he'll have something soft to fall on to. Oh Lord, let him increase in wisdom and experience without t-too much pain or having to come to me for more money.

Subsequent episodes in the series would maintain a similar blend of the profound and the banal. There would be musings on sex, money and mortality, and there would also be plenty of patter about the fading popularity of treacle, the inconvenience posed by the big bollard on Bridge Street, the considerable cachet to be had from being seen out with a full tin of cocktail biscuits, the weight of the dust on the floor and how many 'p's there should be in 'p-p-p-p-pepper'.

Both Arkwright and Granville would be seen doing their best to fight against the suspicion that their life is slipping away. Each one would be battling back in his own distinctive manner.

Arkwright, from one instalment to the next, would seek to defy any creeping thoughts of decrepitude with constant thoughts of pulchritude (a strategy symbolized in one episode by his bid to seduce Nurse Gladys inside the back of a converted hearse). Granville, on the other hand, would respond to his feelings of deprivation with daydreams and bike rides (sounding like a veritable Thoreau bobbing over the cobblestones and fussing over the crusty cobs).

Arkwright's favourite way of lifting his sagging spirits is by flirting with Nurse Gladys, who, it soon becomes clear, rather relishes the routine of resisting his advances:

ARKWRIGHT: There's a cold front coming in from the Atlantic. You ought to g-get something a bit warmer around your chest. Like a hot shopkeeper.

GLADYS: And what makes you think *you're* more appealing than an extra vest?

ARKWRIGHT: You're a big bonny lass, y'know. If we don't get engaged soon I won't have time to explore all of you, will I?

GLADYS: Have you tried loosening your collar?

ARKWRIGHT: No, no, no. What *I* want to do is to t-try loosening *yours!* Do you know, I've never looked down a s-state registered nurse?

GLADYS: It's that shop that's doing it to you. You're stuck in there all day, every day, breathing in that spicy mixture of firelighters and lavatory cleaners.

ARKWRIGHT: Look, why d-don't we get *engaged?* Then I could give you a discount!

GLADYS: Why don't we just stop as we are – having a laugh and a joke with you goosing me occasionally? When I'm not looking![113]

It does not take too long before the two of them are sharing their own little private language composed of shopping and sexuality, coupling thoughts relating to copulation with words referring to commodities:

GLADYS: Have you got one of them nice big round cottage loaves?

ARKWRIGHT: No, but you have.

GLADYS: That'll do!
ARKWRIGHT: All I've got is a small wrapped Wonder Roll.
GLADYS: Save it for me.
ARKWRIGHT: It's yours any time you want it. Well, you know
              that, I've told you that before.[114]

There are times when he seems a little bit too desperate, such as the occasion when he pops up outside her bedroom window (ARKWRIGHT: 'Er, just passing.' GLADYS: 'On a *ladder?*'), but he usually recognizes the rules of their relationship, which are there for her to make and for him to break. 'I reckon w-we could make a go of it,' he reflects at one point, 'once she stops kicking me in the groin.'

It was equally inevitable, as the series progressed, that Granville's readiness to dream of a better life, and Arkwright's fear of seeing his current life get worse, would regularly spark some classic *Steptoe & Son*-style exchanges:

GRANVILLE: *[Dreamily]* Happiness is a game for two players.
ARKWRIGHT: You used to like t-train spotting. What
              happened to your train spotting?
GRANVILLE: I wish we'd still got an empire.
ARKWRIGHT: Yes. A p-pity they pulled that down, wasn't it?
GRANVILLE: I'd have liked to spend the monsoon season
              with a Eurasian mistress. Y'know: come back
              after a hard day flogging the natives, and there
              she is, waiting...
ARKWRIGHT: Yes, with almond eyes and 83 relatives on the
              borrow.
GRANVILLE: *[Slicing potatoes]* It's not that I want to be
              promiscuous. Well, yes it *is*, really, but I can't
              afford it. I'd settle for one, nerve-tingling,
              affair...
ARKWRIGHT: Hey, w-watch what you're doing with them
              chips – they're 7p each now, y'know!
GRANVILLE: Yeah, before I settle down for good, I'd like to
              have a spot of colour in me life.

ARKWRIGHT: Yeah, and when they turn up, them coloured
                         spots, you'll be sorry!
GRANVILLE: I'd like to tame some very spoilt, very rich,
                         young woman, y'know: 'HEIRESS ELOPES
                         WITH SHOPKEEPER'S ASSISTANT'.
ARKWRIGHT: Is *that* what you want to be, eh? An international
                         playboy on the Riviera circuit?
GRANVILLE: Yes.
ARKWRIGHT: What? And throw up the only agency around
                         here for Vac Sweep??[115]

Something that seems to capture the contrast in their characters, on a regular basis, concerns their mutual fear of the ferociously resistant spring clip that has to be encountered whenever there is another note to put in the till. It threatens Arkwright with commercial castration every time that it snaps at his money-loving fingers, while, for Granville, it harbours a hazard that symbolizes castration on every other conceivable level.

Arkwright tries to treat it as a kind of classical challenge, a great enemy to overcome by 'j-jiggling it about a bit', whereas Granville regards it as a sign of how stunted his life still is, obliging him, over and over again, to grapple with a mere metal spring when he could and should be grappling with experienced women, exotic cultures and complex philosophical conundrums. For the former, it is just one of those onerous things in life that any grown-up has to face up to and survive, while for the latter it is one of those things that a young man should surely be free to shun in favour of having some proper fun:

GRANVILLE: If you're going to risk that vicious spring clip I
                         don't want to look. You just tell me when it's
                         all over.
ARKWRIGHT: Oh, don't be daft! You only have to j-jiggle it
                         a bit!

[He forces the note under the clip and then snatches his hand out just before the spring snaps back down]

70

GRANVILLE: One of these days your reactions are going to get slower. Now, have you any instructions – do you want your fingers burying or cremated?

ARKWRIGHT: I want them round your earhole if you don't get something done in this shop![116]

With the spring clip representing the closest thing to real danger from one day to the next, the episodes flowed by low on incident but high on humour. Arkwright would get stuck with Spoonerisms ('Don't crit there siticizing!'[117]) when he would have much preferred to have got stuck into spooning ('I thought I'd pulled it off this time. Fortunately it's only bruised'[118]), while Granville would trudge through all of his chores thinking of the maxim 'gather ye rosebuds while ye may', only to find, once he was at last free to go out, 'there's nowt left but thorns'.[119] Nurse Gladys, meanwhile, was usually too busy rushing off 'to stick things in people',[120] or look after her housebound mother, to even have time for something as tamely titillating as sharing a spot of tea from the safety of the front room.

There were no hugs, no tears and no lessons. There was just Arkwright's brief monologue at the end of each week, delivered from outside his shop in the moonlight, mulling over what little had happened to Granville, Nurse Gladys and himself, but always leaving the loose ends loose:

That G-Granville, you might know he'd f-fall on his feet. Or on this particular occasion on his head. Trust him! Mind you, I think I can trust him with her. That's one of the advantages of a sh-sheltered upbringing. You haven't got the know-how to muscle in on your uncle's territory. Oh, and w-what territory: them lovely rolling acres! Part of the national heritage is G-Gladys Emmanuel. Oh God, don't let the socialists n-nationalize her![121]

Probably the most impressive and memorable episode was the penultimate one in the series, because it blended all of the various themes and relationships together in a particularly vivid and interesting way. Entitled 'Well Catered Funeral', it featured all of the usual elements relating to sex, money, family and mortality while also telling an entertaining tale, at a pleasant, leisurely pace.

It begins with the news that one of Arkwright's oldest friends, a nut-brown ale-loving fellow called Parsloe, has passed away. 'He went very quick at the end,' reflects one local gossip. 'He went v-very quick at both ends,' reflects Arkwright.

The fact that poor Parsloe was last seen in the shop as recently as last Tuesday, looking 'as large as life', prompts Granville to ponder, yet again, the injustices of existence. 'What's so large about life?' he mutters miserably, parking a 2lb packet of sugar down on the counter. 'So far my life has been about three foot nine. It's had no magic nor magnificence about it!'

Talk of another person's demise (and the tangled love-life that he left behind) serves only to spark thoughts of his own existential angst:

Why is it I never get involved in these powerful little human dramas, eh? I mean, it's not as though I'm not available. I mean, you'd think the word would get about that here I am on the threshold of manhood, willing to be coaxed out of me bicycle clips. I mean, I could be lured away from stacking carrots by the first determined, mature woman to come along.

Arkwright, in contrast, is merely cheered by the fact that he has been charged with the task of arranging the catering for after the funeral, having received a generous posthumous payment from Parsloe for some boiled ham and buns. There is even the prospect of adding some Eccles cakes to the spread.

The more that Granville reflects on the idea of mortality, however, the more rattled and restless he becomes:

GRANVILLE: Where are we *going* with our lives? Eh? I mean, the struggle – what's it all in aid of? The morning of a funeral, Uncle, should give you some moments of concern.

[He hops up and sits on the counter]

ARKWRIGHT: Well don't sit on the penny chews!

GRANVILLE: I mean, where is it all *leading* to?

ARKWRIGHT: Look, p-people don't want to eat a penny chew when it's been s-sat on!

GRANVILLE: Haven't you ever stopped to consider about the *quality* of life?

ARKWRIGHT: I would do if I had to eat that penny chew! Look at it – it's all bent!

GRANVILLE: Look: *[rings doorbell]* do you know what that sound is? Do you know what that *is?*

ARKWRIGHT: Yes, I do. It's the fight bell. It means s-seconds out and let's get some m-money in the blue corner.

GRANVILLE: No. That is *life* passing us by! That is *mortality*. Old age. Sickness. Death.

ARKWRIGHT: Ah, that reminds me: we're getting very low on moth balls.

GRANVILLE: 'Ask not for whom the bell tolls, it tolls for thee.'

[The telephone starts ringing]

ARKWRIGHT: Just as long as it d-doesn't try to reverse the charges, that's all.

No matter how long the debate goes on, however, Granville's search for common ground with his uncle only finds common chasms. The more that he states his aim to suck out all the marrow of life, Arkwright's mind turns to the marrows on sale in the shop:

GRANVILLE: There's a whole world outside that door that I've never even sampled!

ARKWRIGHT: You've nearly had the wrappers off that M-Maureen once or twice!

GRANVILLE: I'm not talking about *that*. I'm talking about adventure, romance, the arts! I mean to say: when did we last have a natter about, er, despair in the works of Dostoevsky?

ARKWRIGHT:	*[Sarcastically]* Oh, it m-must be *ages!*
GRANVILLE:	What do you think of modern theatre?
ARKWRIGHT:	Filth!
GRANVILLE:	You see? What *can* we talk about?
ARKWRIGHT:	*LIFE*, you dozy prong! Life! It's all going on out there. Up and down the street. In and out the windows. It's not in *books!* You've got your head f-full of intellectual f-fluff.
GRANVILLE:	It's an intellectual world.
ARKWRIGHT:	And look where it's got us. Where's my tea?

Nervously leaving Granville behind in temporary charge of the shop (ARKWRIGHT: 'It's my business that's at risk if you ruin it, isn't it?' GRANVILLE: 'What, in one morning?' ARKWRIGHT: 'World War T-Two started in one morning – and look what *that* did to the grocery business!'), Arkwright sets off for the funeral, where he hopes the neutral ground in church will enable him to negotiate a pact with Nurse Gladys Emmanuel. His hopes of impressing her, however, fall badly flat once the collection plate is passed around. Having come out with only a roll of notes in his pocket, he disgraces himself by insisting on taking back some change.

Gladys, though appalled, still agrees to join Arkwright and Granville for supper in the back room of the shop, where, sitting around a table boasting plates of sliced bread, sausage rolls, pickled onions and half-bottles of pale ale, they actually resemble the unconventional nuclear family to which, deep down, each one of them knows that they belong:

ARKWRIGHT:	It's been a funny old day.
GRANVILLE:	Aye, it has for me an' all. That shop bell has never stopped ringing. Half the time it was you.
ARKWRIGHT:	I told you, I d-don't like to be away from the shop for too long.
GLADYS:	Oh, in that case, what's all this loose chat you've been giving me about going on honeymoon?
ARKWRIGHT:	Oh well, there are *some* things for which I'm willing to make an exception. *[He proffers*

	her a pickle fork] Have you had an onion tonight, yet?
GLADYS:	*[Grimacing]* No! *[Returning to her theme]* What *sort* of exception?
GRANVILLE:	Ah, now's your chance, Nurse! The world is your oyster! He'll take you anywhere – within cycling distance!
ARKWRIGHT:	Listen, why don't you g-go out and enjoy yourself, eh, Granville, eh? Or go out anyway! You're always squawking about never having any time off.
GRANVILLE:	The rest of the day's me own? Look at that *[points at his watch]* – it's nearly bedtime!
ARKWRIGHT:	*[Looking excitedly at Gladys]* That's true!
GLADYS:	Not round here it isn't! Not if I don't get a decent honeymoon!
ARKWRIGHT:	Oh, all right, well, where do you want to go then?
GLADYS:	Tahiti. But I'm open to suggestions. What did *you* have in mind?
ARKWRIGHT:	Well, I thought we might, er, b-borrow Dickie Jowett's boat and cruise the inland waterways.
GLADYS:	Where exactly?
ARKWRIGHT:	Well, I quite favour the stretch of canal between here and M-Mulberry Street.

[Gladys scowls and takes a swig of ale]

ARKWRIGHT:	Well, don't go all National Health about it! I mean, it's all *water*, in't it?
GLADYS:	How can you tell? It's such a mucky colour! And if we got all the way to exotic Mulberry Street, you'd barely be able to hear the shop bell!

The unofficial family meeting then breaks up, with Gladys going home to check on her mother ('I'm making no promises,' she calls out when

Arkwright urges her to 'hurry back') and Granville wandering off dolefully on his own down the dark and deserted street ('Sometimes, if you're lucky, you can find all sorts of moths to watch'). It is the first little hint, however, that these three characters, trapped together in the same little corner of town, can cope with each other, in spite of all the little niggles, rather well.

The series then came to a close, on 26 March, with Arkwright entering into an uncharacteristically bold but ill-advised experiment with modern self-service shopping (turning the store into 'an Aladdin's cave choc-a-block with the irresistible treasures of an advanced c-consumer society!') It was, of course, never going to work (far from becoming the intended 'c-c-c-customer trap', the cluttered new central display serves only as a 'little grotto for shoplifters'), and, before the dust has been allowed to re-settle, Arkwright is left on his own in his usual place to have the final say:

> That c-central display is coming down tomorrow. The run-free tights with the s-special offer on the back will be tucked away where they belong – next to the meat paste. Them apples will get sold eventually I suppose. They'll just go soft, that's all. Well, after all, that's life, isn't it? To hell with s-self-service, I say. Tomorrow we start with a new motto: 'G-God help those who help themselves!'

The series had received a mixed reaction from the critics. By far the most negative opinion had been that of *The Guardian*'s Peter Fiddick, who, after watching the first two episodes, subjected the show to a strikingly dismissive critique.

Fiddick claimed that Roy Clarke 'seems to have two styles': one being 'cohesive, integrated, all the jokes welling from the situation, strikingly original and very funny' (*Last of the Summer Wine* was cited as an example) and the other (which he felt *Open All Hours* epitomized) 'composed of what one can only call gag-shows, situation comedy in which the situation is not so much the foundation for the comedy, more the estate agents' blurbs'. He went on to say that, as far as this new show was concerned, 'all the viewer can do is sit there and watch the gags being fed into the machine. All the actor can do is hope to pick them off, one at a time.' He concluded acidly: 'I won't say I didn't laugh. In half an hour of well-seasoned jokes, you can't get it all wrong. But I will say I felt I could have written it myself.'[122]

'That was normal for me,' the always self-deprecating Roy Clarke would later say. 'I always get bad reviews!'[123]

It was, as premature dismissals of a sitcom go, an exceptionally patronizing piece of work, especially as Fiddick – a very able television critic but, contrary to his boast, no writer of comedy – was experienced enough to know better. It was, nonetheless, soon eclipsed by several more measured and generous accounts, including one by Hazel Holt in *The Stage*, who lamented the fact that this 'delightfully idiosyncratic' sitcom had been 'sadly neglected' by many of her colleagues,[124] and another by Fiddick's *Guardian* colleague Nancy Banks-Smith, who wrote after the third episode that she found the show 'a comedy series of considerable charm'.[125]

The most positive feedback came from among the ordinary viewing public. Averaging approximately 6 million viewers per week (with a high of 7.5 million and a low of 4.8 million)[126] – which was, by the standards of BBC2 at that time, an above-average-sized audience – the show also received what was a generally very warm response from the in-house surveys that the BBC conducted. Two formal audience research reports were produced and distributed internally at the time – one based on a panel being questioned about the first episode in the series, and the other one about the final episode – and both of them suggested that the show had been a success.

Responding to the opening edition, it was noted that, of those who had graded the programme in terms of its overall quality, the majority were split between awarding it a 'B' or an 'A', with the next largest group opting for an 'A+' – which, when added up and evaluated, was calculated as giving the show a 'Reaction Index' (the scale of appreciation) of 66.[127] As the BBC's traditional average Reaction Index for an entertainment programme was about 63,[128] this represented a reasonably solid start.

Moving on to summarize the various responses, the report said that the episode had 'amused the bulk of the reporting audience, who appreciated the "original" basic idea and somewhat "earthy" comedy ("not a word or situation wasted") arising from Arkwright's interest in the attractive district nurse'. There was also said to be widespread praise for the performances of the cast (with the 'first class' Ronnie Barker being 'ably supported' by David Jason and Lynda Baron), as well as nostalgic affection for the corner shop situation (which was said to have given a 'life-like impression of a "chock-a-block" grocer's from "pre-supermarket days"').

On the negative side, just over a quarter of the sample were 'slightly disappointed' that the show, though 'good for a few laughs', did 'not quite match *Porridge* or other series in which Ronnie Barker had appeared', while a small minority complained about the fact that the programme 'had no real plot' and was too reliant on 'vulgar' humour ('Oh dear, an awful lot of gazing at female bottoms and knickers'). There was also a 'handful' of viewers who found Arkwright's stutter 'rather tasteless' and considered it merely 'a sign of paucity of material' (although the BBC only actually received two letters of complaint about the speech impediment, and Barker, much to his relief, had a complimentary letter from a family of five stutterers who told him they had spent days after each episode laughing about it and sending each other up).[129]

In general, however, the majority of the panel seemed keen to applaud. 'This,' concluded the report, 'was evidently quite a promising start to a series which several, looking forward to next week's episode, were apparently already convinced was "bound to be a winner".'[130]

The second report, on the closing episode, was even more encouraging. Scoring an excellent Reaction Index of 72, the opening comments were eye-catchingly enthusiastic:

> Tonight's episode, the sixth and last, brought the series to a successful conclusion. The preoccupations of Arkwright the grocer, his nephew Granville and Nurse Gladys Emmanuel proved a rich vein of comedy for writer Roy Clarke; a large majority of the sample finding it very funny: 'a breath of fresh air, simply superb', 'real honest-to-goodness entertainment'. One reason for the favourable response was the unusual nature of the relationship between the characters, different from the normal pattern of domestic situation comedy. Moreover, the setting in a corner shop

and not too unbelievable situations materially increased the humour. The dialogue was witty and crisp, several of the reporting audience also remarking on its consistency: 'keeps the same high standard from week to week', 'I always look forward to this and I've never yet been disappointed', 'there's always plenty of laughs'.[131]

There was still, inevitably, a tiny minority who found some faults. One or two protested that the humour was too predictable, and 'tried too hard for laughs'. Another complained that the sitcom 'lacked a certain something', although he or she was uncertain as to what that certain something actually was, saying merely that there was 'something missing – it doesn't sparkle like a comedy show should'.[132]

The vast majority of the responses, however, were full of admiration for all aspects of the production. These panellists declared that they were 'delighted with all three principals', not only for their individual performances but also for their ability to serve as foils for each other: 'Lynda Baron and David Jason are a perfect match for Ronnie Barker'. Jason, in particular, attracted plenty of praise, with many judging him 'the surprise of the series' and 'the find of the show' because of the pleasure they derived from 'watching his personality develop over the weeks to the stage where he was no longer overshadowed by Ronnie Barker'.[133]

There was also, once again, a great deal of appreciation for the context of the comedy, with the nostalgic element still very evident. 'The appearance of the shop itself,' noted the report, 'seemed to coincide very well with what those reporting remembered of their local store: "it's so like the one that used to be on the corner of my street, just a nice big muddle", "glad we saw it from the outside as well". Criticism of [this aspect of] the production was virtually non-existent.'[134]

The conclusion was very positive, even though the report strained hard to seem scrupulously fair and balanced:

Viewers were asked their opinion of the series (55% saw five or six, 33% three or four and 12% one or two) and, although a tiny number would not welcome further visits to Arkwright's shop as the idea, they felt, lacked sufficient depth to carry even six episodes, there was evidently a strong current of feeling that the idea was well worth exploiting further: 'another series is a must – there's so much potential in it', 'please can we have more, this was the highlight of my week's viewing'.[135]

With positive public feedback like this (even, in fact, with much more ambivalent feedback than this), countless BBC sitcoms in the past had coasted to being commissioned for a second series. This show, buoyed by this kind of audience response, certainly had good cause to look forward with confidence. *Open All Hours*, in spite of the lack of publicity, had managed to build up a strongly promising following, and looked quite capable of consolidating on this initial success.

There was, however, a problem. The powers-that-be at the BBC wanted Ronnie Barker to do something else. They wanted him to make another series of *Porridge*.

Open All Hours, they agreed, had proven itself to be a perfectly amiable and admirable new sitcom on BBC2, but, they pointed out, this was an increasingly competitive time in British television, and the BBC needed its biggest stars in its biggest shows – and that, for Ronnie Barker, meant returning to *Porridge* on BBC1.

Roy Clarke was not consulted. 'I'm a journeyman hack,' he later said without any hint of bitterness. 'By the time things are in production, I'm on to something else. I very rarely went into the BBC physically, so generally I was unaware of what was going on with any of these things. I only ever heard after the fact.'[136]

Ronnie Barker was invited into the discussions, but, it seemed to him, only as a matter of courtesy. He could sense that most minds had already been made up.

Neither Barker nor Clarke (nor, indeed, the rest of the cast and the crew) was happy about the decision. It seemed, after all, to have been set up as a self-fulfilling prophesy, because a new BBC2 sitcom was only ever going to attract a modest BBC2 audience, and was thus fated to look like a minor comedy offering.

The deal, however, was not really open for debate, and Barker, though frustrated, was proud enough of *Porridge* to respect the logic of the policy. Norman Stanley Fletcher was coming back, and Arkwright, once again, was going to be left out in the cold.

CHAPTER FIVE

The Longest Lunch Break

Ap-ply-ply your brakes, Granville!

The one time, during the whole of his prolonged absence from the corner shop, that Arkwright could be glimpsed in public was, improbably enough, when he met the Queen Mother. The occasion was the 1980 Royal Variety Performance at the London Palladium. Ronnie Barker, dressed in a flunkey's uniform, was waiting in the foyer to greet the royal visitor in the guise of Arkwright. 'Your puh-puh-programme, Your Majesty,' he stuttered. 'Lovely, Mr Arkwright,' she replied with a beaming smile. 'That'll be two guineas, please,' he added. Slightly startled, she looked down at her sparkly little evening bag and said, 'I don't think I have any money on me.' Barker nodded sympathetically and assured her that the bill would be sent on to Clarence House – 'VAT added!'[137]

It was a smart little stunt, and it also served to show that *Open All Hours* was still very much alive in the mind of at least one very important viewer, but it did nothing to appease those who had been waiting so long for another series. Like the white dot on an old television screen, the show had been shrinking into the distance as everyone associated with it moved on while it remained stuck back in 1976.

Ronnie Barker, for example, had duly made a return to *Porridge* for a third series in 1977, but then continued playing Fletcher in the 'sequel' sitcom *Going Straight* in 1978, as well as the movie version of *Porridge* in 1979. These projects, combined with his regular *Two Ronnies* commitments, meant that Barker had no real time for Arkwright during the latter part of the 1970s.

The other members of the cast were similarly busy. David Jason, in particular, was finding himself increasingly in demand elsewhere, first as the star of his own ITV sitcom, *A Sharp Intake of Breath*, which ran for four series between 1977 and 1981, and then, from 1981, in the BBC's *Only Fools and Horses*. The irony was that he had only been chosen for the latter show (he was actually fifth in line for the part[138]) after its producer/director, Ray Butt, had chanced upon an old episode of *Open All Hours* and been so impressed with Jason's performance as Granville that he decided to cast him as Del Boy.

Lynda Baron, meanwhile, was also working on numerous other productions, the most notable of which, as far as television was concerned, being the 1980 ITV sitcom *Grundy*, in which she appeared alongside Harry H. Corbett (in what turned out to be his last major role before his premature death in 1982). On the other side of the camera, Sydney Lotterby was immersed in a succession of significant and time-consuming projects, including Barker's own *Porridge* and *Going Straight*, as well as the first series of *Yes Minister* and *Butterflies* (both of them starting in 1980).

Roy Clarke, however, was probably the busiest one of all. Aside from being solely responsible for all of the scripts for the ongoing *Last of the Summer Wine*, which was returning every year to start another series, he was also writing a new sitcom called *Rosie* (which had evolved out of *The Growing Pains of PC Penrose*), which would run for four series between 1977 and 1981, and another one called *Potter*, which starred Arthur Lowe (until his death, after which he was replaced by Robin Bailey) and would run for three series from 1979 until 1983.

Everyone from *Open All Hours*, therefore, was now doing very well indeed. It was this, however, that seemed to be making the return of *Open All Hours* so difficult. Nobody had a space for it in their diary.

'I suppose that was the only reason,' Roy Clarke would later say. 'I assumed, at the time, that other people just had a lot of other things to do. Ronnie, certainly, was that busy, and David was doing other things, so I guess that explains why the break was so long. But I'm only speculating. I don't know for sure. I did as I was told. They either wanted something next month or next year or later still, or they didn't want it at all. I just waited to be asked.'[139]

'That was indeed the only reason for the delay,' Jimmy Gilbert would confirm. 'It was simply down to the fact that everyone was too busy doing other things.'[140]

What made the prospect of *Open All Hours* making a return, even if all of the old team suddenly became available again, seem so much bleaker was the fact that there was no-one at the BBC who was strongly inclined to champion its cause. It was not that the show had enemies. It was just that it did not have good enough friends.

There were many executives who wanted plenty more series of *Porridge* or post-*Porridge* spin-offs, because that had become a brand that commanded the biggest prime-time following. There were also just as many who wanted to ensure that Roy Clarke was not left too drained by other projects to maintain the high standards that he was setting with *Last of the Summer Wine*, which itself was fast becoming another major ratings winner. *Open All Hours*, as a consequence, just seemed to slip from some executives' minds.

Someone over at the commercial wing of the BBC did think that it was at least worth commissioning a 'novelization' of the first series of episodes (a fairly common practice in the pre-home video age), and Christine Sparks' *Open All Hours* duly went into print early in 1981,[141] but that was as far as any activity went. There were no plans to bring the show back to the screen.

There was, ironically, more interest in the sitcom at this time among programme-makers in America than there was from its own British broadcaster. The Americans, however, did not want to show it there. What they wanted to do was to 'adapt' it for a US audience.

The format rights were secured soon after the first British series had been broadcast (thanks in large part to the efforts of Bernie Brillstein, a very effective agent, manager and 'TV packager' who would later rise to greater prominence as the co-founder, with Brad Grey, of Brillstein-Grey Entertainment, which was responsible for such successes as *The Larry Sanders Show* and *The Sopranos*). Produced by Brillstein, the US version would be written by a large team overseen by the duo of Tom Patchett and Jay Tarses (who had previously worked on, among other projects, *The Bob Newhart Show*).

Entitled *Open All Night*, it was adapted in the most predictable American way, shifting the location from a corner shop in a suburb of Doncaster to a small convenience store in a suburb of Los Angeles, and changing the characters from Arkwright, his nephew Granville and his girlfriend Nurse Gladys to a 7-Eleven manager called Gordon Feester (played by George Dzundza as 'a good man trying to get by'[142]), his flaky wife Gretchen (Susan Tyrrell) and her dim-witted teenage stepson Terry (Sam Whipple). An African–American character – Robin, the philosophical night manager, played by the ex-American footballer Bubba Smith – was also added to the cast, as well as a pair of loveable and permanently peckish African–American police officers.

Making more use of the opportunity to feature plenty of one-off, and sometimes star, guest appearances (the chat show host David Letterman was one such celebrity 'customer') than it did of the chance to explore the interaction between the regular characters, it was a very different kind of sitcom to its British inspiration, relying on a conveyor belt of cold and unrelated gags to keep the audience entertained.

The most telling difference was the apparent aversion that the American show had to suggesting that any of its characters might not be, at least in essence, sweet-hearted and likeable people. In place of the chronically irascible Arkwright's money-grabbing misanthropy, for example, was the eminently huggable Feester's mild tetchiness, and instead of relying on Arkwright's amoral deviousness to solve certain problems, Feester was left to rely largely on a mixture of luck, love and the kindness of strangers.

The nearest that *Open All Night* came to matching some of the comical bite of *Open All Hours* was in the awkward relationship between Feester and his feckless stepson Terry, which reversed the Arkwright–Granville master–slave dynamic by making Feester keen on keeping Terry *out* of the family business:

FEESTER:	Get cleaned up, will you? It's almost time for your shift.
TERRY:	Six to six-fifteen? Some shift!
FEESTER:	Well, if you want eventually to be night manager, that's how you start.

84

TERRY:	Fifteen minutes at a time? You'll be *dead* before I get a whole shift!
FEESTER:	Exactly!
TERRY:	Short hours and doodly-squat wages!
FEESTER:	A dollar for fifteen minutes. That's pretty good pay for a buffoon!
TERRY:	Who are you calling a buffoon?
FEESTER:	You!
TERRY:	Just checking.[143]

First broadcast on the ABC network on 28 November 1981 as a mid-season replacement for another cancelled show, it was praised by many of the critics (and won an award for its writing), but failed to perform well enough in the ratings, and was itself cancelled after 13 episodes in March 1982. The idea, however, of using a format in which a potentially endless procession of people could come, cue up a gag and then go away again certainly impressed quite a few producers at the time, and it was at least apt, if seemingly coincidental, that two of the show's best writers, David Isaacs and Ken Levine, would return to the conceit when they were recruited to work on *Cheers* (1982–93).

The fate of the original *Open All Hours*, on the other hand, took an unexpected turn for the better towards the end of the 1970s. The catalyst for this came not from America but Australia.

The reason was that, early on in 1979, Ronnie Barker and Ronnie Corbett decided to spend the best part of the year together, with their respective families, in Australia, where, among other things, they were to make a special edition of *The Two Ronnies* for the Nine Network. Meanwhile, back in Britain, the BBC found itself without any new material from its two stars, so it decided to fill the gap by repeating the first series of *Open All Hours*, only this time on BBC1.

Shown during April and May of 1979, it attracted much larger weekly audiences (with a peak of 12.2 million[144]) than it had done three years earlier on BBC2, thus appearing to vindicate Ronnie Barker's belief that it had been in the wrong place at the right time. Although there was still no great groundswell of support for the show inside the Corporation, the combination of the excellent audience figures with the positive feedback convinced Jimmy Gilbert, who by this stage was the BBC's head of light entertainment, that the sitcom deserved another chance.

On 18 January 1980, therefore, Roy Clarke was asked to write a second series.[145] His fee would be £2700 per script (he was getting £3000 for *Last of the Summer Wine*), with Ronnie Barker earning £4000 (a huge amount for the BBC in those days, and at least twice as much as most of its other leading sitcom stars were receiving[146]), David Jason £950 and Lynda Baron £550 per episode.[147]

Both Clarke and Barker were pleased to have the chance, as soon as their diaries would allow it, to reunite the team and finally revive *Open All Hours*, but it was David Jason's eagerness to resume his role as Barker's sidekick that really underlined what a strong bond still tied everyone involved together. Jason, after all, was now – with one starring vehicle just behind him and another one just ahead – well on his way to emerging from out of Barker's ample shadow, and many other ambitious actors in his position might have passed on the chance to go back to playing a supporting role, but Jason did not hesitate.

He had grown closer to the man he called 'The Guv'nor' during the making of the first series. After each Sunday recording, the two of them would set off together to unwind at a little bistro near the Victoria and Albert Museum, where they shared a bottle of the house wine – 'battery acid', Barker dubbed it,[148] although they never struggled to finish it off – and made each other laugh. It was not long before Jason was also visiting Barker and his family for dinner, and their friendship continued to blossom as they sought each other out in their leisure hours.

It was a similar process at work, where the two of them, along with Lynda Baron and the rest of the crew, took great pleasure in being together. 'It's amazing,' Barker said one day in the rehearsal room. 'What do you mean?' Jason had replied. 'Look at us,' Barker explained. 'We're getting paid just to make ourselves laugh. It's not a bad life, is it?'[149] That was very much the mood of the whole team, and it was a major reason why Jason, like the others, was so pleased to come back to the corner shop.

There were, of course, a few concerns about how best to re-commence things after such an extended absence. Society, since 1976, seemed to have moved on – from the Winter of Discontent to the first spring of yuppiedom; and so had politics – from Labour to the Conservatives, from Butskellism to Thatcherism; as had popular culture – from punk to the new romantics, from family entertainment to alternative comedy.

Roy Clarke soon came to the conclusion, however, that it was better to leave the world of *Open All Hours* where it was. In an era that was dominated like never before by the big and impersonal supermarkets and the coldly anonymous shopping malls, the show's mildly nostalgic otherness (which had obviously been evident right from the start, but had now been lent another nuance by the fact that the new Prime Minister was herself the daughter of a Grantham grocer) would only add to the humour. There was also a certain degree of stubbornly unfashionable realism about the decision: contrary to the lazy city-centric assumptions of the time (let alone the over-generalizing popular histories about the era that would follow), there *were* still places like Arkwright's shop and little neighbourhood sprinkled all over Britain, and particularly in the old industrial northern towns, so the second series of *Open All Hours* was hardly betraying the present by seeming to be stuck in the past.

Once he had started writing – he had been given a deadline of 31 May 1980 to submit all the scripts – the old familiar feel for the situation flowed freely. One script – the seventh – would end up being rejected as 'unsuitable' and an alternative had to be written,[150] but otherwise the process was a straightforward and enjoyable experience. Clarke soon had the corner shop peopled by more quirkily representative customers from all areas of Arkwright Country, and it was as if the 'CLOSED' sign had not been on display since 1976.

When it came to the actors, however, there was a certain amount of anxiety about hiding the passage of time. Ronnie Barker did not have too much of a problem – all that he needed to do, to resume playing a character who was no longer quite so much older than himself, was to use a little less make-up and a slightly greyer and more natural-looking false moustache. David Jason, on the other hand, faced a rather more testing kind of challenge.

When he had first played Granville, in the pilot episode, he was 33, while the character was said to have been 25. By the time that the second series was set to be filmed, Jason would be almost 41 with greying hair and a bald patch, while Granville was still supposed to be a boyish-looking man whose age was thought to be 'thirty-ish'. It was obvious, therefore, that a certain amount of 'help' would be needed to make the portrayal still ring true.

After experimenting with various options in the make-up room, it was decided to pin a hairpiece at the back of his crown and then dye the rest of his own hair a suitable shade of black. Once a few more tricks of the trade had been applied to freshen up his face, he was ready once again to play the errand boy who is never allowed to grow up.

With their personal preparation complete, it was time for Sydney Lotterby to take the team back up to Yorkshire for another session of location filming. Lasting from 20 January to 1 February 1981, most of the shooting took place, as before, outside Helen Ibbotson's Beautique at 15 Lister Avenue, on the corner of Scarth Avenue, in Balby, and across the road at number 32 (which now served as Nurse Gladys's residence[151]).

It was always a hectic schedule, but never without plenty of laughter. 'It makes life easy, you know, if people are nice,' Lynda Baron later recalled. 'And if they're also clever, then it makes your job very easy as well.'[152] The average day involved filming enough footage for two episodes, with sometimes the arc lights still glaring as late as midnight. The BBC had found an empty house for sale nearby that served as the staff canteen on the ground floor. Barker and Jason shared one bedroom upstairs as their dressing room, while Lynda Baron was left to occupy the other.

The production team ensured that the salon was turned very swiftly into a grocer's, with not only the windows being clogged up with sundry cans and cartons and cola bottles, but also the pavement outside partially covered with everything from spuds, swedes and tomatoes to spades, shovels and Tupperware containers. Within a few hours it looked as though the wily old shopkeeper had never been away.

Almost all of the local inhabitants got used to seeing the crew and cast turning their street corner into Arkwright's cosy little world. There was only one, rather endearing, exception: an elderly local man often used to venture inside the shop to buy a box of matches, which someone from the crew would hand him, and then, once he had wandered off out again on his way, the filming would resume.

There was, once again, a great sense of camaraderie among the cast and crew, with the principal three actors relishing the opportunity to socialize together after each day's work. 'We were three mates,' Ronnie Barker would say. Lynda Baron agreed: 'Once you're working away, you become a family. And we did get on really, really well. But how could you *not* get on with two such *silly* men?'[153] They would meet up for dinner, drink plenty of wine, and generally relax and laugh. 'The three of us swapped anecdotes and experiences, teased each other, did a lot of talking and some damage to the *vin rouge*,' Barker later recalled. 'Lynda had this stock line when debates started: "No-one ever beats me in an argument, so don't try." David and I did try, though.'[154]

The very popular Sydney Lotterby, Barker revealed with great affection, 'would never eat with us. I asked him, "What do you do for dinner?" And he said, "Whisky and peanuts." But occasionally you could cajole him to come to dinner if it was a special occasion.'[155]

There were only a few isolated inconveniences. Inevitably, given the busy schedule, there were times when the actors were obliged to brave the bracing Balby weather for a late-night shoot, such as the time when Ronnie Barker had to spend what felt like an eternity lying down in a gutter with a dustbin on his head ('I think that's the coldest I've ever been in my life'[156]), and the odd occasion around midnight when a nearby resident would shout out from his bedroom window to ask how much longer the noise was going to last.

The only genuinely disturbing disruption the team ever encountered was when David Jason, while filming another night-time scene outside the shop, found himself face to face with a stranger armed with a knife. 'Suddenly,' he would later recall, 'a large middle-aged figure in dark, shabby clothing had come striding past the camera and was now standing right in front of me, brandishing a long, serrated blade and bawling meaninglessly. Funny how a certain kind of calm can descend on you in a situation like that. I suddenly looked at this man rather quizzically and said "Was there something you wanted?"'[157] A few moments later, two members of the crew managed to bundle the man off the set and police were called to the scene. 'The poor bloke turned out to live nearby and to be a fully paid-up member of the bewildered,' Jason explained. '[He] was just out and about with his bread knife. As you are.'[158]

Once the filming had finished, the team returned to London to prepare for the studio recordings. Rehearsals, as usual, took place at the 'Acton Hilton' from the last week in February.

Everyone was highly professional, concentrating hard during the first couple of days to ensure that the basic things were done properly so that they had something solid on which to build. Kathy Staff, who was back playing the gossipy Mrs Blewett, would later recall how impressed she was by the way that Ronnie Barker developed each episode's performance:

> Ronnie Barker's professionalism was a revelation. At the first 'plotting', he had to know exactly where everything was in that shop. 'Now where's the tea? Where's the sugar kept? Where's the butter?' And he had it all blocked in his mind, so he knew exactly whether to turn this way or that way. That is a real professional.[159]

Lynda Baron was similarly impressive. Thanks to her photographic memory, she was always the first to be word perfect after the initial day of reading and blocking. 'Lynda would come in the next morning,' David Jason would recall, 'and she would have absorbed everything from the previous day and be able to work without a script, while Ronnie and I were still fumbling with bits of paper and looking confused. Needless to say she was also DLP (dead line perfect), unlike me, who was still prone to the occasional gentle paraphrase.'[160]

Later on in the process, Barker, in particular, would find time for a certain amount of improvisation, using his stutter to explore the rhythms of the script and listen for the best of all the potential comic moments. Although Roy Clarke put Arkwright's stutters down on paper, Barker would often move them during rehearsals, sometimes elsewhere in the same line and sometimes in another line entirely, depending on what worked best for the ears rather than the eyes.

An example from this period is a remark in the seventh episode of the second series. The actual script went as follows:

> Hey up, he stair-stutters as well. It's bad enough having a slair-slight impediment in English. But what it must be like having to go through life stuttering in a foreign tair-tongue.[161]

After Barker had worked on it in rehearsal, however, it went like this:

> Oh dear, h-he stair-stutters as well. Oh dear, imagine. I mean, it's bad enough having a slair-slair-slair, it's bad enough having a slair-slair-slair, it's bad enough having a slair-slight impediment in English. But imag-imagine stair-stuttering your way through a fair-foreign tair-tongue.[162]

'It helped that Ronnie was a bit of a writer himself,' Sydney Lotterby would reflect. 'If he ever thought that something wasn't quite right about a script, he would take it home with him, and then the next morning he'd bring it back and it would be brilliant.'[163]

The other actors would also be trying out various minor revisions and elisions, respecting the script but also exploring the possibility of the odd alteration. Roy Clarke always gave his blessing to such experimentations. 'It had to feel right for them,' he later said. 'They were the ones who had to perform it.'[164]

There was still time for some light-hearted socializing during these sessions, especially at lunchtime. On the top floor of the building was a canteen, where, as David Jason would put it, there was a choice of 'egg, chips and beans, or chips, egg and beans, egg, chips and sausage, or sausage, egg, chips and beans'.[165] It was only a slight exaggeration, but the pull of the place had much more to do with the convivial mood rather than the limited menu. With so many top BBC shows being rehearsed in the same block, it was not at all out of the ordinary for stars from the likes of *Yes Minister*, *Juliet Bravo*, *Terry and June*, *The Hitchhiker's Guide to the Galaxy*, *Blake's 7*, *It Ain't Half Hot Mum*, *To the Manor Born* and countless others to congregate in the canteen for a break, and the cast of *Open All Hours* were happy to join them all. 'If you could time your lunch break to coincide with the arrival of the girls from Pan's People in their rehearsal leotards,' David Jason later recalled, 'you considered yourself doubly refreshed.'[166]

The set designers, meanwhile, were now able to reconstruct the inside of the shop without any real anxieties about provoking accusations of advertising. As Sydney Lotterby would recall:

There had only been one incident in the previous series. In one of the very first episodes, Ronnie or David – I can't remember which – was holding a cardboard box, and stamped right across it was the brand name. [It was actually Ronnie Barker, midway through the first episode, 'Full of Mysterious Promise', and the box bore the brand name Lucozade.] And it was almost in close-up. And my boss, Jimmy Gilbert, had said, 'Can you avoid this sort of thing from now onwards? There have been a few *words* about it…' But after a while no-one seemed to bother about it. There were so many products on show I think they all just blended into the background.[167]

The studio recordings commenced from Sunday 22 February, either in Studio 3 or 8 at Television Centre. The routine was the same as before: rehearsals from 10.30am to 6pm, followed by dinner, the warm-up and then the actual recording in front of a live audience from 8pm to 10pm.

The only moment of distraction came when the actors first stepped on to the studio set, which by this time was well on the way to being filled with all of Arkwright's essential comestibles. Bacon, Sydney Lotterby would recall, was a common problem:

Being a corner shop, there was always ham or bacon on the set. Now Ronnie, of course, was prone to being rather large, and therefore he wasn't allowed things like bacon and cheeses and biscuits and things of that sort inside his house. But on Sunday mornings in the studio, both he and David would slice off some bacon and get the prop boys to cook it for them. I'd come in and find them standing there stuffing themselves with bacon sandwiches before we rehearsed!'[168]

Everyone had his or her own way of preparing for a performance. Ronnie Barker, for example, liked to have a brief period after dinner when he could shut his eyes, focus on his lines and get himself ready to play Arkwright, but he also enjoyed watching furtively from the wings as Felix Bowness warmed up the audience. The others would join him shortly before they were due to be led out in front of the cameras.

Once the recording was over, the audience would depart, the crew cleared the set and the lights went out. This was the procedure, once a week, until all of the episodes were completed.

There was nothing left to do after that but wait, once again, for the show to be screened. Would people remember it? Would people want to return to it? Would people still laugh at it? All the team could do was hope.

CHAPTER SIX

Series Two

Ah! You hear that little tinkle?
Now THAT'S real!

It was a strange situation for a sitcom. Early in 1981, eight years after its pilot episode and five years after its first full series, *Open All Hours* was finally back on the screen – and it was still being treated by some as if it were an entirely new programme.

The Times, for example, billed the belated arrival of the second series as a 'new' Ronnie Barker vehicle, linking it to the contemporaneous launch of Ronnie Corbett's new sitcom, *Sorry!*[169] Similarly, *The Observer* listings described the show as 'a new comedy series from reliable *Last of the Summer Wine* writer Roy Clarke', as if he had just added a brand new string to his bow.[170] Whether this was due to ignorance, carelessness or forgetfulness, it certainly created the impression that *Open All Hours* was going to have to introduce itself, and prove itself, all over again to the Great British Public.

In today's hype-driven broadcasting climate, the imminent arrival of an existing sitcom, returning after a long break and featuring a major and much-loved star, would be treated to several weeks (at least) of pre-publicity, with everything from high-profile TV, radio, print and internet interviews to innumerable niche marketing campaigns and an eye-catching amount of tie-in merchandise, but, back in the early 1980s, there was next to nothing. The second series of *Open All Hours* was thus left to creep back on to the screen so quietly that its sudden presence probably struck some casual viewers as quite a surprise.

The one thing in its favour was that it was now to be shown, as Ronnie Barker had always wanted, on BBC1. It was scheduled for Sunday evenings at 7.15pm, in a shoulder shrug of a slot that was not the best for a mainstream sitcom (following straight on from *Songs of Praise*, with many people's moods now turning glumly to thoughts of getting ready for the return to work or the start of school on Monday), but at least it more or less guaranteed an audience of about three times, or more, the size the show might have expected on BBC2.

It started on 1 March, looking more or less as it had done, to those who could remember, five years before. The opening sequence had been re-filmed for the new series, with only a few minor concessions to acknowledge the passing of time. The corner shop was still subjected to a bird's eye view, and there were still two women walking past (although one of them, in a nod to changing fashions, was now wearing trousers instead of a skirt), the dreaded old delivery bike was still stuck by the kerb, and there was still the same desperately eclectic exhibition of groceries and sundry provisions on the pavement outside the premises. Only the prices displayed on the windows had altered: 'Heinz Soups, 36p' 'OXO Cubes, 27p' 'Firelighters, 15p'.

Rather like the two figures in a weather clock, Arkwright and Granville had swapped their order of appearance, with Granville now the first one out, either sweeping the floor or sometimes painting new prices and promotions in white on the window, followed shortly after by his uncle, standing just under a sign for Bird's Angel Delight, sniffing the early morning air for potential sales. It was, reassuringly for its fans, the same situation as before.

Running for seven episodes, rather than six, for this second series, the sitcom gleefully reprised many of the previous themes and conceits. There was, for example, the usual terror of taking on the till with its jaw-like snap action and its spiteful spring clip ('I'm going to open that up one of these mornings,' says Granville with a shiver, 'and find it full of loose fingers!'[171]), and the ancient delivery bike ('It's totally clapped out!'[172]) and Arkwright's legendary stinginess (ARKWRIGHT: 'It's not the money that counts, it's the thought.' GRANVILLE: 'How come you never think of anything worth more than a pound?'[173]), and his Sisyphean struggle to complete some of his sentences ('Eh, close yer mouth, there's

95

a double-decker bu-bu-bu-, there's a d-d-double, th-there's a d-d-double, there's a d-d-d-double, oh, don't bother, it'll have gone!'[174]).

There was also another procession of quirky customers (including a swarm of choking smokers and a woman whose shopping list is determined by the barks of her dog), and another cluster of classic Roy Clarke lines (for example, 'Her features never seemed to know the value of team work'[175]). Plots were still largely minimal or entirely absent, and the comedy mainly came, once again, from the interaction between the key characters.

Arkwright seemed, if anything, an even more ruthless selling machine than he did in the previous series, announcing edicts like an evangelist for the Protestant work ethic ('The Shopkeeper's First Commandment: "Thou shalt not be motionless"'[176]), explaining away his many acts of cynicism ('You c-can't afford s-scruples when you've over-bought!'[177]), dragging dilatory customers over the threshold and into the shop ('It's amazing, y'know, isn't it? You stock your shop with all kinds of imaginable luxuries, and still they d-dither on the doorstep!'[178]), and proving himself such a master of the dark arts of persuasion that he even sells cigarettes to non-smokers ('I mean, *I'm* a non-smoker myself and *I* smoke them. I find it g-gives you something to do with your h-hands'[179]). It was thanks to Ronnie Barker's artfully vulnerable acting that the character remained, in spite of his many seemingly irredeemable flaws, strangely amiable.

Granville, on the other hand, is still a Walter Mitty in a pinny, a dreamer on a delivery bike whose desperate desire for a better life seems destined to be defeated. From the very first episode, he is complaining about 'the difference in lifestyle between somebody like me and Frank Sinatra', and it is not long before he is fantasizing about 'cruising down the main drag in Las Vegas' and recreating Gene Kelly's dance routine from *Singin' in the Rain*. 'Before you let your mind wander,' he is warned, 'just make sure it's not too weak to be out on its own,'[180] but still the dreaming goes on. As with Barker's portrayal of Arkwright, it is largely down to David Jason (along with Roy Clarke's artful lines) that Granville remains endearingly sweet rather than irritatingly soft.

The strongest theme running like a thread throughout the whole series – and actually providing the sitcom with an additional element of soap opera – was the slow and still not entirely certain evolution of the relationship between Arkwright and Nurse Gladys Emmanuel. It was made clear, right from the first episode, that this dynamic was going to dominate, because it was quickly revealed that, at some point since these two characters had last been seen on the screen, Gladys had finally relented and agreed to get engaged to Arkwright:

ARKWRIGHT: How would you f-fancy a f-fun-filled fortnight in a sunny little corner of the room above me shop?

GLADYS: You're all mouth and trousers.

ARKWRIGHT: N-Not necessarily in that order.

[He cackles and moves to tickle her on the hips]

GLADYS: Keep away! Don't start grappling in the street!

ARKWRIGHT: You're all right – they all know we're g-going to be married.

GLADYS: They're not all invited to the dress rehearsal!

ARKWRIGHT: W-Well, what would you take for a swollen chest?

GLADYS: More than you'd pay.[181]

It did not take much longer, however, for the prospects of further progress to seem less than propitious. One problem was the unseen but obdurate presence within the Emmanuel home of Gladys's elderly mother, whom Arkwright rightly perceives to be a long-term threat to his chances of nudging the nurse all the way to the church: 'She can't stand me, y'know. She sits up there in her pink woolly bed jacket, spitting biscuit crumbs, doing this impersonation of someone who's going to live forever.'[182]

Another problem was that it was obvious, as Granville would never tire of telling his money-mad uncle, that Gladys was never going to tolerate sharing her husband with a shop:

GRANVILLE: I don't know why you don't give that up as a bad job. She's never going to marry you.

ARKWRIGHT:	We're engaged – why shouldn't she?
GRANVILLE:	Because your interests are not broad enough.
ARKWRIGHT:	Listen, she's broad enough for both of us.
GRANVILLE:	She wants a bit more out of life than somebody who can calculate percentages in his head.
ARKWRIGHT:	That's just a knack with me, that. I've been kn-knackered with that since birth.[183]

There would, as a consequence, be plenty of crises in the relationship, caused time and again by Arkwright's apparent inability to convince Gladys that his passion for her is even greater than it is for maximizing profits. There was, for example, the occasion when he surprised her by volunteering to take her off to a hotel for the night, only to spoil the effect by choosing a place about a hundred yards away where he could keep a beady eye on his shop via a pair of binoculars. There was also the time when he promised to expand his commercial concerns in order to provide Gladys with the funds for a future full of fun and luxury, but then could only bear to expand as far as sending out a few more goods in the back of a clapped-out ice-cream van.

What would stop Gladys from washing her hands of this tight-fisted materialist was the realization that, deep down, he was genuinely determined to make her his wife. She might have to work hard at deciphering his garbled declarations of devotion, translating his clumsy shop talk into something sounding more like the language of love, but he would certainly remind her – and even surprise her – often enough about his eagerness to lead her down the aisle:

GLADYS:	Have you really thought about it?
ARKWRIGHT:	You must be joking! That's all I ever *do* is th-think about it. I'll give you an example of how *much* I th-think about it: I was in the shop the other day – ay, you must promise not to repeat this...
GLADYS:	Get on with it!
ARKWRIGHT:	No, *promise!*
GLADYS:	Get *on* with it!

ARKWRIGHT: I was just serving Mrs Ellis with six ounces of
                        s-smoked bacon –
GLADYS: I love the association of ideas – me and bacon!
ARKWRIGHT: You haven't h-heard the worst yet.
GLADYS: What did you do?
ARKWRIGHT: Well, I didn't realize until after she'd gone: I let
                        her w-walk out through that door with six
                        ounces of p-prime smoked bacon!
GLADYS: What had you done?
ARKWRIGHT: I'd only ch-charged her for four![184]

She rolls her eyes and groans at such graceless stabs at romance, but
there is also just enough of a hint, behind the world-weary pose, that
she really quite likes the old rogue. There is still some distance for the
couple to go – she will need to be sure of his soul before he can be
certain of her body – but the partnership, in all of its current
imperfection, seems permanent.

Granville, meanwhile, is growing into more and more of an
unfulfilled figure with each passing episode. Although, by this stage, he
has been 'promoted' by Arkwright to the lofty non-position of 'Assistant
Manager', and is now free to paint new prices and promotions on the
front of the two shop windows (until, that is, his uncle barks out the
inevitable words: 'G-Granville, f-fetch a cloth!'), he is still deeply
dissatisfied about being stuck inside the shop.

'I feel ridiculous at my age,' he moans. 'Look at me: the virgin
grocer!'[185] Apart from a fleeting flirtation with the divorcée who delivers
the milk, he spends most of each day far away from females of a similar
age, rooted to the spot until Arkwright finally deigns to stop the clock:
'By the time I get where all the girls are it's like arriving late at the
market: all the best goods have been snapped up and all that's left is the
over-ripe stuff that everyone's been prodding and poking about.'[186]

Arkwright's response to his nephew's restlessness is to distract the
brain by keeping the body busy ('I know your sort: if I didn't t-turf you
out of bed of a morning you'd be lying around there gone seven!'[187])
and the bedroom cold ('Do you realize how many unnatural practices
are directly attributable to c-central heating?'[188]), while protesting that
his surrogate parenting does not deserve to be blamed:

GRANVILLE: Ooh, can I have a bun?

ARKWRIGHT: Of course you can have a bun. There are more than enough. Have I ever d-deprived you of anything?

GRANVILLE: Only a satisfactory love life.

ARKWRIGHT: Eat your bun. All right, are they?

GRANVILLE: *Mmm,* lovely. I didn't think you'd let me have one.

ARKWRIGHT: Oh, Granville, y-you *wound* me at times, y'know.

GRANVILLE: Oh yeah, like when?

ARKWRIGHT: Well, the time I s-sat on your bicycle clips springs to mind. How's the cream – is it nice in those?

GRANVILLE: *Mmmm,* it's lovely.

ARKWRIGHT: I'm not *really* mean to you, am I?

GRANVILLE: No, not to me. To everybody.

ARKWRIGHT: That's just a f-f-façade, that is. Remember, I b-brought you up from this high. *[He holds a hand level with Granville's left armpit]* Admittedly n-not very far.

GRANVILLE: All right, no need to rub it in. I know I'm too small for elegant women.

ARKWRIGHT: Yes, but l-look on the bright side, lad: you're just the right size for a nice sh-shop bike, aren't you, eh? *[He picks up a toilet roll decorated with 'inspirational' observations]* Here, you're getting all s-sticky, here, have a piece of this.

GRANVILLE: You're being very agreeable today.

ARKWRIGHT: Well, a little th-thoughtfulness never comes amiss.

GRANVILLE: Is that what it says there? *[Squints at sheet of toilet paper]*

ARKWRIGHT: N-No, *I* said that. No, here it says: 'A thought for today – Don't forget that y-yesterday was the tomorrow you worried about the day before yesterday'.

GRANVILLE: I don't get that.

ARKWRIGHT: No. Well, you get that. *[Hands him a sheet]* Here you are – wipe your hands. That'll be 50p exactly, please.

GRANVILLE: What – just for one bun??

ARKWRIGHT: No, no – and the toilet roll as well. Don't moan – I've knocked f-five pee off for you![189]

The greatest problem for Granville is that Arkwright hates change – he is still reeling from the realization that his new suit, which is otherwise identical to his old suit, now has a fly that zips instead of buttons – and the prospect of Granville being allowed to grow up represents, for Arkwright, too much change for change's sake. True, he is not best pleased to see Gladys, embracing the idea of being part of a budding family unit, sometimes offering Granville maternal comfort by pressing his head to her breasts ('You leave him alone,' she protests. 'Alone?' Arkwright replies. 'He's *not* alone, is he – he's got two friends in there with him!'[190]), but, deep down, he is terrified of any disruption to the status quo:

ARKWRIGHT: One day, Granville, all this will be y-yours, lock-lock-lock-lock-lock stock and barrel. I'm always telling you this.

GRANVILLE: Yes, I know – every time I ask for a rise. *[He starts sweeping the shop floor]* Anyway, supposing I wanted to get married…

[Arkwright, on hearing this, flies across the room and grabs Granville by the neck of his tank top]

ARKWRIGHT: *MARRIED?!?* Why sh-should *you* want to get *married?* What have you been up to?

GRANVILLE: No, no, I haven't been up to anything!

ARKWRIGHT: *Tell me!* I don't l-let you out until nine o'clock, you shouldn't have had *time!*

GRANVILLE: I *haven't* had time![191]

STILL OPEN ALL HOURS

Arkwright is fully prepared to combine the roles of guardian and gaoler if it means it will keep his nephew comfortably dumb (GRANVILLE: 'When am I going to start burning the candle at both ends?' ARKWRIGHT: 'There are *some* ends, G-Granville, where the last thing you want is a blister'). It is clear, nonetheless, that even some of the customers (even some of the odd ones) are starting to notice the effects on Granville of his rudely arrested development:

MRS BLEWETT: Granville, you're a bag of nerves!

GRANVILLE: Yes, I know, I'm sorry, it's me age. I've just reached that stage in my life when you're supposed to be all sexual tension and raw edges. You know, you try to talk to people and they think you're weird.

MRS BLEWETT: Calm yourself, Granville. Nobody thinks you're weird.

GRANVILLE: *[Wiping a trio of tea cakes with a cloth]* Yes, they do, they *do!* I mean, you try to have a frank conversation about things that really matter –

MRS BLEWETT: *[Spotting the tea cakes]* 'Ere! I'm not having *them!* They've been kicked all over the floor!

GRANVILLE: No, no, I'm not going to sell these to you, Mrs Blewett. That's unhygienic. I'll sell these to Mrs Tattershall. *[Gesturing with one of the tea cakes]* Why is it that people can never *communicate* deeper than talking about, well, the Government, or her at number 17 and 'will she find true happiness with her new fitted carpet?'

MRS BLEWETT: Oh, I don't think she stands a cat in hell's chance. For a start, it clashes with her three piece suite! Now, what she should have done in my opinion –

GRANVILLE: There you go! *Listen* to you! Mrs Blewett, we have known each other for ages. You have had seven children. Therefore you are a woman of wide human experience.

MRS BLEWETT: Not *so* damned wide! They were all from the same stable!

GRANVILLE: But I respect your experience, Mrs Blewett. I'd be fascinated to hear about it. *[Holding her hand]* All females to me are a magical mystery…

MRS BLEWETT: Don't be *stupid*, Granville! Give me a packet of them jam tarts.

GRANVILLE: If you'd just explain to me why it is never possible for people just to *talk* to me!

MRS BLEWETT: Because you're *WEIRD!*[192]

It was actually one of Granville's many fraying threads of neuroticism that ran through the centre of the final storyline in the series. Entitled 'St Albert's Day', it focused on Granville's obsession with finding out the identity of his father.

His dogged curiosity about the question had been evident in most of the previous episodes. A throwaway remark by Arkwright, light-heartedly suggesting that Granville's father might be a 'H-Hungarian' because 'he certainly dropped a goulash with yer mother',[193] is enough to start the wheels whirring in the young man's head:

GRANVILLE: Do you reckon he *was* Hungarian? I mean, she must have loved him, mustn't she, to have kept his identity a secret like she did?

ARKWRIGHT: Perhaps she c-couldn't pronounce it.

GRANVILLE: Yeah. Just think, if she hadn't met him, I wouldn't have been here.

ARKWRIGHT: You're not s-supposed to be here now – you're supposed to be out delivering!

GRANVILLE: No, it makes you think, though, doesn't it, eh? I mean, what a narrow line there is between who gets born and who doesn't get born. Just think: I could have been one of the nameless unborn.

ARKWRIGHT: D-Don't worry – I would've th-thought of something to call you![194]

By the time that the final episode comes around, therefore, Granville's genealogical fancies ('We may be *small*, us Hungarians, but we're neat, and we make wonderful horsemen!') have reached fever pitch. It only takes the arrival of a mysterious-looking foreigner to get him leaping to wild conclusions.

Arkwright – who, along with the local handyman, is distracted at the time by the need to stop the shop front door from sticking shut – is not even sure at first of the nationality of the stranger (HANDYMAN: 'He's one of those unpronounceable backward mob where no tourist ever goes twice.' ARKWRIGHT: 'Oh. W-Welsh is he?'), but, once it transpires that he is probably Hungarian, even Arkwright, worn down by having to endure so many instances of what he has come to dub Granville's 'I wonder who me father was days', starts to get suspicious. Wandering into the back room, he surveys his nephew, partly hidden behind his pinny, and cannot resist scrutinizing his features:

ARKWRIGHT: You don't *l-look* Hungarian.
GRANVILLE: Dressed like this I don't even look human! I think I *do* look Hungarian.
ARKWRIGHT: All right, well, where abouts, then? Where abouts do you think you look H-Hungarian? Is it your elbow or what? Nothing that sh-shows looks Hungarian.
GRANVILLE: I got, er, y'know, the, er, high cheek bones.
ARKWRIGHT: How could someone of *your* size have *high* cheek bones?? You've only j-just got *low* cheek bones!
GRANVILLE: Anyway, the milk woman reckons I've got gypsy-looking eyes.
ARKWRIGHT: Oh, yeah? Neither taxed nor insured, I know!
GRANVILLE: No, some days I just *feel* Hungarian.
ARKWRIGHT: You were f-feeling the milk woman when I caught you!

Once the stranger has come into the shop, however, Arkwright's anxiety about possible returning fathers is made worse by his more general fear about foreigners ('j-just standing there, looking foreign'), and he worries that he might be in the presence of an exotic shoplifter. Needing to find an excuse for Granville to check his pockets, Arkwright improvises hurriedly and manages to convince the visitor that such a brusque intrusion is one of the rituals associated with the ancient half-holiday called 'St Albert's Day'.

Having sent the Hungarian away feeling thoroughly befuddled ('He's fluent in rubbish,' mutters Granville, almost admiringly, of his scheming uncle. 'He speaks it like a native'), Arkwright has to cover his tracks as quickly as possible:

GRANVILLE: You thought he was my father, didn't you?

ARKWRIGHT: Never c-crossed me mind.

GRANVILLE: Look at me when you're lying to me!

ARKWRIGHT: What's for d-dinner?

GRANVILLE: Never mind what's for d-d-dinner! You *did*, you thought he was me father, didn't you, eh? Ha, 'St Albert's Day'!

Realizing that the fleeting exposure to the 'f-foreign fella' has left his nephew even more unsettled than usual, Arkwright resolves to do something about it. Confiding in Nurse Gladys, he persuades her to conspire with him in 'a little w-white lie' to rid him once and for all of his Hungarian obsession.

Joining Granville for a cup of tea, they plant the seed that he might have been spawned by royal loins, reminiscing about the time, supposedly nine months before Granville was born, when King George VI, complete with his stutter, came up to Leeds with 'a lot of f-foreign dignitaries'. The ever-impressionable Granville, upon hearing this, begins to look excited as Arkwright and Gladys pretend to ponder the presence of 'an English duke' ('a little fella' with 'gypsy eyes') who popped up to Doncaster for the races. Once the detail is added about his mother, who was waitressing at the races at the time, and went missing for a couple of days only to reappear with 'a big s-secret smile' on her face and clutching two 'enormous tins of Royal Doncaster B-Butterscotch' close to her chest, Granville's excited eyes are practically popping out of their sockets. 'I've *always* liked butterscotch!' he exclaims desperately.

Suddenly, all thoughts of Hungary have floated far away, because Arkwright is glancing back and forth appreciatively between a bank note and his nephew's face, and Granville is rubbing the inside of his shirt cuffs just like Prince Charles and saying 'one' when he really means 'I'. Relieved that Granville is at least dreaming in English once again, Arkwright wastes no time at all in urging his protégé back into his bicycle clips to attend to Mrs Horner's overflow.

It is, then, more or less as it always was, and it leaves Arkwright with one more monologue before the run is over:

> I wonder how much I lost to that damned door. Oh well, some days you just have to take the rough with the rough. It's been a funny St Albert's Day. I wonder if that Hungarian found his girl. 'Girl'. Ha ha. She'd be a right old boiler by now! Oh Lord, let me make that money back tomorrow. And perhaps extra for a rainy day. And please, Lord, try and change our Granville's mind. He's going to look ridiculous with a monocle.

The series was left to slip quietly away by the critics, who had seemed disinclined to discuss it throughout its seven-episode stay, but, in terms of viewing figures, the return of *Open All Hours* had been a great success. Averaging an audience of 11 million per week,[195] the show had been one of the BBC's most consistent performers (faring particularly well, rather intriguingly, in the south, east and west,[196] where, perhaps, its 'northern-ness' was seen as somewhat exotic), and, once again, the internal feedback had been very positive.

'I've always wanted,' said Ronnie Barker, 'to play one
of those guys who runs a little shop that sells everything'.

Sydney Lotterby, the show's much-admired producer/director.

The site chosen to serve as Arkwright's corner shop was
Helen Ibbotson's hairdresser's in the Doncaster suburb of Balby.

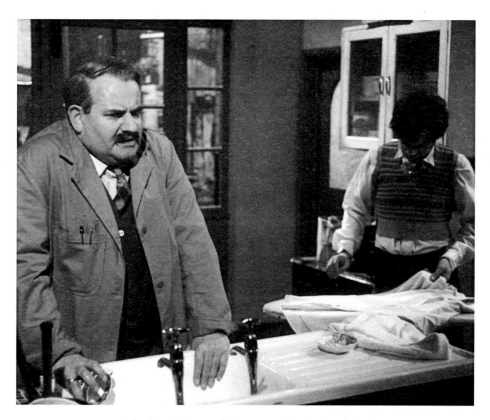

The beginning of the trapped relationship:
Arkwright and Granville in the 1973 pilot episode.

Arkwright with the original Nurse Gladys Emmanuel,
Sheila Brennan: 'It was just a joy to work with him,'
she said. 'He was such a generous actor'.

Yootha Joyce as one of Arkwright's earliest customers, the disreputable matriarch Mrs Scully. 'Would you get me half a bottle of sherry for our Claudine?' she asks. 'Well,' he replies, 'it sounds a fair exchange'.

Arkwright returns for the first series of *Open All Hours* in 1976.

Ready for business:
Lynda Baron arrives as
the new Nurse Gladys.

Lynda Baron in the
1960s: 'TV's
glamorous satire girl'.

Granville's romantic opportunities rarely stretch beyond a brief flirt with the alluring milk woman (played by Barbara Flynn).

The maternal touch: 'Come out of there, Granville!'

Arkwright waits in vain for the nurse-shaped bed warmer that he craves.

'We were meant for each other,' gasps the grappling grocer.
'A man with a s-stutter needs a big target to make love to!'

The master at work: Arkwright confuses a pedant
with a correctly spelt tin of baked beans.

The servant at work: Granville takes a breather from his despised delivery bike.

Three friends on location in Balby. 'How could you *not* get on with two such *silly* men?' reflected Lynda Baron.

Difficult customers: the nosy Mrs Blewett (Kathy Staff)...

the indecisive Mavis (Maggie Ollerenshaw)...

the dog-doting Mrs Tattersall…

…and the frightening Mrs Featherstone (Stephanie Cole).

An intrusion: Granville, who might be half-Hungarian,
encounters a proper whole Hungarian in 'St Albert's Day'.

An extraction: while Granville buries his head in a book,
his uncle steals a sausage in 'The New Suit'.

A happy family: Jason, Baron, warm-up man Bobby Bragg and Barker on the set for the fourth and final series in 1985.

'Here's Ronnie B,' Bobby Bragg recalls, 'improving one of my gags!'

Still Open All Hours: Lynda Baron and Sir David Jason are joined by new recruit James Baxter back in Balby in 2013.

Will Arkwright live on forever? 'I'm going to have a damned good try!'

PART
THREE

We've got to grab the casual customer.
Let me get me claws on him.

CHAPTER SEVEN

Arkwright Country

That's a lot of sky to be a shopkeeper under.

After watching *Open All Hours* for two series, viewers had come to feel that they knew its milieu. From the first sight of that dark grey little road, with its row of red-bricked bay-windowed houses completed by the cluttered shop on the corner, it was easy for people to associate it, via memory or myth, with their own notion of northern England.

It had arrived, as a pilot, in the same year that Ridley Scott's Hovis commercial first reached the television screen, and together the two of them seemed to nourish a powerfully nostalgic vision of the north. It might not have been an entirely accurate vision, and certainly not a comprehensive one, but, nonetheless, it touched the right nerve and set the right tone.

The Hovis commercial – which featured a small boy (dressed just like Granville in a cloth cap and pinny) pushing a big delivery bike laden with loaves up the steep cobblestoned street of a northern town, while the strains of Dvorak's 'New World' Symphony, arranged for a brass band, accompanied each weary huff and puff – was an open invitation to the national imagination, the best bit of past-prodding since, well, unsliced bread. Itself something of a musical echo of Peter Skellern's 1972 single 'You're A Lady' (in which the Bury-born singer was accompanied by the Hanwell brass band), this commercial wormed its way into viewers' heads and simply refused to wriggle away.

The advert was not actually filmed in the north of England at all. It was filmed on Gold Hill in Shaftesbury, Dorset. It *seemed* northern, though, and that was what mattered. A knowingly evocative snapshot of a popular cultural idea, it summoned up a whole inventory of memories, from cricket grounds to collieries, from taciturn farmers to brusque businessmen, from muck to brass, which summed up a traditional impression of the northern landscape.

Open All Hours, which also began with the same slow, mournful sound of a brass instrument, seemed to have a similar effect. There was the traditional-looking street – this time an authentic northern street – and the scattering of well-lagged Lowry-like passers-by, and the cosy-looking corner shop, and the stout, crusty-looking shopkeeper. At a time when many consumers were beginning to realize what a Faustian pact they had blundered into by forsaking the old little grocer for the new big supermarket – gaining more bargains but losing the sense of belonging – the familiar, intimate, organic sight of Arkwright's humble emporium represented quite a warm and welcoming sight.

Even the well-established brands on show in the shop window – Neville's Bread, Terry's Chocolate, White's Lemonade, Bird's Custard Powder, Will's Gold Flake Cigarettes, Nugget Boot Polish, Stone's Ginger Wine, Reckitt's Blue, Tartan Special Ale, Victory V Lozenges, PG Tips and Maid Marian tinned drinks – had a resonance that reminded one of a time or place where things seemed much more closely knit and deeply rooted.

Where was Arkwright's supposed to exist? To Roy Clarke, as the writer, it suggested somewhere in South Yorkshire close to where he had grown up. 'It was Doncaster,' he later said, 'and I guess, more specifically, a place called Thorne.'[197]

More generally, to other northerners, it could have suggested anywhere from Goldthorpe to Garstang, from Kirkstall to Carnforth, from next door to the neighbouring county. Many people merely had to look out through their window. To southerners, on the other hand, it could have fitted in fairly neatly somewhere or other on their own romanticized map of the north – turn right at the Coronation Street cobbles, turn right again at the top of Hovis Hill, turn left when you see the Railway Children and then go straight on down, past where Kes is flying over his field, until you reach the solitary shop on the street corner.

It did not really matter, so long as somewhere between the show and the viewer a strong enough connection was made. People begin to bond with a sitcom not just because of what the sitcom gives to them but also because of what they bring to it. Like two hands brought together for a loud round of applause, the strong combination of viewer and viewed is a mark of real sitcom success. The more that people watched the world of *Open All Hours*, therefore, the more that it meant to them, because viewers believed in it, thought about it and wanted to see more of what they imagined might be going on inside.

All great sitcoms inspire such curiosity among their most avid admirers. Whether it is the Walmington-on-Sea of *Dad's Army* or the Torquay of *Fawlty Towers*, the Shepherd's Bush of *Steptoe & Son* or the East Cheam of *Hancock's Half Hour*, the locale becomes part and parcel of the appeal. Unlike in lesser examples of the genre, where the characters are only cared about, if at all, for each isolated half hour in which they happen to appear, the best sitcoms create characters who live on in the mind between the times when they are seen on the screen, making one wonder about where they go, what they do and who they meet.

Open All Hours was such a sitcom. It was not just about a shop. It was not just about a street. It was also about a way of life.

It nudged one into associating the characters with the people one actually knew. It led one to compare the location with the sort of places that some of one's own friends and family had graced.

It was here, therefore, in this unnamed northern town, that viewers would be encouraged to imagine the kind of people who inhabited its houses. One or two were seen each week in certain scenes, but the broader community was represented mainly by the gossip that went back and forth across the shop counter. This was the basic way that viewers came to acquire their understanding of what Arkwright Country was probably like.

There were, for example, the numerous remarks about those locals who were deemed to be somewhat dubious and louche, such as 'Her at number 10' (who is 'still swapping' with 'Her at number 8'[198]); and another suspected *femme fatale* at number 75 (who, according to her neighbours, has had a carpet-fitter camped there 'for three weeks'[199]); and the man down the road whose simple needs merely require the strength 'to blow the froth off another barmaid';[200] and, most notoriously of all, the married woman at number 87 (who has been known to play

Scrabble deep into the night with a succession of lodgers until one of them spells out a four-letter word[201]. Mrs Moffat, meanwhile, represents a more discreet type of suburban sybarite, slipping off to Chesterfield to indulge in a spot of vice ('You'd never have thought it – she looked such a q-q-quiet little woman in that hat'[202]).

Then there was the obvious opprobrium for the large and unruly family of Mrs Scully, a fag-puffing, heavy-drinking, thickly made-up matriarch (whose *chic* high heels were described in Roy Clarke's script as akin to 'a lick of paint on a disaster area'[203]) who continues to defend all of those who happen to share her surname. There is, for example, her work-shy husband, who spends most of his time curled up in bed with the cat ('He likes to put his feet on it'); and their son, Newton, newly released from his latest spell inside (MRS SCULLY: 'It's all right, he's going straight this time.' ARKWRIGHT: 'Aye, he always does – straight for someone's till!'); and their daughter, Claudine, who is very unlucky in love ('Her young man's just broke it off'); and their youngest son, who, she boasts, has just embarked on a promising writing career ('He's nearly *covered* the lavvy wall!').[204]

Worse still, at least as far as Arkwright is concerned, are the characters who appear reluctant to spend the cash that he is so keen to get in his grasp, such as Mrs Braddock, who dares to ask him to cash a cheque ('M-My pleasure, Mrs Bounce, er, B-Braddock')[205]; Mrs Henderson, who prefers to poke the produce rather than purchase it ('She's got an index finger which is v-very detrimental to a sliced loaf, she has. Which might of course explain the rather pained expression on the face of M-Mr Henderson, I suppose')[206]; and the weary worker who has to be frog-marched from the bus stop just to get him into the shop ('I've heard things about this place. Why do you think I tiptoe past this shop every morning?'[207]). This is how Arkwright divides the community in terms of the haves and the have-nots: the haves have already been had, while the have-nots, much to his chagrin, are still holding out. 'It's amazing, y'know, isn't it?' he grumbles. 'You stock your shop with all kinds of imaginable luxuries, and still they d-dither on the doorstep!'[208]

Other, somewhat more pliable, local figures are more notable for their various little idiosyncrasies. There is, for example, the smugly pious Wesley Cosgrave, a long-term boil sufferer whose buttock-based

affliction 'inhibits his organ playing',[209] and the even more smugly
pious Mr Wilkinson ('It's a great burden, Granville, being holier than
everybody else. But I enjoy it'[210]), who only needs to hear people
talking of eggs to launch into a sermon about impure thoughts ('You
start thinking about eggs and the next thing you know you'll be
encouraging your mind to dwell on the reproductive cycle! You'll not
find the four letter word "eggs" on *my* shopping list, Granville!'[211]).
There is also the poor customer at number 11, whose groceries always
end up going to the person at number 111 because Arkwright has
'started s-stuttering in writing now';[212] the woman with the 'af-f-f-
fliction' who is stuck inside number 16;[213] Mr McIntyre, who is
sometimes confused with a 'creepy, crawly, slimy thing' when he comes
in for his embrocation;[214] as well as the silently suffering Vera, who is
enduring a seemingly endless delay for her hysterectomy operation
('I'm still waiting for a bed'[215]).

Vera, in fact, is one of the community's many essential gatekeepers
of gossip, in the sense that she, like the rest of them, likes to stand and
hold the gate wide open and let all of the gossip flow through:

VERA:	Is he out of danger yet, then?
ARKWRIGHT:	Well, I d-don't know about that. He's back with the gas company.
VERA:	He's tried it once before to my knowledge. Took an overdose.
ARKWRIGHT:	Aye. Of l-laxative. Oh dear, what a terrible way to go. Or at least k-keep going.
VERA:	Well, he tried a bit harder this time. He'd have done it an' all if his clothes line hadn't broke.
ARKWRIGHT:	Well, you see, that's the trouble. They w-will p-purchase from these supermarkets, won't they? *[He reaches for one of his own clothes lines]* Now if he'd bought *that*, y'see, that-that's reinforced all the way through. *That* wouldn't have let him down at the last minute!
VERA:	I'll have two pound of King Edward's, please.[216]

Vera's exchanges with another local woman, Mrs Ellis, show how the pure gossip gets processed as it moves along on its circuitous route:

MRS ELLIS: Did you see him from Harrison's? Parked outside 87 again! I'm not kidding, he does more with a gammy leg than most blokes do with two.

VERA: Ah, well, they're all the same, these short men. They're always havin' to prove themselves. There was him from the new housing estate –

MRS ELLIS: Napoleon.

VERA: Oh, I don't know what he were called. But he always wore them fancy boots.

ARKWRIGHT: Yeah. Earnshaw.

VERA: Eh?

ARKWRIGHT: Earnshaw. L-Lived in Eastfield Road. Presumably after he escaped from St Helena.[217]

Working in tandem with the gossips are the local storytellers, who, while not serving such a directly informative function, do nonetheless help to put some quirkiness and colour into each prosaic day. The elderly, homburg-hatted, treacle-loving Freddie is one such garrulous figure:

FREDDIE: I want a large pad of writing paper.

ARKWRIGHT: Hey, you must have been retired longer than I thought, Freddie, if you've used up all that C-Coal Board stationery already! *[He gets a pad]* Here you are, here's a nice one, l-look at that.

FREDDIE: Is that the biggest you've got?

ARKWRIGHT: Listen, the next size to that is a roll of wallpaper!

FREDDIE: Well, it'll do for a start. I'm going to write me war memoirs.

ARKWRIGHT: Oh well, you'll need a p-packet of postcards, won't you?

FREDDIE:	'A View from the Home Front: An absorbing personal record'. I was there, you know, on the night they bombed Tomlinson Street.
ARKWRIGHT:	Yeah, I'll never know what Göring had against Tomlinson Street. Unless it was that Hy-Hygienic Fisheries, y'know – perhaps he found out about the shape of Percy's chips. *[Points at the pad]* That'll be 43p, come on.
FREDDIE:	I feel it's a duty to record it all for posterity.
ARKWRIGHT:	Yeah.
FREDDIE:	My entire role in the whole affair.
ARKWRIGHT:	Yeah, well, I w-wondered why you were up so early this morning. What are you going to do this afternoon – World War Three?
FREDDIE:	It came to me in a dream. This voice said: 'Freddie, why don't you write your war memoirs?' Up to that I hadn't even thought of it.
ARKWRIGHT:	Well, y-you don't, do you? Did you recognize the voice? Whose was it?
FREDDIE:	Well, at first I thought it must be God.
ARKWRIGHT:	Yes, well, you would at that time of night.
FREDDIE:	But it turned out to be Mr Samuelson from Gordon Street.
ARKWRIGHT:	*What?* Him with the…him with the horse and cart??
FREDDIE:	Yes.
ARKWRIGHT:	Well, I'm surprised you thought *he* was God with the vocabulary *he's* got! Unless he was talking about that place d-down the road from Gomorrah.
FREDDIE:	Sodom?
ARKWRIGHT:	Exactly, that's what I say![218]

Not everyone in the area has sufficient leisure time to indulge in this kind of idle anecdotalism. There are plenty of labourers around but, clocked in and generally confined behind the factory gates, they are glimpsed only fleetingly inside the shop on the corner. The only ones who spend a minute or so gathered around the bacon slicer are Messrs Glastonbury, Raffertree and Ellis along with their assorted co-workers, taking their regular and intensive smoking break. 'There's a lot of effort goes into c-coughing like that, y'know,' Arkwright says admiringly as the ash starts to settle after their departure. 'If I could harness all that energy I could h-heat this place for a week!'[219]

A few of Arkwright's fellow local tradesmen will also sometimes flit in and out of view, usually in the vain hope of avoiding being beaten down and bullied by Arkwright. There is, for example, the bread man, who continues to indulge in his 'ungovernable lust for speed' at the expense of Arkwright's Eccles cakes ('When he brakes like that all the currants finish up at one end!'[220]) and is always dangerously close to bagging an unintentionally boosted order ('I'll have a dozen dair-dair-date, a dozen dair-dair-date, I'll have a dozen dair-dair-d-date and walnut. And *don't* think that's three dozen I've just ordered!';[221] there is also the moustachioed, wide-lapelled, smooth-talking car salesman George Innes, whose encounters with Arkwright are always destined to end in the spilling of his own bitter tears (INNES: 'Oh, no, we're not going to have a thoroughly boring old argument about money, are we?' ARKWRIGHT: '*I'm* not. I'm going to have a thoroughly *enjoyable* argument about money!'[222]); and Mr E. T. Bickerdyke, the rather seedy 'door-to-door tailor' with his off-the-peg wares ('What have you got that's r-rugged, and hard-wearing and tough, apart from Mrs Bickerdyke?'[223]), who is disappointed to find that even when he raises the subject of sex Arkwright remains stubbornly focused upon sales (BICKERDYKE: 'Are you still knocking off the district nurse?' ARKWRIGHT: 'Are you still knocking off a big discount for cash?'[224]).

It is Neville, the balding, stubble-chinned, plainly enervated second-hand goods salesman, who probably most dreads a visit from Arkwright. 'Just window-shopping, are you?' he inquires with a world-weary sigh. 'I am at these prices,' Arkwright replies, while still eyeing ominously all of the potential knock-downs that he can negotiate once inside.[225] Poor Neville, realizing that the relentlessly hard-bargaining encounter will drain him of what precious little energy he still possesses, does what he can to resist ('Look, I'll tell you what I'll do, I'll give you a pound, in your hand, just to take your custom to another shop'[226]), but still ends up meekly acceding to Arkwright's wishes:

ARKWRIGHT: I am looking for a new washing machine.

NEVILLE: A *new* one? You??

ARKWRIGHT: Aye. Big, and glossy, and n-new. To be delivered immediately.

NEVILLE: Oh, well, in that case, come inside, come inside! *[He checks himself]* To be delivered *immediately?*

ARKWRIGHT: Aye, immediately. Only *delivered*, mind. You needn't think I'm going to *buy* one at this sort of m-money!

NEVILLE: I might have known.

ARKWRIGHT: I just want it *delivered*, y'see. In f-full view of the street. We take it in carefully through the shop door, and then wh-whip it out through the back, you sneak round the side and then p-pick it up again. In return for which, I'm about to undertake something more m-modest in the re-conditioned line.

NEVILLE: What?

ARKWRIGHT: A second-hand one, you c-custard![227]

Beyond the bustle of business, there is also the suggestion of sex, or at least a hint of harmless flirtation, courtesy of the younger women who live in the area. Aside from Nurse Gladys, with her long legs and generous breasts, who commands the special attention of Arkwright himself, there are numerous other members of the opposite sex who can count on being observed, admired or objectified.

One of them is Gloria, who will sometimes wiggle past the shop in her peachy pink trousers just when Granville is painting up the special 'bargains' on the window ('Y'know, during the war,' Arkwright is moved to reminisce, 'Herbert Ogden spent a who-who-whole week's wages on a land girl with a wiggle like that from Darlington. All he got were a t-ttip for what to do with his broccoli'[228]). There is also the still-young but excitingly experienced milk woman, whose early morning visits, bearing bottles of fresh milk, reduce Granville to a gibbering wreck who can barely keep control of his pints (ARKWRIGHT: 'How do you s-sleep standing up?' GRANVILLE: 'I'm not sleeping. I'm dreaming. You think life has passed you by, and then all of a sudden something magical happens, and you find yourself…sweeping up broken milk bottles'[229]); and the girl who works at the petrol pumps (offering 'a future filled with unlimited free football badges'[230]) has a similarly beguiling effect on young and impressionable delivery boys, sometimes making them pedal blindly straight into parked cars and road works.

There are also many more mature women either on view or mentioned in dispatches, and, indeed, one of the most interesting aspects of Arkwright Country, and one of the most admirable aspects of *Open All Hours* as well, is the prominence given to women of all ages. Roy Clarke, as a writer, had always shown an unusual willingness, and ability, to create plenty of notable roles for talented female actors – indeed, he and his fellow Yorkshireman Alan Bennett seemed at times during this period to be the only British men interested, in a calm, modest and unobtrusive way, in making women (particularly more mature women) visible and interesting on the screen – and *Open All Hours*, like *Last of the Summer Wine*, soon became a kind of love letter to the tough but tender-hearted working-class women who knocked northern men into shape.

'It does seem to be a thing of mine,' Roy Clarke later reflected. 'I've got this great respect for tough northern ladies. I admire them, because they keep the whole show on the road. And they always emerge in my sitcoms.'[231] They are the ones, it is clear, who keep Arkwright Country going, because they are the ones who manage all of the men.

They might sometimes be hard and domineering in their treatment of their spouses, but it only takes a brief look at how some of the men behave when they are let out on their own to realize that, without the whip continually being cracked back at home, they would either spend all day curled up fast asleep on the couch or else be causing chaos around the town. The sloth-like, droopy-eyed Winston, for instance, is a prime example of the species; only allowed out for running repairs of DIY-related wounds, and exuding an air of a little boy lost in his underused overalls, his moans never suggest a spirit that has been unfairly caged:

ARKWRIGHT: Oh dear, w-wounded again, Winston? What's she got you doing now?

WINSTON: I'm building another blinkin' bookcase, aren't I!

ARKWRIGHT: Oh, it's a wonderful m-mind-broadening thing, this second marriage of yours, int'it? *[He reaches for the plasters]* What do you want – a large or a small?

WINSTON: I'd better have a large.

ARKWRIGHT: Oh, it's a big bookshelf, is it? Here you are, then, let's have your finger, come on.

[He tends to the wound]

WINSTON: Steady, it hurts!

ARKWRIGHT: Yeah, well, it's a good thing it's n-not your drinking hand, int'it?

WINSTON: You must be joking! *Drinking* hand? What practice does *that* get these days? When I tell her I feel like a drink she says, 'Oh, good, now maybe you'll get on with building cocktail cabinet!'

ARKWRIGHT: H-Have you told her y-you're a mechanical idiot?

WINSTON: She won't listen. Do you know what she wanted me to do on our honeymoon?

ARKWRIGHT: Now you're not supposed to give away cabinet secrets, are you!

WINSTON: She wanted me to prove how much I loved her by re-doing the bathroom with self-adhesive tiles. *Self-adhesive tiles!* Have you used 'em?

ARKWRIGHT: No.

WINSTON: I were up till two o'clock trying to let go of her nightie![232]

It is people like these – the gossips, the gadflies, the misfits and mischief makers, the businessmen and the bores, the disciplinarians and the drones – who together made up what now seemed to regular viewers, after watching a pilot and two full series, like Arkwright's Country. Each new customer entering the shop, each new address that was mentioned, each new figure that was discussed, each new scandal that was savoured, added another little detail, another bit of local colour to be stored away in the mind.

It was the beauty of being a television viewer in those pre-home recording days. The head was your hard drive, the heart was your software. There were many frustrations in that era, but this was, at least when considered in retrospect, a positive and creative consequence of the condition. One had to think, and dream, and marry the memory with the imagination. Once something was gone from the screen, if it mattered, it was stored inside one's head. That was where it all lived on.

Open All Hours was watched. It was also remembered. That was why, in spite of the gaps between series, it held on to such a loyal audience.

The most vivid of all its inhabitants, of course, were those who were seen, centre screen, week after week. When fans sat back in the show's absence, therefore, and reflected on what they had absorbed, what most fuelled their fascination was the trio who dominated each episode: Arkwright, Granville and Nurse Gladys.

CHAPTER EIGHT

The Inner Circle

I think if the average man had been
r-responsible for shaping his own end,
then things would've t-turned out
a lot better looking.

The very heart of Arkwright Country, the comic core of its appeal, consisted of the triangle that encompassed both Arkwright and Granville inside the shop on the corner and Nurse Gladys Emmanuel in the house across the road. It was the interaction between these three characters that really made the context come alive.

Arkwright, of course, was the dominant figure as the shopkeeper, but Granville gave him another dimension in terms of family, while Gladys did the same in terms of love, lust and romance. It was mixing these elements together that made the trio seem more than the sum of its parts.

Arkwright himself was certainly a hugely vivid and powerful comic creation. From the first time that he came into view, hovering over the merchandise and fussing about the need to 'f-f-fetch a cloth', he seemed more like someone who had stepped on to the screen from the street rather than a figure that had been imposed on it by the format.

Like all great sitcom characters, he was just familiar enough to summon up similar types from one's own life, and just distinctive enough to make one appreciate him as unique. Once he had lodged himself in the mind and been animated in the imagination, he lived on between the episodes, and inspired people to ponder his past and his personality.

It certainly seemed as though this figure, given the lived-in look of the shop and his own deeply ingrained commitment to extracting cash from the local community, had come from a long line of hardworking grocers. That grubby-looking brown coat had something heraldic about it, as if it had originated in a corner shop near Camelot and then been handed down to each Arkwright brave enough to reach out and put a hand into the fearsome till.

His twice-married father ('He never g-got anything right the first time'[233]) appears to have influenced his own fierce commitment to maintaining the family business. We never hear anything about a mother, who presumably was too meek to emerge very often from the murk of the back room. The father, however, was clearly a workaholic who instilled the same materialistic values into his son.

The same could not be said of Arkwright's now-deceased sister (or, to be more accurate, half-sister: 'We never did find out which half'[234]), whose first name was never mentioned but whose unconventional exploits are a frequent point of reference. A remarkable number of people around town still seem to remember her all too clearly (Nurse Gladys, for example, can recall many telling details, although, to be polite, she limits herself to the insight that Ms Arkwright always sported 'very striking earrings'[235]), with men especially beaming brightly at the mention of her name, although they all suddenly fall silent when Granville appears within hearing distance.

Arkwright's own attitude towards his 'wild and rebellious'[236] sibling seems ambivalent at best. Although he will sometimes insist that they had always been on good terms ('She always used to wave to me as she went past in a g-gentleman's car. Sometimes with both feet'[237]'), and acknowledges that she did exhibit a few of the more orthodox family traits ('She was always game for a bargain, w-were my sister. If anyone knew how to get a bit knocked off, she did'[238]), his many barbed remarks about her promiscuous past suggest that he not only disapproved of her lack of principles but also, in his heart of hearts, envied her unfettered pursuit of pleasure.

No clues are given as to the origins of Arkwright's stutter, but, if he ever suffered as a result of being stuck with it, the trace of the trauma has long since worn away. Granville may tease him about it from time to time, but, on those rare occasions when an outsider acknowledges its existence, he appears genuinely startled to think that someone finds it at all significant:

ARKWRIGHT: Ah, ma-ma-ma-
STRANGER: 'Mare'?
ARKWRIGHT: M-M-M-Morning! Would you let me finish speaking, please?
STRANGER: Are you having treatment for that?
ARKWRIGHT: For what?
STRANGER: Your impediment.
ARKWRIGHT: *I* haven't got an *im-im-im-impediment!!* [*Pointing at Granville*] The only im-impediment I've got is *h-him!*[239]

Granville is the major puzzle in his life. The nephew who has become, in all but name, an adopted son, is a problem that Arkwright prefers to ponder rather than solve, like a much-revolved Rubik's cube. He has his occasional theories about the young man's 'peculiar' attitude – 'I reckon it's the fluoride they put in the toothpaste, I think it's imbalancing your hormones a bit, or maybe you're not quite regular enough with yer sher, with yer sher-sher, with yer shaving'[240] – but he usually settles for a sigh and a shrug. Simultaneously infuriated and intrigued by Granville's apparent inability, or disinclination, to be more like himself, Arkwright remains rattled by the failure to keep him completely under his control.

Part surrogate father and part surreptitious gaoler, he boasts about how he got the boy started in the shop at the tender age of ten, and then bought him a delivery bike the following year ('to d-develop his muscles'[241]), and cultivated him as a protégé ('It'll all be yours, one day, lad!'[242]), but he also has to resort to all kinds of schemes and stunts (from nipping romantic relationships cruelly in the bud to withholding details about his parentage) to ensure that this would-be free spirit stays stuck in his place. Without Granville there is no successor, and no shop, so Arkwright cannot afford to release him, even though doing so would at least promise a quieter life.

Arkwright does not have much time to contemplate any kind of life beyond the daily grind inside the corner shop. He has not, by his own admission, been away from this site for so much as a single night since 1957, and even then it was only because he needed to have his appendix taken out.

Rooted contentedly to the spot, he secretes his savings in an old OXO tin, his ready cash rolled up tightly in his pocket and his surplus stock stashed in the room out the back. His curiosity about the world outside his window is limited to the question of what quantity of people could become his customers.

He has little time for any current affairs beyond those that are gossiped about inside his corner shop. 'It's a p-public duty these days to keep yourself ill-informed,'[243] he says proudly, and he always does his best to honour this obligation, turning off Radio 4 just before the news starts ('You've no idea what benefit I derive from that regular daily not listening to the news'[244]).

He is an unashamedly insular man – 'sanity begins at home'[245] – who only welcomes intrusion from anywhere outside when there is a strong prospect of it ending up with cash being exchanged in his direction. A proud Little Englander, who longs to see the restoration of 'a bit of English sanity to English streets',[246] he can get quite evangelical about the virtues of boredom, which he believes is the key to keeping people out of mischief.

He does not indulge in any kind of formal exercise, having long since graduated from the onerous job of delivery biking duties, but he seems to keep himself fairly fit simply by pursuing Nurse Gladys, following customers around his shop and clashing on a regular basis with the cash register. He is seldom ill, and copes with any excessive stress by following the soothing ritual of going off to 's-spit polish yer boots',[247] although he does confess to experiencing certain minor psychosomatic maladies during times of financial insecurity: 'At the thought of the erosion into me profit margin, me fingers lost all sense of grip.'[248]

He believes in God, as a sort of Great Shopkeeper in the Sky, and has a little chat to him every evening as he starts getting ready to shut. His only prayers, however, tend to involve requests for better prospects for money and sex.

Culture is largely a foreign country to him. Although he was once rather partial to the charms of Ava Gardner ('We used to say if you're going to 'ave a gardener, she's the one to 'ave'[249]), he is deeply suspicious of the cinema, and is particularly critical of Ken Russell's permissive productions, which he thinks bring Granville out in spots.[250] He does possess an ancient gramophone player and a selection of 78 vinyl records, which he keeps in his bedroom in the hope of luring a woman upstairs with a scratchy siren's song, but he has long seemed disinclined to modernize his selections: 'I went down to get the latest Engle-Engle-ber-ber-ber-Engleber-ber-ter-humper-dom-pom-per-dink, but, by the time I managed to say it, they'd sold out!'[251]

He is, if anything, even more averse to the idea of higher education, regarding it as a poor substitute for picking up practical experience on the shop floor. 'Think on, you, think on,' he warns Granville as the young man laments his lack of formal learning. 'Some people *h-have* to go to university! You know, the way their parents are fixed, they've no choice, poor devils. Look at that Joan, look at that Joan, look at that, look at that Jo-Jo-Joan Bakewell! Look at her! And all them other fairy lights! Whereas if they'd had a *decent* job, and started work at 14, they'd be as right as you and me!'[252]

He respects the law, but remains profoundly doubtful of those who are supposed to interpret and enforce it. 'If you put all the m-magistrates in this country nose to tail,' he ponders, 'I wonder if they'd f-finally get a clearer view of their responsibilities?'[253]

An avid reader of the *Daily Express*, which he studies when seated in the comfort of his easy chair out in the back room, his political views are clearly to the right of centre, but mainly because he wants politics to keep itself separate from economics. He has no real problems with the State so long as it stops sticking its snout into the marketplace.

State-management of certain industries, as a consequence, is one thing that is guaranteed to get this independent shopkeeper hot and bothered. He fears that everything from his firelighters to his fiancée is in danger of being nationalized.

Anything that smacks of corporate commerce or pushy paternalism has him shivering under his overalls: 'F-Fancy the Americans p-paying all that money for Disneyland when they could have had Marxism for nothing!'[254]; 'The Workers' Revolutionary Party claims that there are concentration camps ready and waiting all over this country. They must mean B-Butlins!'[255]

He is also no friend of the organized left. 'The "extreme left",' he reflects. 'That's all we ever hear about, int'it? "The Extreme Left". Funny expression that, isn't it? "The Extreme Left". It's like a lot of leftovers, isn't it? It's like all them little bits at the end of a p-party that nobody wants. Come to think of it, that's not far off the truth'.[256]

The one thing that seems to really absorb him during his tabloid tutorials are the stories about saucy young women. 'This paper is full of y-young ladies' upper attributes,'[257] he complains unconvincingly. He refuses, however, to swap his tabloid of choice for a broadsheet with a bit more substance: 'I don't think I could handle more substance than this!'[258]

It is when the paper is put down and the customers come in that he is well and truly in his element. Facing anyone across his counter, he is the master of his art, able to badger and beguile most customers into buying whatever it is that he most wants to sell.

His ability is rather less reliable when it comes to speculating on the market. He is certainly prepared to back his own judgement when it comes to taking a gamble – 'I've got a flair for this sort of work, y'know. When I'm on the threshold of a reasonable profit a r-razor sharp instinct takes over'[259] – but he often has to sign off with a loss.

The only major dream that Arkwright still has, apart from that of a much better day of sales, concerns the eventual capture of his ideal woman. Described variously as possessing 'a huge chest and a backside like a school bus',[260] and 'looking like a very attractive heavy goods vehicle',[261] and offering 'a lot of eastern promise behind that faint flavour of cocoa',[262] the fantasy is made flesh in the form of Nurse Gladys Emmanuel.

Plying her with shop-soiled run-free tights and confectionery that has crept past its sell-by date, and regularly crossing the road to ogle her breasts, legs and bottom, he harbours an ardour for her so strong that it seeps into every aspect of his beloved shop, causing him to think of her whenever he squeezes a soft bap, caresses a melon or contemplates opening a competitively priced bottle of wine: 'I have to keep my hands at room temperature in case I ever have to decant any of that sparkling, f-full-bodied white, known locally as Nurse Gladys Emmanuel.'[263]

Vowing to marry her in an instant, if only she will accept an instant that coincides with a Bank Holiday, he waits and watches her movements with interest. Until she weakens and relents, he is content to settle for selling, and sees no reason to stop: GRANVILLE: 'Do you think you're going to live forever?' ARKWRIGHT: 'Well, I'm going to have a damned good try!'[264]

Nurse Gladys Emmanuel herself, meanwhile, remains firmly the mistress of her own fate. She might tolerate Arkwright first as a friend and then as a fiancé, and sometimes tempt him into trying a more daring approach to his life, but she is a woman who is determined to stay in control.

Viewers still knew nothing, after two series, about her background, other than the fact that she lives with her elderly mother (who is destined to remain an unseen character in the same comic tradition as Captain Mainwaring's 'Elizabeth' and Arthur Daley's ''er indoors'), and has a sister (also fated never to be glimpsed on the screen) who lives somewhere close to Wesley Cosgrave. She has never been without her admirers, as the threatened return of Chalky White served to confirm, but her love life, at present, seems fairly happily on hold.

Gladys is a woman of simple, practical tastes, spending most of her time in her smart nurse's uniform ('with her black bag neatly laundered and her b-blouse tightly packed'[265]), rushing from one patient to the next in her trusty old white Morris Minor. Strikingly industrious, she is used to putting others before herself, and, even after she has completed the last of her calls for the day, she still feels obliged to fuss over her mother before she can think of settling down and having a rest. The nearest that she seems to get to a treat are the two large tea cakes that she sometimes orders from Arkwright.

There is a semi-repressed desire for pleasure and adventure beating away in her breast – she quite fancies one day having a honeymoon in Tahiti – as well as, judging by her willingness to cradle Granville's head in her chest, a craving to allow a maternal concern to come out. She is, nonetheless, too busy to give in to her instincts, and too wary to allow Arkwright's wooing to progress any further.

They make, in many ways, a most peculiar couple. She, for example, prefers to relax with a glass of good wine and a decent meal, whereas he is happy enough with a glass of lager and 'a s-salted peanut'.[266] Similarly, she likes to unwind by watching medically based soap operas while he likes to unwind by watching his shop. She is also certain that she will be better protected against a cold front coming in from the Atlantic by an extra vest rather than a 'hot shopkeeper'.[267] Surely most importantly of all, she puts herself, and her pocket, right at the back of her priorities, while he puts himself, and his pocket, right at the front.

She knows, however, that he might – just might – meet her needs, and she is sure that she has his measure. She is aware, for example, that he has wandering hands, but she is also aware that she only needs to shout 'BURGLARS!' and his hands will be back around his wallet 'like greased lightning'.[268]

She can also see straight through the more romantic of his requests. When he claims, for example, that he would happily have her wearing a red dress, sporting a red rose in her hair, 'doing a flamenco', she realizes, straight away, that, if they married, 'within 24 hours you'd have me in an apron with curlers in me hair doing a casserole!'[269]

Whereas Arkwright wants her to remain more or less the same, only much nearer in a physical sense to him, she wants him to change. She will not relent until he becomes a better uncle to Granville, a more thoughtful partner to her, and a more compassionate member of the community. She also, most ambitiously of all, wants to make him care more about pleasure than profit: 'I'll develop his spending muscle if it's the last thing I do.'[270]

The more that Arkwright and Nurse Gladys think of themselves as a couple, however, the more that Granville is treated by them as their surrogate son. He might be 25 years old, or a little more, and impatient for independence, but he still identifies with his image as an orphan, and still feeds off the sympathy that his position provokes.

The circumstances that led to Granville's emergence into the world remain a matter of intense speculation, not least for Granville himself. He might have been conceived during the night that his mother spent in Clayburn's haystack,[271] but, then again, it could just as plausibly have occurred on one of her countless other nocturnal assignations.

He does not know much about his mother, who presumably died when he was just a child, and cannot even remember what she looked like. Arkwright volunteers the odd tantalizing detail – sometimes, by his standards, reasonably pleasant (such as the fact that she was 'big, beautiful and buxom'[272] and 'kind, loving and generous – no sense at all!'[273] and 'down to earth – a bit too often for her own good, but she meant well'[274]), and sometimes not ('Your mother never used her head for business. Q-Quite the reverse, in fact'[275]) – but Granville rarely welcomes his input:

ARKWRIGHT: You're just the same as your mother was: happiness is h-horizontal.

GRANVILLE: Why are you always so *rude* about your own sister?

ARKWRIGHT: No, don't misunderstand me, some people l-loved her dearly. Others used to get it on discount.

GRANVILLE: Oh, *look* –

ARKWRIGHT: *No*, that's only a joke. It's only a *joke*. Her one fault, maybe, was that she was inclined to be a little over-f-friendly.

GRANVILLE: If you didn't like her, why do you keep her photograph, eh?

ARKWRIGHT: I didn't say that I didn't *like* her! No, she always had a r-ready smile, and she certainly *enjoyed* life…[276]

Sadly, Granville knows even less about his father (GRANVILLE: 'I would've liked to have known my father.' ARKWRIGHT: 'Yes. S-So would your mother!'[277]). According to his mother, his father 'died in an accident',[278] but he remains unsure, and would clearly love to find out much more.

His uncle, once again, is of little help. The often-asked question, 'What was my father like?' usually elicits little more than a disparaging line like 'Lightning'.[279] On one occasion, for example, Granville's readiness to wonder whether his father, like himself, 'liked to linger in bed' prompts Arkwright to reply acidly: 'He didn't linger long in your mother's, did he? He was up before she got his name!'[280]

There is, of course, the long-running rumour that the mystery man hailed from Hungary,[281] but it is unclear how reliable this information really is. Granville rather likes the idea that, by the standards of his local neighbourhood, he might have an unusually rich and distinctive lineage, but Arkwright usually treats the link as no more than a joke.

The uncertainty about his father's identity, however, does not stop Granville from using the thought of him as a source of inspiration. 'I'd like my father to be *proud* of me,' he declares. 'Whoever he was.'[282]

He might moan about all of the things that seem to conspire to keep him stuck in the shop – from the pain caused by his 'knotted calves'[283] to the claim that his free time consists only of 'two hours of daylight every Midsummer's Eve'[284] – and mutter about the strain he endures trying to 'preserve a shred of emotional integrity in this crude commercial environment',[285] but he is still determined to enlighten and improve himself so that, one day, he can fit into the glamorous metropolitan milieu of his dreams.

He is quite the budding autodidact, devouring everything from *Teach Yourself Kung Fu* in no fewer than 98 weekly parts ('If you ask me,' sneers Arkwright, 'you've got more weakly parts now than when you started!'[286]) to a supernatural novel called *The Curse* ('He's reading everything but the *Grocers' Gazette*,'[287] Arkwright complains), forsaking the 'orthodox' *Yorkshire Post* in favour of the suspiciously heterodox *Manchester Guardian* ('That's no place for a formative mind,' cries his uncle. 'They talk about cannabis as if it were ice cream!'[288]), and, although he is practically primed to incline towards the line of least resistance thanks to the study he has made of the double-entry book-keeping system,[289] he is eager to explore anything he can find about art, ethics and philosophy. His musical tastes stretch from soul music to Shirley Bassey, and his fashion aspirations have already seen him startle Arkwright with his extravagant attempts at seeming à la mode ('He s-s-spends a fortune on handmade underwear. You wouldn't believe the places he's got his initials sewn on!'[290]).

He is also waiting to be able to embrace his sense of wanderlust, talking wistfully about one day 'trekking through sun-drenched equatorial Africa',[291] as well as visiting other equally exotic-sounding locations, even though, at present, he is confined to covering the local catchment area on an ancient and overly audible delivery bike. It is almost as if Arkwright realizes that, if he were ever to let his nephew sit behind the wheel of a fully operational van, he might drive off into the distance and disappear from the shop for good.

At the moment, however, Granville's top priority is getting a genuine girlfriend. Finding the female form to be 'more attractively wrapped even than bars of chocolate',[292] he is not particularly fussy, and, indeed, makes a point of professing to 'like girls of all sizes' on the grounds that 'it shows I'm flexible in me taste'.[293]

He has long had a crush on the attractive divorcée who delivers the milk every morning, but, although she likes to tease him ('You poor love. What you need is a sympathetic married woman. Or better still: a sympathetic *ex*-married woman'[294]), and he is always eager to get his hands on her yoghurts, the relationship seems destined to remain platonic – especially as he keeps dropping the pints on the pavement whenever she gets him overly excited.

He also enjoys a little flirt every now and then with the customers, although Arkwright is always there to make sure that nothing too naughty comes from any of the exchanges:

EVA: Hey, I like your Granville. He looks like the kind of young man who'd be reckless enough to do something desperate for the love of a good woman.

[She squeezes Granville's wrist playfully]

ARKWRIGHT: Er, er, G-Granville, f-fetch a cloth – go on! There are some apples in that w-warehouse that need polishing!

GRANVILLE: I always have to go when customers get interesting!

ARKWRIGHT: Go on with yer!![295]

There are numerous other young women who smile when he catches their eye during his trips out on delivery duties, and, even when stationary, his mind will still wander to thoughts of the opposite sex.

'When I think of the tights that have been through my fingers,' he mutters, gazing longingly at a packet of hold-ups, 'it's about time I had one with a leg in it.'[296]

He knows, however, that he is hampered by his image as an errand boy ('How can you look debonair in a flamin' *pinny?*[297]), and hindered by his lack of leisure hours ('I'm stuck here slicing bacon and my life is trickling away'[298]), but he cannot stop thinking about what he is missing (indeed, it would seem very apt, in a Granville-esque way, when a song featuring the lines 'Everybody needs a bosom for a pillow/Everybody needs a bosom' was released in 1997 by a band called, equally aptly, Cornershop[299]). Waiting in vain for a feminist to molest him,[300] his sexual yearnings are sublimated inside the shop, showing themselves in such ways as the sensual manner with which he gently squeezes a couple of packets of sliced bread, or the way that he paints each rounded-looking letter on the window as if it was a peachy posterior.

Arkwright, of course, would much prefer it if Granville abandoned all such dreams and desires and reverted to the innocence, and pliability, of childhood ('You've been a constant worry to me ever since you first went into Y-fronts!'[301]). His response to his nephew's worryingly grocer-phobic pretensions is to hope that it is simply a fleeting phase ('He's at a very funny age'[302]), but he is not above the odd bit of shop-floor sabotage to push the young man back on track. Nurse Gladys, on the other hand, reacts far more sympathetically to Granville's sense of frustration by mothering him as much as she can while urging Arkwright to loosen his grip.

Their three-way exchanges, as a consequence, sound more and more like dysfunctional family conferences:

GLADYS: He works you too hard.
GRANVILLE: Yes. My only consolation is that working helps you to forget that you're an orphan.
GLADYS: Oh, *Granville!*

[She holds his head to her chest just as Arkwright enters the room]

ARKWRIGHT: Hey, what kind of t-t-treatment is *that* for a bad leg?

GLADYS: You load him with too much stuff on that
              bike!

ARKWRIGHT: Look, he scratches his knee a bit and the next
              thing I see he's having his head s-squeezed!

GLADYS: He needs a bit of comfort.

*[Granville, still with his head pressed tightly to
her chest, nods appreciatively]*

ARKWRIGHT: 'Ere, can't you agree without nodding?

[Granville, without looking up, shakes his head repeatedly]

GLADYS: It's dangerous for him on that bike!

ARKWRIGHT: It's a bit risky in *there* with *them* two, I'll tell
              yer!

GLADYS: You've no right sending him out on these dark
              mornings, loaded up like that, half asleep!

ARKWRIGHT: Look, I send him out when I think there's
              v-very little traffic.

GLADYS: *I'm* traffic! I was half asleep myself. I've been up
              all night sitting by the bedside of some poor
              old man.

ARKWRIGHT: Oh! How come you never sit by the bedside of
              this p-poor old man?

GLADYS: Because you're *not* a poor old man. You're a
              tight-fisted old man!

GRANVILLE: That's true! That's true![303]

This, then, was the story so far of the central comic trio whom regular
viewers had come to know and love to watch. Fleshed out a little more
from week to week, they seemed, by this stage, engagingly familiar and
intriguingly believable. Enough interest had been invested in them to
make people curious to see what they did, or failed to do, next.

These three, however, were not the only figures who made the
comic context seem full of flesh and blood. There were also, increasingly,
the regular customers to consider.

CHAPTER NINE

The Customers

Answer that bell!

Every time the bell rang above the shop door, there was the promise of more novelty for the comedy. New figures could come and go, like one-off variations in a familiar fictional riff, but some of them could also return and become a telling part of the texture of the sitcom, adding depth as well as dynamism.

Among those customers who appeared often enough to be deemed semi-regulars were three women: Mrs Blewett, Mrs Parsloe and Mavis. Each, in her own way, contributed some colour to the character of the show.

Mrs Blewett (played by Kathy Staff) represented the nosy loner in every neighbourhood, the tireless seeker-out – and spiller – of local secrets. A sharp-eyed, sour-faced, tart-tongued tittle-tattler, she was strongly reminiscent of Norman Evans' old northern music hall character, Fanny Fairbottom, who was notorious for her regular gossips over the garden wall:

> I knew what *she* was as soon as I saw 'er! Oh yes. That coalman was never away, y'know! I mean, don't tell me it takes thirty-five minutes to deliver two bags of nuts! He's a bad lot. Oh yes. I knew what was goin' on when I saw him shout 'Whoa!' to his horse from her bedroom window.[304]

Mrs Blewett, dressed like a bowl of milkless muesli, blessed with a voice like a rusty foghorn and bearing an expression still etched with the enervating strain of enduring childbirth no fewer than seven separate times, could always be relied on to come up with the same kind of bilious and breathless revelations:

MRS BLEWETT: Did you know they buried old Scrooby last Tuesday?

ARKWRIGHT: Old Sc-Old Sc-Old Sc-*Did* they? Oh, I didn't know he'd died.

MRS BLEWETT: Neither did *she!*

ARKWRIGHT: Oh.

MRS BLEWETT: He sat there on the settee for *three* hours, *staring* at her!

GRANVILLE: Well, he never was very talkative, though, was he? No, I mean, he *wasn't.* I once ran over him on the shop bike, right across his foot, and he never said a word. He just hit me with his crutch. Well, it wasn't *my* fault, I just came round the corner and there he was, trying to strangle this kid.

ARKWRIGHT: Oh, yes, he always knew how to command respect in the young, I'll say that.

MRS BLEWETT: And *he* looks like death across at number 29.

ARKWRIGHT: Oh dear.

MRS BLEWETT: They came at nine o'clock on Thursday night with an ambulance and took him away. They're all expecting him back, but I told her, 'He looks yellow to me – that means kidneys. I wouldn't give you *tuppence* for his kidneys!' How much is your boiled ham?

ARKWRIGHT: Well, it's a b-bit more expensive than his kidneys! But it's a bit of choice stuff – th-they'll never take *that* away in an ambulance!

MRS BLEWETT: I'll have a quarter.

ARKWRIGHT: Right. I th-think you'll enjoy it, Mrs Blewett.

MRS BLEWETT: Aye, I expect so. Hey, and speaking of a bit of choice stuff, have you seen her round at 87 lately?

ARKWRIGHT: 87? Isn't she the one with the, er...
MRS BLEWETT: That's the one, yes!
ARKWRIGHT: How *is* that new lodger?
MRS BLEWETT: Not as fit as she is! I wonder how the husband's
                taking it?
ARKWRIGHT: Well, very infrequently by the sound of it![305]

Neurotically punctilious (she is fiercely opposed to the concept of tight jeans, and demands that her boiled ham be cut 'unemotionally'[306]) and aggressively morbid ('I've seen 'em taken in their fullness and in their prime'[307]), she is particularly exercised by thoughts of her timidly ineffectual husband:

ARKWRIGHT: Morning, Mrs Blewett!
MRS BLEWETT: *Is* it? You wouldn't think so if you had to run
                about after *him*. Sixty-four years old and he
                still can't keep a button on his shirt. I'll have a
                tin of me polish and a bottle of bleach.
ARKWRIGHT: A-no-nother tin of polish, Mrs Blewett?
MRS BLEWETT: Aye, they don't go very far.
ARKWRIGHT: Well, you must have a very nice sh-shiny place
                up there to be miserable in.
MRS BLEWETT: *You'd* be miserable if you lived up there with
                him! If he's not under me feet he's down at that
                British Legion club, trying to drink his way
                back through the Second World War! I
                wouldn't mind but he only got as far as
                Aldershot!
ARKWRIGHT: J-Just you and him now the kids have gone,
                is it?
MRS BLEWETT: More's the pity. He never *was* any help.
ARKWRIGHT: No. How many kids was it?
MRS BLEWETT: Seven.
ARKWRIGHT: Good grief, how much help do you want? At
                least it explains a few of them m-missing
                buttons, doesn't it?[308]

If men tend to irritate her, then it also has to be said that she is hardly a signed-up member of the sisterhood, either. While she resents men for what they fail to do, she resents women for all that they *do* get up to:

MRS BLEWETT: She's always been inclined towards, well, you know...

ARKWRIGHT: Yes, well, she c-certainly gets through a lot of aspirin.

MRS BLEWETT: Yes, I'm not surprised. The only one I blame is her mother. Her mother had the American Army during the war.

ARKWRIGHT: N-Not *all* of them, I trust!

MRS BLEWETT: You'd have *thought* so if you'd lived next door. And it wasn't as though she was good looking! I mean, she had a face like a fit.

ARKWRIGHT: That's true. Although, mind you, I can't quite think what it would've fitted.[309]

Her blathering becomes, after a while, like a kind of white noise to Arkwright, who tries to block most of it out, rather like someone wearing a tin-foil helmet, and just makes what he hopes are commercially encouraging noises:

ARKWRIGHT: Oh. One of those. One of those. T-Two of those. Oh, and another one of those. I think you certainly get through a lot of b-biological detergent in your house, Mrs B-Blewett.

MRS BLEWETT: Ah, it's his collars. He *will* keep running his fingers round his collars.

ARKWRIGHT: Oh, a n-nervous habit. They say him up at the post office is just the same with his lady assistant, you know.

MRS BLEWETT: You can't get 'em clean.

ARKWRIGHT: No.

MRS BLEWETT: I've tried everything. He *is* me husband, after all.

ARKWRIGHT: Well, that's one good reason for running your finger nervously around your collar, I suppose.

MRS BLEWETT: He's always been nervous. He smokes endless cigarettes.

ARKWRIGHT: Oh, p-pity, we d-don't sell that kind. They're too long to get in the shop, y'know?

MRS BLEWETT: If you don't turn your husband out right it reflects on the wife, I always think.

ARKWRIGHT: Oh, yes, you're absolutely right there, Mrs Blewett.[310]

The only hope of selling her anything other than her most basic domestic essentials, Arkwright realizes, is to break into the gossip and play on her self-conscious sense of probity:

ARKWRIGHT: I should have known it all along, because she never d-did buy any.

MRS BLEWETT: Buy any what?

ARKWRIGHT: She never once b-bought one single packet of f-f-fig biscuits. Which, at t-today's reduced prices, they represent a most economical supplement to the household d-diet.

MRS BLEWETT: *Fig biscuits?*

ARKWRIGHT: Yes, the very same, the chaste housewife's indicator: the f-fig biscuit.

MRS BLEWETT: What's so special about fig biscuits?

ARKWRIGHT: Oh, n-nothing that a *customer* would spot, of course. No, it takes a lifetime of sh-shopkeeping nous to spot a connection like that.

MRS BLEWETT: A connection like what?

ARKWRIGHT: Well, the fig connection. The connection between a fig biscuit and honourable womanhood. Don't ask me to explain it, Mrs Blewett, but all I can say is this: you show me a g-grocery list without a fig biscuit and I will show you a housewife of d-doubtful moral

rectitude. *[He starts totting up her bill]* Now,
that's a bottle of bleach and a tin of polish…
MRS BLEWETT: Yes…a-and a packet of fig biscuits.[311]

Mrs Parsloe (Frances Cox), on the other hand, is as taciturn as Mrs Blewett is talkative. Looking eerily like Buster Keaton in drag, she is mainly an observer, usually arriving just in time to witness someone or something that she thinks merits a disapproving stare or a disbelieving shake of the head.

She is on the spot and already scowling, for example, when Arkwright, his movement impeded by an over-tight money belt, is dragged away by Nurse Gladys to see a hypnotherapist. 'They reckon he heals people,' someone explains. 'No, I don't fancy it,' Mrs Parsloe mutters dismissively. 'Not with my back.'[312]

She is there again, even more sour-faced, just when Arkwright is trying to deal with a rare visitor from overseas. '*Foreign*, is he?' she inquires anxiously of Granville. 'Eeee, don't they have some *funny* ways!'[313]

She knows what she likes, which is 'half a dozen pikelets' and not very much else, but, more importantly, she also knows what she dislikes, which is most of what she sees. Arkwright does his best to stretch her sense of tolerance – 'There are more things in heaven and earth, Mrs Parsloe, than are dreamt of in your b-b-back parlour!' – but she remains defiantly dour: 'I've never heard such *rubbish!*'[314]

Unlike the other women who feature fairly regularly in the shop, Mrs Parsloe is as parsimonious with her prose as she is miserly with her money. Whereas many will make their point with wave after wave of words, she will usually settle for a bone-dry and palpably censorious silence.

The bright-eyed and bird-like Mavis (Maggie Ollerenshaw) is, on the other hand, is a much more endearing sort of figure, although, for Arkwright, her presence often represents a peculiar form of torture. Sometimes known, behind her back, as 'Wavy Mavis', she would probably be one of his best and most willing customers if it was not for the fact that she finds it so hard to make up her mind.

This, after all, is a woman who even struggles to explain how she went from being a Miss to a Mrs:

GRANVILLE: Do you mind if I make a suggestion?
MAVIS: Oh, I don't know, really. I couldn't listen to anything my husband wouldn't approve of.
GRANVILLE: No, no, I didn't mean anything like –
MAVIS: On the other hand, even if you're married, my feeling is you're still a person. ...But then I could be wrong.
GRANVILLE: How did you happen to *get* married, Mavis? You know, when you had to say 'Yes' or 'No'. How did you make your mind up then?
MAVIS: I told him I'd think about it.
GRANVILLE: Well, that's not *actually* making your mind up, is it? I mean, what was it about him?
MAVIS: I liked his clean fingernails.
GRANVILLE: Yeah, I know, all right, but it's a very *important* decision, int'it, so, y'know, what finally *decided* you to say 'Yes' or 'No'?
MAVIS: I thought I was pregnant.
GRANVILLE: And were you?
MAVIS: No.[315]

Granville would actually rather like to get closer to Mavis, but it is clear that, for the foreseeable future, the combination of her unseen husband and her ever-present vacillation will frustrate anything that threatens to go further than flirting:

GRANVILLE: Why don't you pop in and have a hot dog?
MAVIS: Oh, well, I'd *like* to, Granville, but I –
GRANVILLE: I know: you are a married woman.
MAVIS: Oh, it's not that. I can never decide whether to put mustard on it or not.[316]

Time and again, she arrives in the shop full of good intentions as a consumer, only to be overwhelmed by her own indecision. Arkwright, sometimes, can succeed in talking her through to completing a transaction:

ARKWRIGHT: Take your time, Mavis. We can't rush a decision
             like this. Large loaf or small?
MAVIS: ...I'll have a large sliced loaf.
ARKWRIGHT: Large sliced loaf.
MAVIS: No... No, I'll take a small one... That'll do
             nicely for us two... Unless his mother comes
             at supper-time.
ARKWRIGHT: And before we've decided w-what's for tea, it
             already *is* supper-time!
MAVIS: *[Missing the sarcasm]* It's the same at our house,
             Mr Arkwright!
ARKWRIGHT: Oh, really?
MAVIS: I'll have a tin of beans.
ARKWRIGHT: A tin of beans, right. Ah, now then: large or
             small?
MAVIS: ...Haven't you anything in between?
ARKWRIGHT: Only a couple of thumbs at the moment.
MAVIS: ...Small.
ARKWRIGHT: That'll be 41p. There we are. A large loaf and a
             tin of beans. You certainly kn-know how to
             plan a meal, Mavis.[317]

More often than not, however, her indecision is final:

MAVIS: I better have a tin of...er...soup.
ARKWRIGHT: One tin of soup, M-Mavis, thank you. L-Large
             or small?
MAVIS: ...Large... No, small.
ARKWRIGHT: Oxtail? Mulliga-Mullitawn-Mulliga-mu-mu-
             mulliga-M-Mulli- Tomato?
MAVIS: Oxtail.
ARKWRIGHT: Oxtail!
MAVIS: ...No, I'd better take tomato.
ARKWRIGHT: Tomato!
MAVIS: Yes... Unless you've got...Scotch broth?

ARKWRIGHT: S-Scotch broth, Mavis? Th-That's very *exotic!* No, I haven't got a *small* tin. I only have a *large* tin.

MAVIS: Oh.

ARKWRIGHT: Well, I c-can't cut them in half, Mavis. It all p-plops out, you see. I'll tell you what I *will* do. I'll sell you one large tin and I'll only charge you for t-two small tins.

MAVIS: Oh, *thank* you, Mr Arkwright!

ARKWRIGHT: There.

MAVIS: I don't know whether I ought to take a tin of luncheon meat.

ARKWRIGHT: Is it on your list?

MAVIS: Yes… But I crossed it out.[318]

The only way that she can be pounced on for a purchase is if a certain amount of alcohol has been consumed:

ARKWRIGHT: Hello, Mavis. Back again?

MAVIS: On second thoughts, Mr Arkwright, I think I'll take the other brand.

ARKWRIGHT: Are you *s-sure*, Mavis?

MAVIS: Yes. I've made me mind up!

ARKWRIGHT: My goodness, you do seem very sure of yourself! Have you been having a little n-nip at the sherry again?

MAVIS: It changes me whole personality. Shopping becomes a completely new experience!

ARKWRIGHT: You naughty thing![319]

It was these kinds of characters who helped the context come to life. They not only provided some of the interactions and exchanges that frequently took the place of any conventional plots, but they also broadened the base of the comic situation.

While viewers could focus on the unofficial family unit at the heart of each episode, they could also wait to be engaged and amused by the latest comings and goings from the greater community that surrounded the core. They brought the full richness of Arkwright Country right into the corner shop. Having lived with them for two whole series, the fans were now keen to see what they would all do next.

PART FOUR

Why k-keep quiet about a good thing, my love?

CHAPTER TEN

Series Three

GRANVILLE: Is there nobody happy round here?
ARKWRIGHT: Would you ask me that when
I've c-cashed up tonight?

The return of *Open All Hours* for a third series in 1982 was supposed to be a run-of-the-mill affair. The vast majority of the metropolitan media had already made up their minds about this particular sitcom: they had decided that it was just a modest example of the genre, barely worthy of any serious attention, and never likely to make much of a mark. What happened next, therefore, would come as quite a shock.

The show (which had only been re-commissioned after John Howard Davies, the BBC's new head of comedy, had decided to postpone a new Roy Clarke/Ronnie Barker sitcom collaboration called *The Magnificent Evans*[320]) was given the same slot as last time – 7.15pm on Sundays – on the same channel – BBC1 – and, once again, its return was largely ignored by the broader media. Despite this, however, 1982 was destined to be the breakthrough year for this sitcom. Without any help or hype, *Open All Hours* would, quite suddenly, go from being just another sitcom to one of the biggest shows on British television.

No-one was predicting it, no-one was expecting it – not even the sitcom's own stars and the team behind the scenes had been harbouring hopes so high. It was, nevertheless, going to happen. It was as if the programme would reach straight out, past all the critics, columnists and the other opinion-formers, and shake the hand of the average viewer. A bond was about to be formed between programme and public that would never really be broken.

There was nothing new, nothing different, about this third series of *Open All Hours*. It had the same themes as before, the same main characters, the same playful aimlessness and the same gentle and droll style of humour. It did, however, 'click' with the country in spectacular fashion as it went on from week to week.

The first episode, which was broadcast on 21 March, slipped on to the screen looking much the same as the previous two series. There, once again, was the bird's eye opening view, with Arkwright in his overalls, Granville with his cloth, the delivery bike on the kerb and the milk float humming past. The only change to the familiar scene was the replacement of the two passers-by with a workman setting off to a job with a ladder over his shoulder (along with a brief freeze-frame to capture the initial expressions of Arkwright and Granville).

There was, however, a quiet confidence about this opening episode, allied to a furtive bit of bite, which was particularly evident in the way that it seemed to make a point of mocking the very kind of modern, modish, metropolitan mentality that had informed the critical indifference to the previous two series. As if to respond head-on to all the old sneers about the show being too cosy, too slow, too safe and too 'old-fashioned', the episode conjured up a character who embodied just such an attitude and provoked an appropriately defiant response.

The scene occurred early on, shortly after Arkwright has endured Granville moaning about the two ancient-looking unsold hurricane lanterns that he has had to sweep around for the past two years. No sooner has the shopkeeper reclaimed some much-needed peace and quiet after his nephew has departed to the back room, he suddenly finds himself being patronized by a pompous new customer who has popped in from somewhere posh:

CUSTOMER: How *delightful!*
ARKWRIGHT: Oh. Always a p-pleasure to see a new face.
CUSTOMER: Oh, I never knew they still existed!
ARKWRIGHT: What, new faces? Oh, yes, yes, you find them just underneath new people's hats.
CUSTOMER: No, not new *faces*. No, these *places* – poky little shops, everything higgledy-piggledy, all scrunched-in! Quaint!

ARKWRIGHT: *[Trying not to show his irritation]* Ah, good. You really think so?

CUSTOMER: Oh, definitely.

ARKWRIGHT: Oh good, because that was just the effect w-we were striving after, y'know. Oh yes. I remember saying to the architect, 'Now look, Sir Hugh,' I said, 'we don't want any of this m-modern rubbish. We'll go strictly for q-quaint.'

CUSTOMER: Oh, I love the *smell!* What *is* it, do you think?

ARKWRIGHT: Well, you've c-come on a bad day, y'see, we get a lot of *old* people in here on a Tuesday. Which is fine unless it's been raining, then some of them will s-smell a bit damp, you know.

CUSTOMER: I think it's cough drops, tobacco and paraffin!

ARKWRIGHT: That's right. And that's only the women.

CUSTOMER: *[Disapprovingly]* I, er, see you're still selling things unwrapped.

ARKWRIGHT: That's a v-vicious rumour, madam! I've never even *appeared* in the sh-shop unwrapped!

CUSTOMER: Mind you, they do look tempting little cakes. I might have *risked* a couple had you had some *tongs*. Don't you *use* tongs?

ARKWRIGHT: Of *course* we use tongs, madam! Oh, I am *notorious* on the tongs. But usually I just save them for the summer months, you see, because they are marvellous instruments for swatting flies.

[He pretends to swat one and then takes the tongs towards the cakes]

ARKWRIGHT: Which cake – one of those, did you want, or one of those?

CUSTOMER: *[Grimacing]* No, no, thank you! Really I only came in looking for French cigarettes. I don't suppose you have any *French* cigarettes?

ARKWRIGHT: No. But we have English ones you can s-smoke with a foreign accent.

146

CUSTOMER: I only smoke the French.
ARKWRIGHT: Best thing that could happen to them.

She heads to the door, still unaware of the sneers that she has been eliciting from this 'quaint' little shopkeeper, but, as she pauses for a few more patronizing remarks, Arkwright cannot resist now treating her with the sarcasm that her snobbery so richly deserves:

CUSTOMER: Oh, I remember a shop like this when I was a child!
ARKWRIGHT: Yes, yes, so do I. This is it.
CUSTOMER: Of course, it's long since been condemned.
ARKWRIGHT: Well, as a matter of actual f-fact, we are on the very verge of the same thing ourselves, you know.
CUSTOMER: *Really?*
ARKWRIGHT: Oh yes. On account of the frats.
CUSTOMER: The *frats?*
ARKWRIGHT: Yes. Oh, they're everywhere, you know. They get under your skirting boards, and your floorboards, into your c-cavity walls. My God, you've had it if they get into your cavity walls, y'know.
CUSTOMER: I'm surprised a property of this age *has* cavity walls.
ARKWRIGHT: Well, we didn't have cavity walls until the damn f-frats got in, y'see.
CUSTOMER: What *are* these frats?
ARKWRIGHT: Frats? Oh, they are a nasty cross between a f-ferret and a rat.
CUSTOMER: A ferret and a rat??
ARKWRIGHT: Yes.
CUSTOMER: *[Alarmed]* And do they…inter-breed?
ARKWRIGHT: Inter-breed? Do they? That's all they ever *do* do! Night and day! It only takes a jiffy, they tell me. Actually, it happened first by accident,

when two of the little creatures tried to force
themselves through the same narrow aperture,
you know, and, er... *[puts hands together
violently]* like *that,* you see. Well, of course,
once having got the knack...

CUSTOMER: The knack?

ARKWRIGHT: Yes, the knack of producing frats. Or as we say
locally, 'fraternization'.

CUSTOMER: And, er, you have them here?

ARKWRIGHT: Oh, we've got them everywhere, they're
spreading like wild frats.

CUSTOMER: But surely if there was an epidemic... I mean,
the *health* authorities would –

ARKWRIGHT: No, no, no, they d-daren't risk a panic, you see.
Oh, no, they just send someone along to
b-bore a couple of holes in your walls and t-tell
you you've got nothing. You see, the trouble is,
officially, th-the problem d-doesn't exist.

CUSTOMER: What does one do?

ARKWRIGHT: One acquires a frat detector. Something that
burns economically on a low light. A little
pleasant yellow flame which turns green the
moment the frats appear.

[He bends down and picks up one of the old hurricane lanterns]

ARKWRIGHT: That's one.

*[She studies it carefully. Granville emerges from the back room just in
time to see her being ushered to the door, having bought not one but
both of the wretched lanterns]*

ARKWRIGHT: Do call again for frat oil, won't you! *[He shuts
the door]* 'Quaint'? What does she mean,
q-quaint? I'll give her *Q-QUAINT!!!*

It was, in sum, a much sharper, more caustic, scene than usual for this
sitcom, and, at least in retrospect, it seemed to signal a fresh and

healthy sense of self-respect. While the odd critic, like this one-off customer, might peer into the show and turn up his or her nose at its supposed air of antiquity, the sitcom understood, and respected, its regular clientele, and was determined to keep giving them precisely what they wanted.

The series went on to do just that. Nothing was broken, so nothing needed to be fixed. Except the cash register. The cash register *did* need fixing, but that was why it was left as it was:

ARKWRIGHT: I'm going to have to s-slacken that spring off, it's no good.
GRANVILLE: Well, you keep *saying* that, but you never *do!*
ARKWRIGHT: Ah, well, you see, these little p-pound notes, Granville, I mean, they've been swapped around and passed from hand to hand all their little lives, haven't they? They've never known a s-stable home. And it's up to us to keep them snug and cosy now that they're here.[321]

The delivery bike also required some tender loving care, so that, too, remained neglected:

GRANVILLE: Why don't you face it – that old shop bike is *CLAPPED OUT!!*
ARKWRIGHT: Listen, a drop of oil and a few adjustments, that's all it needs. Come and attend to these ladies – I'll f-fix your bike for you!
GRANVILLE: It needs more than that old oil can. It needs Aladdin's lamp![322]

All was as it should be in Arkwright Country. The sleepy neighbourhood, the dissatisfied women, the hapless men, the cheeky children, the gossips and the grumblers, the tried and tested range of traditional domestic essentials, and the variety of unwashed and stationary motorized vehicles into whose backs Granville's bike seemed drawn like a magnet: they were all there, always present but not always correct.

149

Arkwright himself, when not bridling at the supercilious witterings of snobbish interlopers from the city, seemed much the same as he had always been. There he was, as usual, in hot pursuit of profits, bringing in dubious but cheap products and then devising new ways to ship them back out at inflated prices.

Even the prospect of a spot of local rivalry does nothing to undermine his self-confidence as a salesman:

CUSTOMER: Is it a good brand?

ARKWRIGHT: Well, it's been v-very well-behaved on the shelves. *[He hands her a tin of stewing steak]* Of course it's a g-good brand! How long do you think I would last if I s-started selling *rubbish* round here? If you want to b-buy *rubbish* you go round to my c-competitor round the corner!

CUSTOMER: Well, he's less than you are on several items.

ARKWRIGHT: Well, he's only f-five foot one. He can afford to be.

CUSTOMER: He has regular reductions.

ARKWRIGHT: I know. And look what it's done to him. He needs a stepladder to look over his counter!

CUSTOMER: He's always polite.

ARKWRIGHT: 'Smarmy' you mean. *Smarmy!* He's the t-type that wears Brylcreem on his teeth! That is not his own smile, y'know. That's one they can h-hire from the G-Grocers' Federation. I wouldn't mind, but it doesn't even fit him! If you observe closely, you will find he's wearing the smile of a m-much larger person! Oh, I haven't anything against the man personally. I mean, don't misunderstand me, outside office hours he's probably absolutely r-repulsive. But I mean, he's s-so s-small he can't be all that repulsive, can he? Although he does t-try, doesn't he? *[Looks at the stewing steak that is still*

in her hand] Are you going to buy that tin
or are you going to bring it up to body
temperature?[323]

He might well, in most senses, be stuck in his ways, but his business
brain remains just as ruthless and restless as those belonging to even the
biggest of his supermarket competitors. Here he is, for example, using
sex to sell (or at least getting a local girl to model as 'Little Miss Arkwright
Stores 1982'[324]), deliberately misspelling 'SPECIOL' on the window so
as to lure the pedants into his lair,[325] shifting over-stocked ginger cake by
'regretfully' responding to the 'unprecedented demand' by limiting
customers to one packet each,[326] and offering to sell directions to nearby
streets to strangers who come in to make an innocent inquiry.[327]

He is also as quick as any megastore manager to deny any
responsibility for whatever complaints happen to arrive. Arkwright, it
is clear, can be modern when it suits him.

His corner shop is not a denial of contemporary life. It is still,
comedically, an integral part of it:

CUSTOMER: I don't know why I come in here to be insulted.
ARKWRIGHT: Well, because it's *convenient*, isn't it? Look how
far you'd have to go to be insulted if there
wasn't a corner shop here, eh? You'd have to go
right up the Co-Op, wouldn't you![328]

The shop was also still serving the sitcom well as a situation, refreshing
its close-knit community from time to time with a few new customers
to come through the door and help fuel the humour. This third series
(which would have featured Kathy Staff again as Mrs Blewett, had her
commitment to the ITV soap *Crossroads* not prevented her from
participating[329]) would introduce a couple more semi-regular members
of the corner shop's clientele: Cyril – a tall, woolly-hatted, lugubrious
but strangely loose-tongued fellow (played by the endearingly artful
comic actor Tom Mennard) blessed with 'the s-silent tread of a Yorkshire
C-County Cricket supporter'[330]; and Mrs Featherstone – a black-
dressed, bleak-faced, recently bereaved housewife (portrayed with

clever severity by Stephanie Cole), whose almost Olympian capacity for misery means that she has taken to widowhood with an ease that borders on relish.

Cyril's problem is that he is not only naturally impressionable, but also that he is exceptionally impressionable when it is Arkwright who is creating the impression. In one episode, for example, the shopkeeper seizes on Cyril as the ideal candidate to consume some of the ginger cake that up to this point has been proving frustratingly hard to shift:

ARKWRIGHT: There we are, then, Cyril, there we are: razor blades and o-one ginger cake.

CYRIL: One *ginger cake?* Why the hell should I want one ginger cake?

ARKWRIGHT: Well, I kn-know how you f-feel, Cyril, but I can't possibly let you have any more.

CYRIL: No, I -

ARKWRIGHT: No, no, I swore a solemn oath: one cake p-per customer.

CYRIL: That's the wife's department. Cakes. *I* don't buy *cakes.*

ARKWRIGHT: Well, you buy r-razor blades, don't you?

CYRIL: Well, yes. I don't expect the *wife* to buy *razor blades.*

ARKWRIGHT: Oh, she uses electric, does she?

[Cyril chuckles at this, then thinks for a moment and looks confused]

CYRIL: What do you mean: 'uses electric'? She's not bad-looking, my missus. ...Is she?

ARKWRIGHT: Don't you know?

CYRIL: Well...you get *busy,* don't you?

ARKWRIGHT: Surely you must have n-noticed her around the place?

CYRIL: Well, yes, I would have *noticed* if she'd gone *bad-looking,* wouldn't I? She *used* to be *good-looking.*

ARKWRIGHT: She is still v-very attractive, Cyril.

CYRIL: *[Sounding relieved]* Well, there you are, then! I *knew* she was!

ARKWRIGHT: Not a very c-close relationship, is it, eh?

CYRIL: Well, you get your own interests.

ARKWRIGHT: Yes. Tell me, Cyril, once upon a time, didn't you ever have, er, s-similar interests?

CYRIL: Well, of course we did! *[He grins saucily]* Naturally! Certainly! Well, you *do*, don't you? In the beginning.

ARKWRIGHT: Mmm. Now, when you first w-went on your honeymoon, a-and she started to allow you to practise those little p-p-practices that you practise... Well, when you came back after a fortnight, it wasn't compulsory to *stop*, y'know? You are a *life* member.

CYRIL: I *know*, you fool!

ARKWRIGHT: You just s-slipped back into your old ways, though, didn't you?

CYRIL: Well, I've got me allotment. And she bakes a lot for the church.

ARKWRIGHT: Oh yes... Does she? Where does she get her *flour* from – she don't come to me for *flour!*

CYRIL: I think the vicar lets her have it. There's somebody what lets him have it wholesale.

ARKWRIGHT: Oh, I see, that's how you g-get to heaven, is it? Mind you, there is another way, you know, Cyril.

CYRIL: What?

ARKWRIGHT: Of getting a l-little bit of h-heaven. Don't you ever wish that you er...could put a bit of s-sparkle back into your marriage?

CYRIL: Well, of course. But where do you find the golden key?

ARKWRIGHT: Funny you should say that, Cyril.

[He places a packet of ginger cake on the counter]

CYRIL: *Ginger cake???*
ARKWRIGHT: *Jamaican* g-ginger cake. From the land of the thr-throbbing d-drums. Land of the tropical heat. Land of the... *[he mimes smoking a spliff].*
CYRIL: Woodbines?
ARKWRIGHT: Not *Woodbines*, no! A m-much *stronger* weed. Something to s-set your blood racing! Something you can either smoke or...*sprinkle* into your home cooking...in accordance with ancient v-voodoo recipes.
CYRIL: Isn't it illegal? What *effect* does it have?
ARKWRIGHT: What effect does it have? Well, you can throw away all of your p-powdered rhino horn for a start! Still, I know *you*, Cyril.

[He moves to put the ginger cake back on the pile]

CYRIL: Where are you going with that?
ARKWRIGHT: No, you won't be able to keep your mouth shut, will you? You'll want to be known down the allotments as the man who introduced them all to g-ginger cake as a marital aid, won't you?

[Cyril smacks some coins down on the counter]

CYRIL: *[Whispering]* I shan't say a word![331]

Mrs Featherstone, meanwhile, has so many problems that, by comparison, she makes Cyril seem quite normal. Besides making being miserable seem like a noble vocation, she also has a pair of under-used eyebrows and a redundant top lip, a belligerent sense of scepticism ('I'm not a religious woman but I find if you say "No" to everything you can hardly tell the difference'[332]), a very strict respect for all kinds of social, political and sporting hierarchies ('I mean, you wouldn't ask Kevin Keegan in for a game of blow football, would you?'[333]), and extremely specific requirements when it comes to buying freshly sliced cooked meats ('It's nothing personal, it's just that I could never bring meself to buy anything unwrapped from today's liberated young people'[334]).

Even when the reassuringly mature Arkwright is serving her corned beef, she remains a model of misanthropic caution:

MRS FEATHERSTONE: I'll take two ounces.

ARKWRIGHT: Right.

MRS FEATHERSTONE: You don't need so much now there's no man in the house.

ARKWRIGHT: No, no, I suppose not, not in quantity, no. Still, now you should be *s-spoiling* yourself with a few little l-luxury items.

MRS FEATHERSTONE: Not after a lifetime's scrimping and saving.

ARKWRIGHT: Oh. Well, p-put it this way: after a lifetime's s-scrimping and saving you should be able to *afford* a few little luxury items!

MRS FEATHERSTONE: Oh, I've got a bit tucked away.

ARKWRIGHT: Yes. You k-keep it tucked away, Mrs Featherstone.

MRS FEATHERSTONE: I intend to!

ARKWRIGHT: Yes, I can tell that by your expression.

MRS FEATHERSTONE: And, of course, I had him insured. It brought me a lump sum.

ARKWRIGHT: Oh, yes, it's very sad. It brings a l-lump sum to the throat, doesn't it?

MRS FEATHERSTONE: *[Brightly]* I suppose financially I've never been as well off.

ARKWRIGHT: That's true, of course, that's very true. But mind you – how long will it last if you keep l-lashing out on two ounces of corned beef like this?

MRS FEATHERSTONE: I shall continue living simply.

ARKWRIGHT: *[Sarcastically]* Ah, you have no idea how that sort of c-common sense warms the heart of a sh-shopkeeper![335]

Such customers, however, would always take second place to the two central characters in the shop, whose frustrations continue to dominate each episode. It is clear, right from the first episode in this series, that Arkwright and Granville, stuck together in this situation, are just as odd a couple as they have always been:

ARKWRIGHT: Do you realize w-what it d-does to a shopkeeper to t-turn down a sale?

GRANVILLE: Aye, I know what it does to *you*. You get nasty with people.

ARKWRIGHT: That is a s-secondary symptom. The *first* thing that happens to me is m-me top lip g-goes numb. It does, it goes absolutely l-lifeless, it just lies there, as dead as if it had been n-nationalized. And me moustache loses all of its lustre.

GRANVILLE: Hah – it's looked like that for years!

ARKWRIGHT: Never! It's been very lively in its time has this moustache! No, it's me *lips*, where rigor mortis s-suddenly sets in!

GRANVILLE: Well, they're due for a rest, anyway.

ARKWRIGHT: It's not funny, Granville! It's a hell of a place for something to die on you – right under your v-very nose! A very peculiar sensation, and I-I-I-I h-have d-d-difficulty f-f-formulating my words.

GRANVILLE: *Really?* I'm sure it's not noticeable.

ARKWRIGHT: Me finger ends get all c-constricted.

GRANVILLE: Have you tried taking them out the pockets?

ARKWRIGHT: I don't g-go around with me hands in me p-pockets!

GRANVILLE: Oh no, not *your* pockets. Other people's pockets.

ARKWRIGHT: Listen, you: if you w-want to succeed in business, you have to have a s-streak of ruthlessness.

GRANVILLE: Aye. Either that or a rich wife.

ARKWRIGHT: You couldn't get a rich wife if you didn't have a r-ruthless streak. The size of your streak you'll be lucky to get any wife at all!

GRANVILLE: Well, *you* haven't got one yet, have you, eh?

ARKWRIGHT: No, I haven't, but I've got one on order, though, haven't I? It's just a question of arranging delivery.[336]

Granville has at least broadened his appeal as an object of maternal affection, as he is now far more adept at eliciting pity for his plight as the poor orphan boy of the corner shop. Not only is he still mothered by Nurse Gladys, but he can also now rely on regular hugs from Mavis ('Every time I see him I just want to cuddle him'[337]), while he continues to long for a furtive affair with the now spoken-for milk woman (or, failing that, a fleeting tryst with such customers as Wendy or the recently abandoned Julie).

It takes the formidably experienced Mrs Whittington to remind him of how ill-prepared he still is for a proper physical relationship: 'I suppose it's because I've got a big bust,' she reflects as he looks at her needily. 'Things are never what they seem, Granville. Oh, my bosom may look all right when it's all trussed up, but if you was ever there when I let it all loose, lad, it'd scare you to death!'[338]

Indeed, while his big-eyed boyishness still moves most local women to fuss and fret over him as though he is their favourite son, there are a few who are unnerved by his peculiarity and are disinclined to indulge him. It was Mrs Blewett in the previous series who went so far as to label him 'weird', and, in this series, it is Mrs Featherstone who echoes that critical description:

GRANVILLE: We're all alone, Mrs Featherstone, in the end. Sometimes at both ends.

MRS FEATHERSTONE: You see how you are? You-You're *weird!*

GRANVILLE: Weird?

MRS FEATHERSTONE: You *talk* weird![339]

Arkwright continues to claim that he only has his nephew's best interests at heart, insisting that he is only being cruel to be kind as he trains him so that he will be ready 'to one day take over this entire empire'.[340] Having protected him assiduously from the enervating effects of formal education, and furnished him with the basic requirements of practical life (ARKWRIGHT: 'You've lacked for nothing.' GRANVILLE: 'That's right. That's one thing I *haven't* lacked: nothing. I've had plenty of that!'[341]), he longs to see his protégé start applying himself to the task of being Assistant Deputy Manager: 'It's no good just g-going through life laying back and letting things happen to you – like your mother did!'[342]

The more that Granville tries to wallow in idealism, the more that Arkwright tries to wake him up to materialism:

GRANVILLE: I can't imagine that, somehow, can you? You know – me, being dead?

ARKWRIGHT: G-Get on with it, will yer? If there's any d-dying to be done it's going to be done in your own time!

GRANVILLE: When I go, I want beautiful women tearing their hair. I shall leave instructions for a private funeral, but if the crowd rushes I want you to let them in anyway. And every year on the anniversary of my death, I want a mysterious woman in black to place upon my grave a single flower.

ARKWRIGHT: P-Plain or self-raising?[343]

Even Granville knows, deep down, that he is never going to escape his fate. Arkwright's defence of the order of things might well be lazily illogical ('Well, you wouldn't want *me* to be the errand boy, would you? I mean, how would you feel then, w-working for an errand boy?[344]), but Granville's countless attempts to break out always carry a lack of conviction. Bidding to copy a customer who seems 'cool', for example, he seeks liberation through a change of style ('I've finished with all that clobber. I'm fed up with pinnies and vests. Pinnies and vests can seriously interfere with your social life'[345]), so he improvises by using a cocoa tin lid as a medallion, only to get it stuck – with dispiriting symbolism – inside Arkwright's cash register ('It's got me by the dangler!'[346]).

Arkwright himself, meanwhile, seems no more likely to transcend the trapped relationship. The knowledge that he is engaged indefinitely to Nurse Gladys Emmanuel only adds to his sense of frustration, reminding him on a daily basis of what is so near and yet still so far from his grasp.

There he stands, inside his shop, gazing across the road at her house, reflecting on the fact that she remains there 'alone in that huge bed, with ample room for the s-small private grocer'.[347] Impressed to some extent by her elusiveness ('cuddly but stubborn, bless her'[348]), but rattled by the length of her resistance (ARKWRIGHT: 'Being engaged to you is like having your own piano and not being allowed t-to have a tinkle on it.' GLADYS: 'I wouldn't mind but you're always after the same three notes'[349]), he celebrates each minor victory ('I made a little progress last night with the aid of some Cy-Cyprus sherry. She's still sticking to her principles, but only just'[350]) while reluctantly accepting that he is really no nearer to winning the war ('No, she'll never name the day while she's got her old m-mother living over there with her. It's a pity her mother can't f-find somewhere to go and live p-permanently, y'know. Like heaven, for instance'[351]).

All he can do, throughout this series, is to keep on pushing, pleading and pestering:

ARKWRIGHT: When are we g-going to get married, eh?
GLADYS: You know how things are.
ARKWRIGHT: I d-don't even kn-know *where* things are.
GLADYS: We'll get married as soon as I can see me way clear. *[Looks at goods on the counter]* What are your meringues like?
ARKWRIGHT: I'm not telling you till after we're married! Two can play at that game, y'know!
GLADYS: You silly beggar! Come here, I'm in a hurry!
ARKWRIGHT: So am I! It's very difficult living in this constant s-state of anticipation.
GLADYS: I can get you something for that.

ARKWRIGHT: I've *got* something for that.

GLADYS: In a bottle!

ARKWRIGHT: Oh.

GLADYS: Anyway, it's your own fault. You won't live with me mother and I *can't* leave her.

ARKWRIGHT: Look, she's a dear little f-frail old lady. Course you can leave her – dump her on a park bench and run for it!

GLADYS: Typical! No wonder she can't stand you!

ARKWRIGHT: I don't see how anyone can live with your mother. Your father couldn't s-stick it five minutes, could he?

GLADYS: He didn't walk out on her. He were killed in the war!

ARKWRIGHT: There you are, you see, they'll go to any lengths to avoid her!

GLADYS: Don't be awful!

ARKWRIGHT: Oh, all right.

GLADYS: I mean, she gets so *bored* lying in that lonely bed hour after hour.

ARKWRIGHT: Yes, I kn-know the feeling.[352]

As with previous series, there was one episode in particular that seemed to make more of a mark in the memory. The fifth instalment, entitled 'The Man from Down Under', stood out due to its willingness (in classic sitcom style) to rattle the cages a little by threatening the cohesion of the comic trio.

The future of the cosy *faux* family unit of Arkwright, Gladys and Granville is suddenly placed in danger, at least in the anxious eyes of Arkwright, by the news that Arthur 'Chalky' White, one of Gladys's old admirers, is planning a visit. Now a big success abroad with a business based in Australia, White (who always thought that Gladys looked like Jane Russell 'from the side') is back in Britain to look up old acquaintances, and Arkwright has convinced himself that it is only a matter of time before this self-made man in his 'b-b-big flash car' will roll up across the road and start looking up Nurse Gladys.

Tense and twitchy, he cannot stop himself from watching out for signs of unexpected activity. When, for example, he spots Nurse Gladys, dressed in her uniform, climb inside her Morris Minor and prepare to drive off, he rushes over to interrogate her as to where she might be going:

ARKWRIGHT: Are you *sure* this journey is for m-medicinal purposes only?

GLADYS: Where else would I be going dressed like this?

ARKWRIGHT: Well, you might be combining business with... Oh, dear, I daren't even *think* what you might be combining business with!

GLADYS: I don't know what you're going on about.

ARKWRIGHT: It's just that I get this impression that you've b-been d-doing yourself up a bit.

GLADYS: Cheeky devil! You make me sound like a condemned shed!

[She drives off, leaving Arkwright shouting after her]

ARKWRIGHT: Well, j-just you remember – you're *m-my* condemned shed!!

Back in the shop, it seems appropriate that Arkwright, his thoughts always a simple mixture of money and sex, should be counting coins as he worries about a woman:

ARKWRIGHT: Oh, i-it's no good. It's no good. I used to get m-more pleasure than this out of c-counting money!

GRANVILLE: I don't know what you're worried about – you're the one she's engaged to.

ARKWRIGHT: Yet we've never really c-cemented it, though, have we, eh? *[Looks wistful]* I've done a bit of p-pointing up once or twice.

GRANVILLE: You've got no proof that he's planning to see her.

ARKWRIGHT: Listen, he's always f-fancied her, Granville.

GRANVILLE: Nah, she's probably forgotten all about him.

ARKWRIGHT: Well, then, he'll make sure she remembers him, won't he? Coming round here, b-brown as a nut, doing tricks with his b-boomerang. Probably v-vice-versa and all!

He gets himself into such a state of fevered confusion that he actually agrees to refund Gordon Stackpool the money he spent on an unwanted metric clothes line, thus causing the whole neighbourhood to start speculating about his sanity. 'I thought he was unshakeable,' says one regular customer. 'And then you hear all these stories about him giving money back!'

As if this sudden profligacy is not a sufficient sign of imminent chaos, Arkwright also starts acting as oddly as Granville, forsaking the usual fussing over the small details in favour of pondering the bigger picture. Staring at an overcooked rissole surrounded by a pile of soggy brown chips, he moans just as bitterly as his nephew normally does about the life that he is expected to lead:

ARKWRIGHT: All these years I've w-worked in the shop, man and d-dogsbody, I've always had me *mind* on me work! *[He points to an old picture]* E-Even in m-me Dad's day, back there in that old shop i-in Canal Street, I've always been s-spurred on by the p-profit motive. Either that or a c-clip round the ear or a k-kick up the back yard. If he were alive today he'd t-turn in his grave.

GRANVILLE: Pardon?

ARKWRIGHT: And all because of a lousy Australian!

GRANVILLE: Chalky White is not Australian! Eat your rissole!

ARKWRIGHT: Oh, I c-can't think of f-food at a t-time like this, I'm p-past caring! Haven't you done any carrots?

GRANVILLE: You're past caring but you're not past c-c-c-carrots?

ARKWRIGHT: Well, what kind of a meal is *this* for a f-fighting man? No wonder my m-morale is low!

GRANVILLE: A minute ago you were past caring.

ARKWRIGHT: How do *you* know what I'm past? Perhaps I'm p-past IT!

GRANVILLE: What? Past what?

ARKWRIGHT: It. That's what I'm p-past. *It!*

GRANVILLE: What about 'It'?

ARKWRIGHT: I'm *past* it, *that's* what about it!

GRANVILLE: Rubbish! Look, if you're still hungry when you've finished that, I'll open a nice tin of peaches.

ARKWRIGHT: Are they Australian?

GRANVILLE: No. They are Californian.

ARKWRIGHT: Oh, well, th-that's all right, then. I've always thought there was something strange about them Australians. I think it's all that w-walking about in the street with them little sh-short trousers on. Too much air to the b-brain.

GRANVILLE: You're just jealous.

ARKWRIGHT: Of course I'm j-jealous! I've got a *right* to be jealous! Men don't like other men walking around with their knees bare and rat-tat-tatting on their fiancée's knockers!

Arkwright's fears appear to be confirmed when Granville, sent off for a spot of surveillance, does indeed spot a 'big flash car' parked outside Gladys's house. Horrified, Arkwright persuades his nephew to help him sneak across and let down all of the tyres.

Hearing Gladys and a mystery man emerging from her house, the pair of them duck down for cover as an engine starts up. They are then surprised to see the couple ride off on a motorbike while the car remains static and uninhabited.

Arkwright and Granville flee back to the shop, where the real owner of the car – an angry insurance salesman – soon arrives to complain about the local hooligans who have sabotaged his tyres. Granville manages to confuse and elude him by pretending to be Chinese, and then, hours later, when Gladys finally returns, Arkwright is waiting in his dressing gown to conclude his investigation:

ARKWRIGHT: Wh-Where have you been?

GLADYS: If you *must* know, I've been on an emergency mission to the mother of an old friend!

ARKWRIGHT: I s-saw your 'old friend'! I also saw q-quite a lot of your leg at the same time! Why the m-motorbike? What's the matter with his car?

GLADYS: Whose car?

ARKWRIGHT: Chalky White! Him with the s-space helmet!

GLADYS: That wasn't Chalky White! That was Muriel Hawkins' husband! Muriel's mother's poorly! You jealous great idiot!

ARKWRIGHT: So you haven't *seen* Chalky? You promise?

GLADYS: Oh, I've *seen* him. He called three days ago. And I sent him packing. I've never liked *him*.

ARKWRIGHT: Oh, God bless you, G-Gladys Emmanuel!

[He kisses her warmly on the cheek]

GLADYS: Now, isn't it time silly old fools were in bed?

ARKWRIGHT: I thought you'd n-never ask!

With the rude intrusion averted, the unofficial family unit is left unaffected. Gladys can go home to check on her mother, Granville can reclaim his monopoly on melancholy, and Arkwright, standing sentry-like at the entrance to the shop, can reassure himself that (once the lingering gossip about that one rogue refund has died down) all will soon be back to normal:

Them women all think I've gone daft. Mrs Featherstone certainly thinks I'm daft. That big insurance man with the flash car, he thinks Granville's daft. Mind you, he *is* daft. Yes, the world is mad tonight. But Gladys still belongs to me. If you can call sleeping in different beds 'belonging'. Meanwhile, there's money to be made, Arkwright.

They'll all be trooping into the shop tomorrow to see if I *am* mad. Dad, if you're listening up there: I am once more in control. Ready to hold high the blood-stained banner and pursue the creed of small businessmen everywhere: 'Fleece 'em for every penny they've got!'

After one more episode – a rather less notable affair about dubious fashions and ill-advised ads – the third series came to a close on 25 April 1982. Just like when the run had begun, there had barely been a mention of the sitcom in the papers from week to week, except for one, very significant, regular feature: the TV Top Ten.

While most of the critics had continued to ignore it, *Open All Hours*, during its third series, had consistently been at the top, or very close to it, of the ratings every single week of its run. Peaking at 14.55 million, the show had averaged about 13.3 million viewers per show, frequently out-performing all of the other top attractions on BBC1 (including such hugely popular programmes as *Dallas*, *Top of the Pops*, *The Kenny Everett Television Show* and *Cagney & Lacey*).[353]

Open All Hours, therefore, had more or less risen without trace to become one of the most successful shows of the year, and one of the top-rated sitcoms of the era. The so-called 'gentle', 'little' comedy, which had been under-appreciated and underestimated for so long, was now having the last – and loudest – laugh.

The team was able to celebrate, in a sense, at the end of the year, when they were invited to contribute a mini-episode of their sitcom – alongside similar shorts from *Yes Minister*, *Only Fools and Horses*, *Last of the Summer Wine*, *The Fall and Rise of Reginald Perrin*, *Sorry!* and *Butterflies* – to a Frank Muir-hosted BBC1 festive special (shown on 27 December) entitled *The Funny Side of Christmas*. *Open All Hours* was there, by right, as one of the BBC's biggest shows of the time.

The eight-minute contribution made the most of its brief spell on the screen by exploring how the ultimate shopkeeper would react to being obliged to 'celebrate' the season by refraining from doing any selling. It was thus an artful snapshot of one man's commercial frustration.

It began with a telling absence of action. Arkwright is in his overalls, looking dour and deflated, standing still in an empty shop on Christmas morning. Granville, on the other hand, is in his best and only suit, looking bright and excited, bounding down to greet the day with a smile and a party horn. They are due over at Nurse Gladys Emmanuel's for 'Christmas din-dins'.

Arkwright, however, seems less than keen, admitting that he had hoped that Gladys's mother would be going away for the festive season (GRANVILLE: 'Where to?' ARKWRIGHT: 'Heaven'), and complaining that he not only has to close the shop on this particular Christmas Day but also 'every f-flipping Christmas Day'. Granville, on the other hand, refuses to let his uncle drag down his spirits, as, apart from the festive lunch, he is also looking forward to a teatime assignation with the indecisive but well-meaning 'Wavy Mavis'.

Arkwright's mood is lifted slightly by the arrival of Gladys from across the road:

ARKWRIGHT: Oh! *[Staring at her chest]* Happy Christmas to you both!

GLADYS: *[Ignoring his flirting]* When you come across, will you bring me some icing sugar?

ARKWRIGHT: Icing sugar? *We've got a CUSTOMER, Granville!* Come in, my dear! Icing sugar? Anything for *you*, my dear, anything at all. That'll be 82p – get it out!

GLADYS: I see you're in your usual generous Christmas mood.

ARKWRIGHT: Ah-ah-*ah!* It's usually 89!

[She ignores him and holds her arms out wide for Granville]

GLADYS: Merry Christmas, Granville!
GRANVILLE: Oh, Merry Christmas!

[He gratefully buries his head in her bosom]

ARKWRIGHT: Eh, not that merry! Come out of there!

[He looks up slightly]

GRANVILLE: And the compliments of the season!

[He buries his head again]

166

Arkwright tries to change the subject by asking politely about Gladys's mother, but this only gives Granville the cue to lament his own lack of a mother, which also provides him an excuse to go in for a third nestle in Gladys's bosom. Once he has resurfaced for air, she decides it is time for the would-be family unit to go off to her place for lunch:

GLADYS: Come on, you great Scrooge, leave your money box alone for one day.
ARKWRIGHT: Oh, all right.

[He gazes wistfully at the cash register]

ARKWRIGHT: I *hate* to see it in this condition.
GLADYS: What condition?
ARKWRIGHT: Shut.
GLADYS: Oh, come on!

[She goes out the door]

GRANVILLE: Will you be turning the lights off?
ARKWRIGHT: No, I think maybe I'll leave j-just one on as a sort of beacon for the w-weary customer. A little light shining out for the benefit of some poor lost soul who might still have a few bob in his pocket.

[Granville makes yet another rasp on his party horn before departing after Gladys]

ARKWRIGHT: Oh, that's g-going to get worse before it gets better!

[He moves away reluctantly from the counter]

ARKWRIGHT: All right, Lord, all right, I'll shut for today. All day.

[He takes off his overalls and continues to commune with his creator]

ARKWRIGHT: Now I don't want you to presume, Lord, that I'm t-trying to t-teach you your business, but I

hope you'll remember this little gesture of
mine when it comes to our J-January sales. I
mean, you scratch my back, Lord, you know
what I mean…

[Gladys can be heard shouting: 'Are you coming?']

ARKWRIGHT: I'm coming, love, I'm coming!

[He opens the door, but cannot help looking back one more time]

ARKWRIGHT: Oh, what a wasted opportunity! I must say,
y'know, Lord, I do sometimes wonder why
you considered it necessary to get yourself
born on a b-b-bank holiday!

That was the end of the special episode, and the end of a special year for
the sitcom. Against all the odds, it had made it to the top – and purely
on its own steam.

While television's increasingly methodical managerial class were
concentrating on manipulating the nation's viewing habits, employing
more and more technical and top-down ways to shape, schedule and
sustain standard TV tastes, *Open All Hours* (though dumped into that
shadowy little slot after *Songs of Praise*) achieved that most old-fashioned
but authentic of things: it offered itself up to the public, simply and
straightforwardly, and the public looked at it and loved it.

There was only one surprise left for this sitcom to spring. At the
very moment when it had established itself as one of the nation's *bona
fide* favourites, at the very moment when it had struck up such an
extraordinary sense of momentum, it went ahead and took a three-
year break.

CHAPTER ELEVEN

Out of Stock

*Hey – will you b-bring that milk in
before you c-curdle it?*

There would seem, in retrospect, something almost inevitable, in this strangest of sitcom stories, about *Open All Hours* being dragged back out of the spotlight just when it was set to confirm its status as one of Britain's top television shows. It was like watching one of those old music hall routines in which a man's braces are caught in a door: every time there are a few hard-earned steps of progress, there is a sudden reversal straight back to the start.

The third series of *Open All Hours* was indisputably a hit. Any other sitcom, from this or any other era, would surely have been assured, after that kind of performance, of a rapid return to the screen. Shows that commanded 13 million or more viewers each week were not just tossed aside. *Open All Hours*, however, was the sad exception to the rule.

There was no hidden agenda against it. There was no clandestine clique of critics. It simply continued to fail to capture the imagination of the executives. It was like the trusted but taken-for-granted employee, consistently impressive and effective but always overlooked for a pat on the back, let alone a promotion or pay rise.

Open All Hours remained, in their eyes, that 'nice little show', that 'cosy comedy', that 'gentle sitcom', which was perfectly pleasant in its own humble way, but was never going to be as great and as grand as, say, *Porridge*. The result was that, whenever something new, something deemed more exciting, something that seemed edgier, came along, *Open All Hours* was always the sitcom that was most vulnerable to being cast aside.

It did not help, in this sense, that Roy Clarke, with *Last of the Summer Wine*, already had another sitcom – also set in the north, also considered 'gentle' by the executives – that was by this time firmly established as a fixture on the BBC. If the bosses were only looking for one of these two shows to fill the niche market for quirky Yorkshire sitcoms, then *Last of the Summer Wine*, which began its seventh series at the start of 1983, was always going to be in pole position. While there is no hard evidence in the archives to confirm that such a policy formally existed, it is certainly noticeable how each new series of *Last of the Summer Wine* was practically rubber-stamped from one year to the next, while the future for *Open All Hours* always seemed to hang in the balance.

It also did not help the show's prospects that David Jason was now enjoying so much success elsewhere as the star of *Only Fools and Horses*. Its second series, in 1982, had actually attracted far fewer viewers than *Open All Hours* (about 5 million fewer, on average, in fact[354]), but, with such stand-out recent episodes as 'A Touch of Glass' (in which Del Boy and Rodney ended up watching in helpless horror as the chandelier they are supposed to be cleaning drops down and smashes on the floor), it had captured the imagination of a growing body of fans and charmed the vast majority of the critics, who were now clamouring for more. With another series already commissioned for the autumn of 1983, therefore, few shows of the time seemed to be building up more momentum, and David Jason's time, for the foreseeable future, seemed tied up with this other sitcom.

His mood at the time also seemed better suited to *Only Fools and Horses*, because, although he still genuinely loved working with the team on *Open All Hours*, and still relished sharing scenes with Ronnie Barker, he had grown somewhat frustrated by the way that his own performances had been treated in the previous series. Having now starred in his own shows, where – as a leading man – his opinions carried clout, it was getting harder for him to revert to the more muted role of being merely the supporting player:

> One time, we finished an episode and discovered that we had overrun the thirty-minute mark by several minutes. So we sat in the editing room working out what to leave out in order to trim the

show down to the requisite size. As I sat there, I could see all my funny stuff hitting the cutting-room floor. I had gone very quiet and Ronnie noticed and asked me if I was all right. I said, 'Any jokes that I have are getting cut. All I'm left with is feeding you.'[355]

Ronnie Barker was always quick to reassure Jason, whom he referred to teasingly as 'a great comedy grumbler',[356] about the worth of his work (on one occasion sending him a poem in rhyming couplets that finished with the playful advice: 'The future will provide thy need/Till then be content to be a little feed'[357]), and Jason, in turn, was always just as quick to appreciate what a rare and special chemistry it was that they shared ('It was like playing top tennis,' he would say. 'When you see people playing tennis, it's tennis. But when you see two top players, serving things that you think the other guy can't get and he does and he returns it, I've always likened that to Ronnie and me'[358]). There was, nonetheless, a nagging feeling now that, perhaps, he might have outgrown being that 'little feed', and outgrown being Granville now that he was dominating his own show as Del Boy.

Ronnie Barker, meanwhile, was pondering other projects of his own. Always keenly aware of how fickle some of his fans could be ('For a while people said [of *Open All Hours*], "Very nice, but we like *Porridge*". Then came yet another series and they missed *Open All Hours*'[359]), and always wary about becoming too closely associated with one particular role, he was considering pursuing something new.

A Welsh character – an egotistical photographer called Plantagenet Evans – was one such possibility. Having enjoyed playing a Welshman in one of the episodes of *Seven of One* (Clement and La Frenais' 'I'll Fly You for a Quid'), and having regretted seeing it dismissed as a possible series, he was now developing ideas for a similar sort of pilot (the repeatedly postponed *The Magnificent Evans*, which had been commissioned originally as long ago as July 1981[360]) with Roy Clarke. It was this, combined with his regular work on *The Two Ronnies*, that rendered Barker less inclined to push very hard for a swift return for *Open All Hours*.

The demand for the show, however, was still strong – not only at home but also, and increasingly, abroad. Sales to foreign broadcasters were growing fairly rapidly (especially in Australia and Scandinavia[361]) and, from late 1982, all three existing series had started being shown in the US via a pay-TV cable service called RCTV, a newly formed division of Rockefeller Center Inc.[362] It was hardly on its way to becoming a major international success, but, slowly but surely, *Open All Hours* was forging a foreign following.

It was also holding on to its large band of British fans. Although the wait for a new series went on, there were no signs that the appetite for the sitcom was being sated. The opposite, if anything, was closer to the truth.

No matter what else the cast members did, there were still plenty of members of the public who were eager to ask them when they would be back making more episodes of *Open All Hours*. At a time when remembering a past show required a real engagement of the imagination, rather than just an idle press of the 'On Demand' button on the computer or TV remote, *Open All Hours* remained in many people's minds as the months went on.

If proof of the persistence of its popularity was required, then it arrived early on in 1983, when the third series was repeated, once again at peak time, on BBC1. It performed remarkably well in the ratings, attracting an average of over 10 million viewers each week.[363] This appears to have encouraged the BBC suddenly to consider bringing the sitcom back, and, on 30 March 1983, a fourth series was indeed commissioned, with Roy Clarke being promised £4000 per script (all six of which would have to be submitted by November).[364]

Once again, however, the enthusiasm for the programme among executives seemed notably lacking, because on 15 September 1983 the contract was abruptly cancelled by the BBC's new head of comedy, Gareth Gwenlan, and Roy Clarke was asked to write the eighth series of *Last of the Summer Wine* instead.[365] No reason for the switch is recorded in the various memos preserved in the BBC's archives, but it seems that, not for the first time, the more established sitcom was given preferential treatment in the production schedules.

Better news came the following summer, when, on 2 May 1984, Gareth Gwenlan announced that he was going to re-commission a fourth series of *Open All Hours*, and Roy Clarke was pencilled in to receive a raise to £4500 per episode. This, however, was not quite the end of the problems dogging the proposed new production.

There was still what was referred to internally, with something of a shiver, as 'The *Yes Minister* problem' to be overcome. This referred to the unintended consequences caused by the BBC's efforts to bring back its critically acclaimed political sitcom.

The writers of *Yes Minister*, Antony Jay and Jonathan Lynn, had ended the show in 1982 after three hugely successful series. Although the BBC had asked them to continue, Jay and Lynn, who had always felt undervalued as writers by the Corporation, demanded an unprecedented (by British standards) £10,000 fee between them for each new episode. The BBC had baulked at this figure, pointing out that it would create a dangerous precedent in terms of its regular pay scale for writers, and so Jay and Lynn ended the talks abruptly and moved on to other projects.

In 1984, however, Bill Cotton was promoted to the post of the BBC's director of television, and, being a great admirer of *Yes Minister*, made it one of his priorities to bring the programme back to the screen. He duly held talks with Jay and Lynn, promising to meet their demands – so long as they also delivered a Christmas special in addition to two more series – and *Yes Minister* (soon evolving into *Yes, Prime Minister*) was thus back on BBC1 by the end of the year.[366]

The problem, however, was that the only way that the BBC hoped to prevent this deal encouraging its other major writers from demanding similar pay rises was to keep it a secret. As usual, of course, at a broadcaster as big as the BBC, it did not stay a secret for long.

Within weeks – probably even within days – the news of Jay and Lynn's deal had slipped out of White City and reached the ears of every powerful agent in London, and, as had been feared, the BBC started being deluged with telephone calls and letters demanding higher fees for their own clients. It was thus expected that Sheila Lemon, who was Roy Clarke's agent, would soon be doing the same for him.

On 10 May 1984, shortly after it had been agreed to offer Clarke £4500 per script for the new series of *Open All Hours*, an agitated Tom Rivers (the assistant head of the BBC's copyright department) sent off a memo to the head of light entertainment, John Howard Davies, warning him of the hazards ahead:

I would therefore have expected to have to offer a commissioning fee of £4500.00 for the new *Open All Hours*. However, Sheila Lemon will undoubtedly assume, <u>unless I specifically inform her to the contrary,</u> that the offer is a top fee. We therefore lay ourselves open to charges of bad faith if contracts to such as Roy Clarke are issued with nothing said. How shall I proceed?[367]

This, predictably enough, caused a fair amount of panic within the corridors of power at Television Centre over the course of the next few months, as Rivers' request for help was bounced back and forth in and out of various executives' offices. Michael Grade, the newly installed controller of BBC1, captured the mood well in a memo he distributed to various fellow executives on 6 November:

> I have discussed [Tom Rivers'] memo of 30 October with [the head of light entertainment] and [the head of comedy], and very quickly a serious situation is brewing.
>
> The special case of *Yes Minister* has quickly leaked to every agent in London and we have to assess the situation, which at worst could cost us around £100,000 if we are to play fair with the star sit-com writers; knock-ons in the variety field are inevitable but inestimable. Comedy repeats are going to be too costly if we cannot hold the line. But with news of the Jay & Lynn deal already on the streets, I do not know how we are going to treat fairly the people who were serving us so well (e.g. Roy Clarke, Esmonde & Larbey, Carla Lane, John Sullivan, David Croft/Jimmy Perry/ Jeremy Lloyd).[368]

It was subsequently decided that other writers and their agents would have to be told that the *Yes Minister* deal was indeed a 'special case' which should not be taken as a precedent for other scripts by other writers, 'or even other scripts by Jay and Lynn'. Bill Cotton, it was noted in another memo, accepted, rather dryly, that 'other writers will not like this', and the relevant heads of departments were advised that if any writers 'threaten to turn down our commission' the head of light entertainment should be alerted before any line was drawn by either party.[369]

The result for Roy Clarke of this intense and somewhat chaotic bout of internal deliberations was that he ended up getting offered (in December 1984) an improved fee of £4750 per episode of the fourth series of *Open All Hours*.[370] Pleasantly surprised ('I had no idea any of that was going on!'[371]), he accepted this promptly, and, at long last, the new production was put in motion.

Sydney Lotterby was once again installed as the producer/director, and talks began with the key members of the cast to secure their participation. Ronnie Barker accepted a huge fee (for the time) of £7000 per episode, while David Jason (who still found himself unable to resist another series working alongside 'The Guv'nor') was rewarded for adding to what was already a hectic personal schedule by being awarded £2750 per episode (the same as he was now receiving for starring in *Only Fools and Horses*) and Lynda Baron also accepted the improved sum of £1000 per show.[372]

Although the fourth series would not be shown until the autumn of 1985, it was, unusually, filmed well in advance, with location work being completed in February and March, followed by studio recordings during April and May. The actual reason for the long delay before the broadcasts has long been lost in the mists of time ('I'm afraid I really can't remember,'[373] Sydney Lotterby said when asked), but the most probable explanation is that the BBC did not want to 'waste' the show by screening it during the summer season, when traditionally the average size of the audience tended to shrink, and preferred instead to save it for September when the viewing figures could be expected to be rising back up to a higher level.

As before, the sense of camaraderie in the camp was exceptionally strong from the start. During rehearsal sessions and location shooting, for example, there was always laughter as soon as the actors arrived early each morning: 'We used to exasperate poor Sydney Lotterby,' Lynda Baron would recall, 'because we'd all sit down together and talk at once at breakfast. In the end, he decided to eat at another table on the other side of the room. "I can't cope with you lot at this early hour," he'd say. "I'm off!" Ronnie would say, "We won't talk at once, we'll press an imaginary buzzer when it's our turn." What happened was that we still all talked at once, but were also pressing imaginary buzzers simultaneously. Then there was the time that Ronnie and I couldn't stop laughing, so had to pack up early for the day. It was a wonderful series to work on.'[374]

Stephanie Cole would agree: 'There were so many laughs. And both Ronnie and David were absolute joys to work with. I always had such a wonderful time. It wasn't like work at all. I particularly remember the incredible friendliness and sweetness of the people in whose street we were filming, even though we were disrupting their lives. They were always so lovely and so welcoming.'[375]

Each episode was recorded, once again, on Sundays in Studio 8 at Television Centre. The only change in personnel concerned the warm-up man. Felix Bowness, somewhat ironically, was unavailable to do his usual duties because, by this stage, he was too busy preparing, among other things, for his next spell in front of the cameras as Fred Quilley in *Hi-de-Hi!* (the seventh series of which was due to begin in December).

In his place came a much younger man named Bobby Bragg, a Rochester-born comedian and all-round entertainer who at the time was based in Gillingham in Kent. He had been a friend of David Jason's since the 1970s, but it was a recent performance in pantomime alongside Lynda Baron that had brought him to the attention of Sydney Lotterby as a suitable replacement for Bowness.

It would be, as he later confirmed, 'an incredible learning curve' to find himself, at that relatively early stage in his career, a part of such a special team:

The main thing that I remember of the early days of going in to work on the show was the fact that they were all so on top of their words. Compared to any other sitcom that I was working on at the time, their professionalism was really exceptional. Ronnie and David never, and I *mean* never, fluffed their lines.

And that meant that the more they'd learnt the script, and the better that they'd learnt it, they could go on to take liberties with it. When, for example, the audience reaction was different to what was expected – say a line got a much bigger laugh – they could change and react without even thinking, and play to the strengths of it.[376]

Bragg's existing friendship with David Jason and Lynda Baron helped him to settle quickly into his own role on the show, but Ronnie Barker soon struck up his own rapport with the newcomer:

> I got on with Ronnie B. from the start, and he seemed to take me under his wing a bit. And in spite of all the pressure that he endured, and all of the work and the worry that he put in to get us ready for a studio recording, he would still find the time to listen to my stuff in the breaks, and he would come up to me the following week and say: 'That routine you did about the one-way system on Shepherd's Bush...' And I'd say, 'Yes?' He'd say, 'I loved it, but, listen, if you do it like this...' and he'd proceed to give me four laughs where up to this point I'd got one! It was astonishing that he actually took the trouble and the time to listen to me, who was at the bottom of the ladder, and help me.
>
> He was the most extraordinary man. He always wanted to help you – he was always extremely supportive. Very soon after I'd joined the team he started calling me 'Sir Robert'. He was always incredibly warm and supportive and generous towards me. I never felt that I'd over-stepped the mark or upset him or anything like that. I always felt a huge warmth and kindness from him. I remember that about him more than anything: he was a very, very, generous man.
>
> There was no selfishness about him at all. None of this 'I must get the biggest laugh'. Even when he was acting with David, if Ronnie thought that the best line belonged to David rather than him, and it was a bigger laugh, he would give it to David unhesitatingly. There'd be no preciousness, no pulling rank: 'Oh, *that's* a big laugh, *I'm* having that one!' Ronnie just wanted the show to be as funny as it could possibly be.[377]

This was a quality of Barker's that would also stay in the memory of his fellow cast member Stephanie Cole:

> One of the many things that I learnt from Ronnie was his thoughtfulness for his colleagues. He used to do the most

extraordinarily generous thing. When you're in the studio, for those of us who are in every week, you still get a *bit* nervous, because you're in front of an audience as well as the cameras and that's a difficult technique, but you're used to it. But if you're an actor coming in to do just one episode, it's very, very scary. And so Ronnie would do this thing: if someone coming in was obviously really nervous when they started to do a scene with him, he would deliberately make a mistake. That would break the atmosphere, because they would then relax, and the audience relaxed – they didn't know that Ronnie hardly ever really made a mistake – and the actor would give a good performance. It was an incredible and wonderful and generous thing for Ronnie to do, and, many years later, when I was doing *Waiting for God* – which was one of the first series that I led – if that ever happened in our series when we had a new actor come in then I would do the same thing.[378]

Although most of Bobby Bragg's experiences of the show would come from the night of the recordings, when he was out and about in the studio, he was given the chance to acquire a much greater insight into the whole programme-making process when he was given a brief walk-on part in one of the shows:

I played a customer in one episode ['The Mystical Boudoir of Nurse Gladys Emmanuel']. I only had one line – 'You don't need a guard dog with a till as fierce as that!' – but it was fantastic because it meant that I spent the whole week with all of them, from blocking on the floor with tape in the rehearsal room to actually being in the studio on the recording night. Normally, of course, doing the warm-up, I'd be coming in at about four o'clock for the dress rehearsal, do the run-through and then the recording in the evening, so I'd miss out on all the preparation and detail that went into bringing it to that point. So being in that episode was a wonderful experience.

I would just sit back and listen, watch and learn during rehearsal as David and Ronnie tried to anticipate where the big laughs would come, and then of course the expressions would come in as they developed it off the page. Ronnie, for example, would do the most extraordinary things with props. He'd say, 'We'll need a broom here,' or 'We'll need a set of scales for this,' and he was always very specific about such things. I'd be thinking, 'What the hell is he doing now? Why does he need *that?*' And then, as it developed, you would see this wonderful business that he'd created out of nothing, building it up bit by bit, and thereby finding two, maybe three, laughs on the way up where there would originally only have been one on paper.

Both of them, Ronnie and David, were magnificent actors with an amazing sense of comedy timing. And, even more impressively, they would telegraph each other. I guess it was in part because of their background in the theatre, but also because of the relationship that they had together, they just knew what the other one was thinking. If you were watching close up, you could see the cogs working and you knew that one would instinctively go with the other. It was so fascinating to watch, it really was. I've worked on hundreds of sitcoms since, and I don't think we'll ever see the likes of that again, in the way that it was conceived and constructed. It was truly magical.[379]

One of the many things that impressed Bragg during this week was Ronnie Barker's unquenchable creativity:

He was always thinking, always searching for something new and something better, from the first day to the last. Once they'd done the read-through and were off the page, you'd see Ronnie start to develop it. 'Do you think I should put a stutter in there?' he'd say. 'Or do you think I should hold it until this word?' And to watch him gradually take control of these words on the page, and play with them until he was completely happy with how they worked in action, was very special. And then, on the actual night of recording, he'd sometimes suddenly come up with something else which was completely new, and that would astonish you all over again.

I remember one such instance of this. There was a line in my episode that showed, if you were lucky enough to have been present all week from rehearsals through to the recording, what a genius Ronnie was. The scene had Mrs Parsloe coming in and saying, 'Arkwright, I'll have a large washing up liquid.' So Arkwright says, 'Will there be anything else, Mrs Parsloe?' And she says something like, 'No, that's it,' and on they go with their next lines.

Now, we rehearsed that a thousand times during the week, exactly the same each time, but then on the night, and actually on the first take, Mrs Parsloe came in, said, 'Arkwright, I'll have a large washing up liquid,' and he said, 'Yes, I think I'll join you!' And the whole place erupted. It was a piece of comedy genius that was absolutely spontaneous.

That was a sign of the greatness of Ronnie Barker: that he could think on his feet like that. And the supporting cast were all such pros that they just went with him. It didn't throw them, they took it beautifully and it worked magnificently. And Syd Lotterby kept it in.[380]

Lotterby was another figure whom Bragg came to admire even more once he had witnessed his work during the week:

Syd Lotterby was a great, great director. I remember Ronnie and David spending hours trying to get each shot looking as good as it could be. But Syd, being the great comedy director that he was, never responded with any of this, 'Oh, *I'm* going to shoot it like *this!*' He knew what he was doing, he knew how to make things work, but he liked to collaborate. He would say to Ronnie, 'How do *you* think we should do this? Do you think this should be a two-shot, or do you think I should come around here and do it like this? Which do you think would be funnier?' And they'd discuss it together for hours, trying to make absolutely sure that they got the best shot. Everything was so thought-through, and precise, and beautifully constructed. It was a work of art.[381]

Finally, Bragg was also struck by the democratic spirit of the show's writer, who, like Lotterby, always acted like a genuine team player:

One of the beautiful things about the show was the attitude of Roy Clarke. It's a fact that many other writers of sitcoms are very precious about their lines being spoken exactly on the comma and the full stop – every single word has to be absolutely spot on. Roy Clarke, however, very rarely came to the studio, and, even if he did, if one of the actors wanted to expand on what he'd written originally, and do something a bit different, then he'd have no qualms about that. He'd let them get on with it. Because, great writer that he was, he also had the intelligence to realize that he was working with two great actors, and so, very shrewdly, he gave them their head. So if Ronnie and David decided between them that this particular scene would work better if the order of A, B and C was reversed or mixed up, they would do it, and, if it *did* work better, Roy would have no worries about it.[382]

One of the other remarkable things about the recordings was the freshness and energy of David Jason's performances, because he had gone, without any real break, straight from making the fourth series of *Only Fools and Horses* to making the fourth series of *Open All Hours*. Rather than conserving his energy by reverting to being merely a 'little feed', however, his pride and professionalism saw him hide whatever fatigue he might have been feeling and shine brightly from scene to scene.

The whole process, in fact, had never gone quite so smoothly or so well, with consistently impressive performances from Barker, Jason and Baron, along with some delightful supporting performances from the likes of Stephanie Cole and Tom Mennard. The applause from the studio audience, when the sixth and final episode had been completed, was loud and long and, as all of the cast members stood there taking their bows, there was a genuine sense of satisfaction in what, as a group, they had achieved.

The writing had been crafty, unforced and funny. The acting had been beautifully judged. The direction had been subtly smart and suggestive. It had been a consummate sitcom production.

As always with this show, however, there was an unconventional coda to the comedy. The feedback would be delayed.

Usually, the early episodes would start being broadcast while the latter ones were still being recorded, so the overlap would allow the team to get a sense of how the series was being received. On this occasion, however, there was going to be a gap – an unusually long gap – before any of the shows would reach the screen.

There was, nonetheless, a confident mood inside the studio. This series, everyone felt, was really going to please the public.

CHAPTER TWELVE

Series Four

Nothing so soothes the shopkeeper as the
sound of a w-well-aimed feather flicking
round his comestibles.

It would be well worth the wait. In September 1985, three years after it was last seen on the screen, and four long months after the fourth series was safely in the can, it was finally opened, like one of Arkwright's unlabelled tins, to reveal a sitcom at its best. *Open All Hours* was back, ready to satisfy its most devoted viewers, and pleasantly surprise those who were new.

It was greeted with what by now seemed like the obligatory apathy of the press. Only the *Radio Times* afforded the show even a modest amount of space, and even that tiny push seemed perfunctory. A quote from Lynda Baron – 'I know it would be much more interesting to say that all of the members of the cast fight, but we don't. We all get on extremely well'[383] – would have done nothing to challenge the common opinion among tabloid journalists that there was no point in a belated burst of interest in the sitcom; harmony does not sell papers.

It did not matter quite so much, this time around, to the *Open All Hours* team. The performance of the last series had proven that the show had won a large and loyal following. They were confident that the new series would be found by its core group of fans. They just hoped that even more people would take notice and give it a try.

The series began, at 7.30pm on 1 September 1985, in its usual Sunday evening slot. In keeping with the overall sleepy feel of the day's schedule, it followed a visit by *Songs of Praise* to the Greenbelt Festival in the grounds of Castle Ashby. As before, it was not an ideal mood-setter for a sitcom (homilies before humour, church before a chuckle), but, on the day of rest, at least the show could count on a large proportion of the population probably being at home.

The opening sequence was subtly different this time around, with the show seeming keen to poke fun at its own 'grim up north' image by starting with a vision even glummer and grainier than before. The corner shop was still pictured from a bird's eye level, but it was now seen on a dark and rainy day, with water sliding down the slate-grey roofs into the grimy guttering, and puddles settling on the sides of the street. A different selection of passers-by would wander in and out of shot each week, ranging from a man and wife wrapped up warmly against the wind, to one funereal figure searching for the odd dry spot on which to walk.

Arkwright and Granville were outside the shop as usual – the former (his cash-ready hands tucked safely inside his overall pockets) sniffing the air for customers, the latter (his trusty cloth dangling from the back of his off-white pinny) perched on a set of steps to spell out another promotion. They were where they always were, only now with a few more years washed through them.

Ronnie Barker, beginning in his early forties, had always been evolving easily towards the official age of Arkwright, and now, at 56, had clearly grown fully into the 58-year-old character. With his hair almost entirely white and his body stout and snug inside his overalls, he looked as though he really had been stuck in a corner shop for all of his life. Arkwright's eyes seemed tired and baggy from always being up and about since the early hours, his hands were poised like a gunslinger to grab any coin or commodity, and his feet seemed suited to shuffling the short distance back and forth between the bacon slicer and the till. One could have put him in any old shop in any corner of Britain, and he would have looked right and ready to over-charge.

David Jason, in contrast, had been obliged to work harder to re-inhabit Granville. Whereas the actor, by this stage, was 45, the character was still a shop-worn Peter Pan, a young man stuck somewhere strange between 25 and 35, still with his thick black curly hair, his 1970s tank top and his eternally boyish expression.

It was probably a little jarring, for some viewers, to watch him now as this figure frozen in time, having seen him, only a few months before, as the always vivid and vital Del Boy in *Only Fools and Horses*. As the experienced, street-wise, older brother Del Boy, he was ageing visibly on screen, as the passage of time showed itself more and more in the receding hairline and the expanding waist. As Granville in *Open All Hours*, however, Jason had to keep changing things to keep them looking the same, getting help from the hairpieces and youthful-looking outfits to increase the degree of disguise.

What was far more important than the make-up, of course, was the acting. Jason, like Barker, had more than enough acting technique to transcend any physical anachronisms. Just as the artful Barker had been able to capture Arkwright's crusty canniness even when he had been 12 years younger, so the similarly skilful Jason was now still capable of embodying Granville's sweet-natured boyishness.

Both characters, in this fourth series, would be seen as so desperate to break out of their trapped relationship that each of them was shown placing advertisements in the local paper, seeking someone to come in and force a change in the dull routine. In Granville's case, the request is for a 'soul mate', a young woman who will arrive and enable him to grow up and get a life. In Arkwright's case, the request is for a 'housekeeper', a mature woman whose imminent arrival will arouse enough jealousy in Nurse Gladys to provoke her into getting married.

Granville's advertisement is like a distillation of all his daydreams: 'YOUNG EXECUTIVE IN THE RETAIL TRADE WITH OWN FLAT AND FIRM'S TRANSPORT SEEKS LADY COMPANION. GENEROUS NATURE MORE IMPORTANT THAN LOOKS. EXPERIENCE NOT NECESSARY IF WILLING TO LEARN'. Arkwright's response ('So th-that's his caper, is it? Right, if he wants a woman, I'll g-get him a *woman!*') is like a crystallization of his cruelty.

Not since the first episode of *Steptoe & Son*, when young Harold arranges to meet a girl only for old Albert to sabotage the assignation by putting the clock forward an hour and fooling his son into thinking that he has been snubbed (HAROLD: 'Who did she think she was?' ALBERT: 'That's women for you'),[384] has there been such a cold and cynical example of one creature trapped in the sitcom cage ensuring that the other one stays imprisoned alongside him. Here was Granville at his most vulnerable, and Arkwright at his most devious, playing out the classic piece of comic fate.

First, Arkwright finds the hardest, harshest, most foul-mouthed local female available – a barmaid at the nearby White Feathers pub – and bribes her to answer Granville's ad and teach him an unwelcome lesson. When that sinister strategy backfires – 'Sherbet dabs! He actually *f-fancies* her!' – he decides to intervene, hides Granville's best trousers in the ice-cream compartment, and then calls the barmaid to cancel their next date ('Tell him w-what?' he asks, as she screams down the phone. 'Tell him t-to *do* what?? Well, I'll p-pass on the message, but if I c-cut out all the swearing there won't be much of it left, will there?!!'[385]).

Granville is shattered. 'I thought she was the one,' he says, sitting on a box of pears and staring sadly into space. 'It was love at first sight. It started with her sweater and then I gradually grew to love her bit by bit as we walked down the road. And she walked out of my life. Round the corner. Into the oblivion of Stanley Street.'[386]

As if to compound the crime, Arkwright goes and does much the same again a little later in the same series, when Granville becomes obsessed with impressing a new young woman in the area called Stephanie ('with a "ph"'). Arkwright waits until his nephew has won her over, and then, as soon as he gets the chance, wrecks the relationship completely, telling her that Granville has a wife and seven children. 'Now, I don't want you to t-treat him or judge him t-too harshly,' he says, utterly unconvincingly. 'I'll *kill* him if he comes near me again,' she snaps. 'Yes, well,' he replies, smugly, 'that doesn't sound *too* harsh.'[387]

Arkwright's own advertisement, for a live-in housekeeper, is rumbled as a ruse more or less immediately by those who know him best. Granville, once he has been reassured that the only potential spare room above the shop will remain stuffed full of lavatory cleaners, soon works out what his uncle is really up to ('You're a conniving old…man, aren't you, eh?'), while Gladys is even quicker to crack the code ('I know what you're doing – you're trying to rush me into marriage!'). All that Arkwright's plan manages to provoke is Mrs Featherstone, the so-called 'Black Widow', into applying for the position.

There had been portents of such an unwelcome occurrence in earlier episodes. In one, for example, the normally sour-faced misanthrope shocks the shopkeeper by allowing her down-turned mouth to twitch up into something like a smile as she attempts a uniquely saturnine style of flirtation:

ARKWRIGHT: The w-widow Featherstone! And what can we do for *you* that's b-brisk and impersonal and n-not necessarily inexpensive?

MRS FEATHERSTONE: Oh, it'll be inexpensive. I never waste me money. We've got a lot in common. You're the only other one I know with a wonderful non-spending way about you.

ARKWRIGHT: *[Nervously]* Oh, it's just a mask.

MRS FEATHERSTONE: You don't have to be modest! Not with me. Not with...Delphine Featherstone. Who's always admired every move you've never made.

ARKWRIGHT: *[Turning pale]* Yes, well, M-Mrs Featherstone –

MRS FEATHERSTONE: Call me 'Delphine'.

ARKWRIGHT: '*D-Delphine*'? W-We've got some tinned fruit called that somewhere.

MRS FEATHERSTONE: It's not an invitation I flash about lightly.

ARKWRIGHT: Oh, n-no-no, even your husband used to call you 'Mrs Featherstone'.

MRS FEATHERSTONE: I'm not one for familiarity. But then, acquisitiveness such as yours always undermines the resistance of the maturer woman. I hear them gossiping about you.

ARKWRIGHT: Oh, it's-it's a lie!

MRS FEATHERSTONE: 'That Arkwright,' they say. 'Rock hard and mean!' You must be very *proud* the way they all look up to you![388]

It is with real horror, therefore, that Arkwright responds when, following his advertisement, Mrs Featherstone (displaying all of the menacing directness of a money-seeking missile) emerges as the one woman who bids to do his bidding: 'Can you think of anyone better qualified to lighten the burden of a prosperous businessman?' she asks Granville. 'I've always admired the strength of his grip on money. He needs someone by his side. A person of the same sober financial disposition.'

Within seconds of her entering the shop to apply, Arkwright is out and on to the delivery bike, pedalling desperately down the street. 'I'll call again when it's more convenient,' cries out Mrs Featherstone after him, still unaware of the negative impression that she has made.

The two men, then, are left where they were before their respective bids to escape: cornered in the corner shop, facing the same fate. All that their solo efforts have proven is the basic sitcom law that when one door opens, it slams back shut – just as swiftly and fiercely as the cash tray in Arkwright's ancient till.

Both uncle and nephew are stuck where they are, in the shop, in the sitcom, obliged to get on with life here and now. Each one of them will no doubt keep pushing to get out, but both of them know, deep down, that, if push ever comes to shove and the resistance disappears, they would only fall flat on their faces.

What we see in the rest of this series, therefore, is the eternal clash of values and visions between the two people who are rooted beneath one roof. Granville will keep on dreaming, and Arkwright will keep on scheming, but neither of them will ever get where he wants to go.

Granville remains a stand-out study in self-delusion, boasting about his capacity for the more cultured and refined things in life ('I've got the blood of poets and lovers in my veins'[389]), while raging at the delay in realizing his dreams (GRANVILLE: 'Youth is passing me by! Life keeps poking me with its finger!' ARKWRIGHT: 'Yes, your mother had the same problem!'[390]) and reasserting his need to meet his ideal woman (someone 'simple, natural, unaffected, no bra'[391]). His brain is full of 'could've beens', 'should've beens' and 'never beens': 'I could've been anything, couldn't I, eh? I could have been a captain in the paras! Or a one parent family!';[392] 'I've had to suppress all my yearnings to become a fighter pilot';[393] 'I could've been an astronaut!';[394] 'It's very embarrassing for me, y'know, with all these divorces about, to have spent the best years of my life not even being a co-respondent!';[395] 'I've never been on water skis';[396] 'Nouvelle cuisine is an absolute mystery to me';[397] 'Nobody has ever said to me: "Granville, undo my zip, will you?"';[398] 'Other young men my age, y'know, can undo a bra with one hand. Me, I'd have to have an instruction book and a set of illustrations!'[399]

He can always seek succour in Nurse Gladys Emmanuel's ample bosom – particularly when he knows how the sight of such succour infuriates his uncle ('ARKWRIGHT: 'Hey, G-Granville, come out of there!' GLADYS: 'You leave him alone!' ARKWRIGHT: 'He's *not* alone in there, is he? Three in a blouse is one too many!'[400]) – but he is still very much the misfit, and he knows it. There is the odd awkward lunge at the woman who (appropriately enough for someone who is drawn so often to breasts) delivers the milk, partly because, as he admits, 'She thinks I'm inexperienced in the ways of the flesh'[401], but she never takes him seriously ('I think you really need a steady girlfriend, Granville'[402]). There is also an even more desperate bid to attract a member of the opposite sex by posing as what he thinks is an 'executive' (complete with a bowler hat and an umbrella), but, once again, his naivety shows up the sham of trying to be what he is not.

Most of the time he seems content merely to waffle on about how he is 'on the verge' of better things, claiming that he will soon be turning his bedroom into a glamorous 'bachelor pad', with a steady stream of his friends from 'the cocktail set' dropping in regularly for drinks and a squint at his Aubrey Beardsley print, and 'some of the most beautiful women in the world' popping by to be advised on how to improve their collections of porcelain. Such reveries, however, are soon arrested by Arkwright's interventions ('The nearest *you* ever come to porcelain is the lavatory seat!'[403]) and he is sent straight back out on the delivery bike.

Arkwright himself is just as blinkered and driven as before. He is (true to the 'Four Yorkshiremen' tradition) palpably proud of his tough upbringing: 'When I was a lad, early was a lot earlier than it is now!';[404] 'Puberty? There was no such thing as *puberty* when *I* was a lad! It hadn't been invented. We went straight from childhood into heavy labour. There wasn't a *pube* in sight!';[405] 'This was the age of the solid r-rubber tyre, lad – we didn't get the time to get c-cosseted!';[406] 'You think *you* get up early, do you? Let me tell you, in *my* young day, they sometimes g-got us up before we went to bed!';[407] 'Oh, *you* don't know you're born! In *my* young day, errand boys were employed specifically for the purposes of being t-trod on!'[408]

The major thing that keeps him going – apart from the prospect of persuading a 'certain state registered person that it's t-time to start me motor'[409] – is the challenge of making more money. 'You've got to get p-people *grabbing* at what you've got,'[410] he asserts, inspecting the arrangement outside the shop of his parsnips and potatoes. Everything is geared to the day-to-day grind of drawing people in and directing them towards a purchase: 'I *hate* losing f-fully-grown customers! Little ones are different – you don't mind throwing a few of *them* back for later!'[411] Other human beings matter to him only to the extent to which they happen to have a disposable income: 'There you are, m-my dear,' he says to one of them as he guides them back out of the shop, 'call again when you've saved up.'[412]

Each of these two characters, after all this time, remains an enigma to the other. In terms of attitudes to class and culture, sex and mortality, they make no sense at all to each other.

Arkwright cannot understand why Granville, who stands to inherit his shop, is so unwilling to inherit his work ethic. Granville, in turn, cannot understand how Arkwright, who stands to do nothing but keep scrapping for sales, is so closed to the notion that there might be more to life than swapping commodities for coins across a narrow counter.

Every debate that they have is a clash between an unstoppable dreamer and an immovable shopkeeper:

GRANVILLE: Money! All you ever think about is money!

ARKWRIGHT: A man must be allowed his own religious convictions. Fair's fair.

GRANVILLE: Yeah, but what about *people?* Don't you care about *people?*

ARKWRIGHT: People are all v-very well as f-far as they go, but you can't retire on 'em. You can't tuck 'em under your mattress of a night time, can you?[413]

There is never any prospect of progress. There is only the possibility of slight umbrage and minor bruising:

GRANVILLE: What about *passion* and *adventure?*
ARKWRIGHT: Oh, look at her! You've got to learn to *p-pace* yourself in life, G-Granville! You're no good to anyone over-extended, are you? You've g-got to take things as they come. Your mother knew how. She used to t-take anything that come. One day, *all* this will be *yours*, Granville!
GRANVILLE: Huh, no it won't – not if you can find a way to take it with you! We'll have to bury you and this lot in a great big container. You'll never be satisfied with a coffin. You wouldn't let us fasten the lid down for a start. D'you know, it'll be the first time you've ever been closed in daylight? Ha ha ha!
ARKWRIGHT: You're b-bearing up very well for an errand boy in pain.
GRANVILLE: I'm not in pain.

[Arkwright stamps on his foot]

GRANVILLE: *OW!!!*
ARKWRIGHT: You see how much sooner we of the older generation n-notice that sort of thing? Almost t-telepathic, we are![414]

The third point in the comic triangle, the female in this unofficial family unit – Nurse Gladys Emmanuel – is similarly unchanged. Still obliged to look after her elderly mother and still inclined to fend off her fiancé across the road, she continues to concentrate on her job. There is a slightly stronger sense of her maternal feelings for Granville, and (at times) her fondness for Arkwright, but, in general, she remains a duty-driven figure who puts principles before pleasure.

Her relationship with Arkwright, by the fourth series, looks much the same as before, with the fact of their engagement being treated like a green light by Arkwright and an amber light by her. Engagement, for Gladys, is a convenient means of managing her admirer's ardour, an opaque and open-ended process not unlike European federalism. Engagement, for Arkwright, is like an uncompleted transaction, tormenting him throughout every waking hour.

In the first episode, for example, he rushes over excitedly as her white Morris Minor arrives, opens her door and stares longingly at her legs:

ARKWRIGHT: By, that's a t-tonic! Pity it's only available on p-prescription!

GLADYS: Oh, stand back, I haven't time this morning for wrestling with grocers!

ARKWRIGHT: Couldn't you *m-make* time?

GLADYS: There'll be time when we're married. When I've smartened you up a bit.

[He puts his hands on her waist, only for her to remove them again]

GLADYS: And improved your moral standards. And started teaching you this foreign language.

ARKWRIGHT: What f-foreign language?

GLADYS: It's called spending money.

ARKWRIGHT: I can s-spend money when I have to.

GLADYS: I meant without an anaesthetic.

ARKWRIGHT: When *are* we g-going to get married? You know I'd do anything to you. Er, f-for you. I'd even sh-shut the shop early. Well, fairly early.

GLADYS: You know I can't whilst me mother needs me.

ARKWRIGHT: Oh, how is yer mother?

GLADYS: She's fine.

ARKWRIGHT: Hmm, typical. No consideration for other people.

GLADYS: Don't be rotten!

ARKWRIGHT: I'm only joking! I hope she lives till she's 80.

GLADYS: She *is* 80.

ARKWRIGHT: Oh, what a coincidence![415]

It is the same story later on in the series, as Granville departs to the back room while Arkwright tries to ingratiate himself, once again, with Gladys:

GLADYS: Keep your voice down, you old fool!

ARKWRIGHT: He can't hear, he's too busy c-counting his bruises.

GLADYS: And so will you be if you start your nonsense!

ARKWRIGHT: You know, isn't it a shame that s-so much of my nonsense is g-going to waste every day? I mean, you never know how much you've got left, do you? Well, wouldn't it be terrible if I r-ran out of nonsense during our nuptials?

GLADYS: Our what?

ARKWRIGHT: Our n-nuptials. You know, when we're having an afternoon nup? When we go on our honeymoon.

GLADYS: IF we go on our honeymoon! Don't forget the 'if' – that's *most* important!

ARKWRIGHT: Oh, I won't. I'll p-pack everything! No, I mean, where is a man on his honeymoon without his important 'if'?

GLADYS: If you promise to be quiet, you can bring your nonsense, and your 'if', over for a bite of supper and a hand of cards when me mother's asleep.

ARKWRIGHT: Oh, *good*, that's l-lovely. I'll teach you how to play strip snap!

GLADYS: Any talk of *that* nature, my lad, and you'll feel the full force of my knockout whist!

ARKWRIGHT: Ooh, well, *that* would p-put paid to my nonsense![416]

While this romantic saga was being played out, and Granville's quiet desperation was getting increasingly noisy, there was still the usual procession of customers coming in and out of the shop. It was these figures, as usual, who provided the variety from week to week, wandering in to play on the aimlessness at the heart of the sitcom.

As in previous series, there were several new names and faces to ponder, such as the cheerful misandrist Mrs Bickerdyke, whose irregular updates on her indolent husband ('about the same – stupid'[417]) never come as any great surprise; the well-wrapped Mr Halliwell, who appears to be gradually withdrawing from the world into a woollen cocoon; Mr Thorndyke, a would-be guinea pig for new types of marital aids; and Mrs Gillespie, a regular buyer of Ex-Lax. On this occasion, however, it was the more familiar figures who had the most rewarding roles.

Mrs Featherstone, once again, was the most memorable customer, with her new-found fascination for Arkwright only adding to the complexity of her character. Slowly but surely, she seemed to be turning into the 'Anti-Gladys', an alternative female figure whose far more modest-sized bosom was out of bounds to Granville, but whose interest in Arkwright sent him cowering behind the counter. It is listening to her paeans to his parsimony ('I've always held you up as an example to the entire area: "Say what you like about Arkwright, but there's nobody can hold a candle to him when it comes to being mean!"'[418]) that, perversely, spoils his own sense of self-worth.

Cyril was another customer (exceptionally well played, once again, by Tom Mennard) who returned to add some local colour to the context. With his curious mixture of credulousness and caution, he seemed to inspire Arkwright into being even more devious and cruel than usual, like a cat toying with a sleepy field mouse:

ARKWRIGHT: There we go, then, C-Cyril: a quarter of mixed s-sweets.

[Arkwright pours the sweets straight into Cyril's cupped hands]

ARKWRIGHT: Thank you very much.

CYRIL: Just like that? Y-You're going to leave 'em lying in me hand?

ARKWRIGHT: Well, if you want m-more active sweets you'll have to j-jiggle 'em a bit.

CYRIL: Aren't you going to wrap 'em up?

ARKWRIGHT: 'Wrap 'em up?' They *are* w-wrapped up!

CYRIL: *Individually* they're wrapped up, but aren't you going to put them in a *bag?*

ARKWRIGHT: Look, am I, am I overlooking s-something here? I mean, we're not *related* or anything are we? I mean, is there any *f-family* reason why you should expect this s-special treatment?

CYRIL: *A little bag?* Putting some sweets in a *bag.* You call that *special treatment?*

ARKWRIGHT: Well, I suppose it all depends what sort of p-pampered background you're from!

CYRIL: *PAMPERED?!?*

ARKWRIGHT: I can't help wondering what your m-missus must make of all these unreasonable demands. You must be h-hell to live with, Cyril! Still, in my book, the customer is always right. You *shall* have your little bag.

CYRIL: Thank you very much.

[Arkwright produces a small paper bag]

ARKWRIGHT: That'll be another 2-2p, please.

CYRIL: I've heard about you! 'Don't go in that shop,' they said. 'There's a great *brute* in there, it'll have your *arm* off!' I thought they meant a flamin' Alsatian!

ARKWRIGHT: We haven't got the m-money to keep dogs in here, Cyril. My assistant will b-bark on demand.

[Granville, who has just arrived, pauses to yawn]

ARKWRIGHT: There you are, there's one coming up now, look.

GRANVILLE: *[Heading for the back room]* It's a dog's life in here, I can tell you that!

ARKWRIGHT: Never mind that, F-Fido. Come back here and e-explain to this gentleman our policy on l-little bags, will you?

GRANVILLE: Certainly: He won't let me go out with any.

[He shuffles off into the back room]

ARKWRIGHT: You must excuse him, he's not quite awake yet. You know what it is with y-young people, they tend to d-doze off, don't they? R-round about f-fourteen. They wake up in their late thirties.

CYRIL: *ARE YOU GOING TO WRAP THESE UP?*

ARKWRIGHT: Y-You're not interested in ph-philosophy at all, are you? Why don't you stick 'em in your pocket?

CYRIL: I don't want this lot rolling round me pocket!

ARKWRIGHT: Well, they're only *s-sweets*, they're not explosive devices!

CYRIL: 'Pick and Mix' it says there. With Pick and Mix you always get a paper bag. Free!

ARKWRIGHT: Look, he comes in here, groggy with sleep –

CYRIL: *Who's* groggy with sleep?

ARKWRIGHT: YOU ARE! I think it shows g-great spirit w-worrying about a little item like a paper bag when you've got eyes as b-bloodshot as yours, and d-don't tell me they're *always* like that, Cyril!

CYRIL: Like what?

ARKWRIGHT: Have you *seen* your eyes this morning? Here – look here! *[He reaches for one of the small mirrors up on display and hands it to Cyril]* There you are, look – they look like s-stewed rhubarb!

[Cyril studies his reflection while Arkwright takes his note and heads for the till]

GRANVILLE: *[Sotto voce]* You're *rude* to people, you!

ARKWRIGHT: It's one of the few pleasures left to the undeserving p-poor, Granville.

[He puts the note in the till, flinches as it snaps back shut, then returns to the counter where he hands Cyril his change]

ARKWRIGHT: There we are, thank you, C-Cyril. *[Cyril, confused, offers him a note]* No, no, no, I've taken 49p for the mirror, thank you!
CYRIL: You *what?* That's *outrageous!*
ARKWRIGHT: Look, is it *my* fault you were t-too late for the January sales? They were q-queuing all night, y'know![419]

The most eventful episode was probably the last one in the series (broadcast on 6 October), as it saw the status quo shaken a little harder than it had been for quite some time. Rules were bent, lies were told, tempers were tested and the legendary till was finally threatened with extinction.

Entitled 'The Mystical Boudoir of Nurse Gladys Emmanuel', the action revolved around Arkwright's willingness to risk wrecking his engagement with Gladys in order to get one night of passion with her in her bed. Once again, sex and money commingle because his craving for the former causes him to compromise with the latter.

The episode begins in the early morning, with Arkwright already up and active in the shop, standing by the door and staring over at Gladys's still-darkened bedroom window. 'You'd think, wouldn't you,' he moans, 'if only occasionally I might g-get the opportunity to look at them c-curtains from the other side!'

Even more impatient than usual, he cannot resist slipping across the road and lobbing a few stones up to attract her attention. It works, and she opens up the window, clearly unsurprised to find her fiancé gazing up at her semi-dressed bust:

ARKWRIGHT: By heck! *That's* f-fresh from the oven!
GLADYS: What is it?
ARKWRIGHT: I don't know, but if you've got any to spare, I'll take the lot! I must say, as a g-grocer's fiancée, you couldn't be accused of under-weight p-portions.
GLADYS: Oh shut up, you tomfool, me mother's in the next room, you'll wake her up.

ARKWRIGHT: Nah, she'll not hear owt, she's as deaf as me hat!

GLADYS: She picks up every vibration.

ARKWRIGHT: Oh, that's all we need! My l-love life on radar!

GLADYS: What do you want?

ARKWRIGHT: Ah!

GLADYS: No – forget I ever said that! Just what did you think you might achieve, throwing bricks at my window?

ARKWRIGHT: Just think of it as c-customs and excise, my love. I'm coming up later for a quick body search. I bet I *find* one and all!

GLADYS: Go and have your breakfast! Tch – 'Customs and excise'!

ARKWRIGHT: Ssh! Don't sh-shout it about. I'm working undercover!

GLADYS: Not under *my* cover you're not!

Arkwright is not the only one feeling frustrated. Granville, back in the shop, is tussling once again with the till. This is a fight that has lasted as long as the show, but, in this current series, the intensity of the battle has increased. In an earlier episode, Granville was lucky to have escaped with his manhood intact after a particularly vicious snap-back trapped his trousers in the till.[420] Now, ashen-faced, he has resorted to using a rubber glove on the end of a broom to 'j-jiggle it about' and make it shut. With alarmed customers queuing up to show their sympathy for his plight ('You don't need a guard dog with a till as fierce as that!'), Granville, his nerves frazzled, is finally at the end of his tether.

Arkwright, to begin with, appears as obdurate as ever when the weary old subject is once again broached:

GRANVILLE: When are you going to get me a new till?

ARKWRIGHT: I w-wouldn't part with that till for all the tea in Ch-Ch-Ch…for all the, all the, t-tea in Ch-Ch- British Rail!

GRANVILLE: It's not parting with the till. It's parting with parts of yourself *in* the till that worries me!

It does not take Granville long, however, to realize that, on this particular occasion, a deal might be struck. Arkwright, after all, wants to enlist Granville's help for a spot of 'subter...subter...fufu... fuftersuge...subtafug- a trick!' It is thus a good time, reasons Granville, for a bit of *quid pro quo*:

ARKWRIGHT: Burglars is the answer! The only way I'm going to get into Nurse Gladys's bedroom is when I am on b-b-burglar patrol!

GRANVILLE: *Burglar patrol?* She's never going to fall for *that!*

ARKWRIGHT: No, no, I'm p-perfectly genuine. I'm going to make this neighbourhood safe for state registered nurses to f-flourish in.

GRANVILLE: Huh! She'd be better off with the burglars!

ARKWRIGHT: She's very careless about her own p-personal safety. Why, in the course of her n-nursely duties, she has to go into dark places the very thought of which makes your hair stand on end. Well, on b-both ends! Are you listening to me, G-Granville? We're g-going to make her s-security conscious!

GRANVILLE: *[Mumbling]* Uh-huh.

[Irritated by his indifference, Arkwright grabs him by the ear]

ARKWRIGHT: What are we going to do?

GRANVILLE: *[In pain]* Ah! We're going to make her more se-security conscious!

ARKWRIGHT: That's a good lad. We're going to teach her to get her to lean on her fiancé during the hours of d-darkness.

GRANVILLE: *[Knowingly]* Yeah. *And* we're going to get a new *till!*

ARKWRIGHT: You drive a hard H-Hungarian bargain, you do!

One end of the bargain appears to be honoured remarkably swiftly when an excited-looking salesman drives up outside the shop and presents Granville with 'one multi-function, pre-programmed, electronic, tamper-proof till with print-out facility!' It is large and neat and clean with all kinds of fancy buttons and knobs just waiting to be pressed and pulled, and Granville can hardly wait to get the ultra-modern machine inside the shop. No sooner, however, has he and the salesman transported it over the threshold, than Arkwright's voice can be heard exclaiming: '*HOW MUCH?!?!?*'

The two men re-emerge hurriedly with the new till, and Granville, still sounding fairly hopeful, declares that they are 'going to get a slightly cheaper model'. The salesman duly returns with what he promises as 'basically the same machine' but 'with fewer functions' and at a 'much-reduced price'. Granville, once again, takes it inside excitedly, only for Arkwright's voice to be heard once again shrieking: '*HOW MUCH???*'

Granville and the salesman find themselves back out by the van, loading the machine in the boot. 'Haven't you got anything on special offer?' pants Granville, now sounding more pained than positive. 'But this *was* on special offer,' replies the exasperated salesman. It does not look good on the till front.

Arkwright, meanwhile, is working hard to ensure that the other side of the bargain is now well on its way to fruition. Not only has he rigged up an alarm to startle his regular customers (who are then greeted by a fierce-looking shopkeeper wearing a helmet and wielding a cosh), but he has also ordered Granville to don a drooping hat and dirty raincoat and then dispatched him across the road to 'rattle a few d-dustbins' and 'lurk around the back of the nurse's rear premises looking suspicious'.

It fails dismally, with Granville only managing to get a drenching from next door, and then his next assignation, which requires him to don a pair of 15 denier tights over his head, climb up on a ladder and stare like a ghostly medieval peasant through Gladys's bedroom window, elicits less than the full-blown horror that was expected: 'Go away Granville, I'm busy!!!'

Arkwright, however, has not given up. As he and his nephew edge towards the door of the shop with a long aluminium ladder suspended over their shoulders, Granville is full of jovial cynicism – 'She'll *kill* you!' – while Arkwright (armed with a badly damaged box of Milk Tray under his arm) is full of northern promise: 'What? A lover bearing gifts? No way! She'll be over the moon!'

The enterprise fails when Gladys responds to the sound of a cardboard container of chocolates being tapped on her window by brusquely wrapping the process up: ARKWRIGHT: 'Milk Tray, my love!' GLADYS: 'TIN tray, to you!!!' As Gladys withdraws into her bedroom after hitting the shopkeeper over the head, Arkwright and Granville are left to hold on to the ladder and hope that no injuries come from the sudden setback.

Later on, as Arkwright takes up his usual post in the doorway of his shop, gazing up at the night sky, he reflects on his latest defeat:

Oh dear, it's good to get back to terra f-firma. I thought me end was nigh. It's the best end an' all. It's funny how helpless you feel, dangling inches beneath the area's finest bosom. And n-not a thing you can get a safe hold on. Ha, and believe me, I *did* try! Even in the depths of a very real predicament, I did *try!*

That was the end of the fourth series. As the loud cheers and applause could be heard over the music that closed the show, the camera moved slowly away from the shop, rising back up to a bird's eye height, as Arkwright was pictured picking up boxes and baskets, reluctantly closing for the night. With all of the other buildings in the street masked in darkness, the corner shop, with its windows still bright, now looked a little like an old television set, which switched off once Arkwright was back inside.

The series, just like its three predecessors, had failed to inspire any reaction from the reviewers, and not even the finale would manage much of a mention in the media, but, by this stage, such indifference did not seem to matter. *Open All Hours* was a hit without the hype.

The viewing figures for the fourth series had been genuinely exceptional. Peaking at a massive 18.95 million[421] – beating, quite comfortably, the likes of *EastEnders* and *Coronation Street* and all of the other big shows of the week – and averaging about 17.4 million per episode,[422] the show had delivered one of the strongest performances of the year (and, indeed, the decade) by any television programme on any channel. The achievement, in broadcasting terms, was immense.

It had been a strange and unconventional rise to the top of the British sitcom ranks. There had only been one pilot and four series, comprised of a mere 26 episodes, spread out over no fewer than 12 years. It began without any fanfare, its momentum was interrupted repeatedly, it was never championed by the critics, it was overlooked for any awards and it did not even seem particularly cherished by its own channel.

It was the stealth sitcom. Initially dismissed by some as trivial and transient, it went on, while its detractors' backs were turned, to win the love and loyalty of a remarkably large proportion of the public, and, in turn, earn itself a kind of TV immortality.

The people responsible for it – the writer, the stars and all of the others behind the scenes – were far too modest to crow about it, but, in their own quiet way, they were very proud of what, as a team, they had achieved. Having answered all the questions asked of them, they now had to contend with the one question left of their own: how on earth do we follow that?

PART FIVE

*We don't use words like 'reductions' –
that's for wimps!*

CHAPTER THIRTEEN

The Revival

If it's not broke, don't mend it.

It all started, again, early in 2013, when Roy Clarke took a phone call from David Jason. The actor wanted the writer to create something for him.

It would be wrong, however, to think that this was the first opportunity for a new *Open All Hours* episode. It could, in fact, have happened so much sooner.

It *should* have started again, in a way, about 28 years earlier, because, back in 1984, when Roy Clarke was commissioned to write the fourth series of *Open All Hours*, he was also commissioned to write either a TV special or film that was meant to follow soon after it. In a letter to Clarke's agent, dated 1 November 1984, it was confirmed that the BBC wanted 'a 75-minute film of *Last of the Summer Wine* for delivery after March 1985, and a 75-minute film/special of *Open All Hours* for delivery in September next year and to be made in February or March of the following year [1986]'.[423]

The *Last of the Summer Wine* project went straight ahead and duly reached the screen on New Year's Day 1986, as a 90-minute (rather than 75-minute) special entitled 'Uncle of the Bride'. The *Open All Hours* film, however, failed ever to materialize.

There is not, alas, any formal explanation that has survived in the BBC's archives, and the memories of most of those involved are now blank on the subject. 'I'd actually forgotten all about that,' Roy Clarke would later confess. 'It didn't come to fruition, obviously, but I can't remember why. I'd forgotten it was even initiated!'[424]

One likely, but still speculative, explanation is that Ronnie Barker was starting – very discreetly – to wind down his career (although he would not actually make up his mind to retire until late in 1985, about a year after the special was commissioned, he was already rejecting most of the new projects that he was being offered), and probably no longer had the enthusiasm to embark on an extended special. It might also have been the case that David Jason was now simply too busy to sign up for such an enterprise. It could well have been a combination of the two, but, however it happened, the special ended up being shelved.

The consequence was that *Open All Hours*, yet again, pulled down the shutters just when it was on the verge of making a major advance. Although, after the fourth series, the official word had been that the sitcom 'will return next year – its stars' workloads permitting',[425] nothing else actually arrived. There was no announcement, no farewell, no formal closing of the door. Arkwright went out of business without so much as a wh-whimper, let alone a bang.

Roy Clarke would have happily written another series, but, as he later recalled, no-one ever asked:

It wasn't *my* decision to finish. I always assumed it came down to Ronnie's commitments and David's commitments, because, you know, by that stage it seemed like an astonishing fluke that we'd got Ronnie Barker and David Jason in the same show. And it wasn't a surprise that both of them had plenty of other things to do. But there was no decision to end it on my part. It just didn't come back. And when it comes to decisions I'm always the last to know. Genuinely. To be honest, the writer usually is![426]

Ronnie Barker, after making one more sitcom (the self-written *Clarence*), officially retired in 1987 ('I'd done everything I wanted to do,' he explained. 'I had no ambition left'[427]), leaving David Jason to concentrate on *Only Fools and Horses* and Lynda Baron to spend more time working in the theatre. Roy Clarke, meanwhile, continued writing *Last of the Summer Wine* (which would end up being the world's longest-running sitcom), as well as numerous other projects (such as the very successful *Keeping Up Appearances*).

Open All Hours, however, would still live on in the memory, first with the help of videos and DVDs, and then, from the late 1990s, via increasingly frequent repeats not only on the BBC (where episodes would sometimes still attract as many as 9 million viewers[428]) but also on such nostalgia TV satellite and cable channels as UK Gold (where it would gradually accumulate a whole new generation of fans). It even enjoyed a brief bout of new publicity when, in 2004, it came a very respectable eighth out of 100 in a BBC poll to choose 'Britain's Best Sitcom' (after being championed on screen by one of its biggest fans, the celebrity chef Clarissa Dickson Wright).[429] As an ongoing sitcom, however, *Open All Hours* seemed over; it appeared to be dead.

As if to symbolize its demise, in 2005, with its star's blessing, the BBC donated to the British Stammering Association two of the false moustaches that had been worn by Ronnie Barker in the series. They were auctioned later that year at its annual London conference (and, in what was arguably not the most mature of gestures, one of the successful bidders promptly burnt the item in an ashtray at his table[430]). This was then followed, in 2006, by the sale of one of Arkwright's shop-front signs by Helen Ibbotson. 'I had another one from the first series but I don't know what happened to it,' she said. 'This is the other one they had done for the next three consecutive series and they asked me to look after it in between. Then at the end they told me I could keep it and it's been a nice souvenir. But it's been in the loft for twenty-odd years, so when a customer came in and suggested I might get a bit of money for it, I thought why not?'[431]

This, then, seemed the fate of the show: to be physically dismembered, but fondly remembered. While the souvenirs were sold in the auction houses and on eBay, the scenes and sounds were left to echo in the head.

It came as a complete surprise, therefore, when, in 2013, Roy Clarke picked up the telephone and took that call from David Jason. Somewhat dazed, he listened carefully and found out what had led to this unexpected turn of events.

Jason explained that he had recently met with the BBC's current head of comedy, Mark Freeland, to discuss possible new projects, and he had expressed a wish to work again with one of his favourite writers.

Clarke, understandably, was not only very pleased and flattered but also more than a little taken aback: 'I'd assumed that I was retired! I mean, I'd been in that frame of mind for several years. And so it came completely out of the blue for me.'[432]

The irony is, however, that this call resulted in the two men collaborating initially not on a revival of their hugely successful old show, but on a completely new sitcom. 'What we actually started on, after that chat, was a project that had nothing at all to do with *Open All Hours*,' Clarke would later reveal. 'It was another idea entirely. So I got a script done, we had some meetings, and then people didn't seem too keen on the idea. So I assumed that was that.'[433]

It was soon after this that Clarke received another call from Jason, explaining that he had now met up with Freeland again, 'and during the conversation I happened to say that one of the things that mystified me was wondering whatever happened to Granville'.[434] Clarke, immediately, was intrigued: 'Funnily enough,' he replied, '*I've* often wondered what happened to Granville, too.'[435]

The two old friends (Jason now aged 73 and Clarke 83) agreed that it was worth them trying to find out, so Clarke, with a mixture of excitement and trepidation, started work immediately on developing ideas for a new script of *Open All Hours*. 'I *was* fearful,' the writer later admitted, 'because it had been such a success and it was remembered so fondly – and in my area where I live people were always referring to it – so you deserve to have a few nerves about tampering with a thing like that. Yes, there was a great deal of unease.'[436]

There was not even any guarantee that the BBC was going to commission it. Mark Freeland, when Jason first suggested it, had been guarded in his response, merely describing the proposal (in that non-committal phrase so beloved by TV executives) as 'interesting'.

It was clear that there was going to be quite a wait before a proper decision was made. 'It's a corporate system, so it wasn't just a case of "do it". It had to go through a process,' Jason later explained, noting that, as is the custom these days, research was going to be conducted 'to see if it was an animal of its time' or something that still had contemporary appeal.[437]

The portents, in one sense, were unusually propitious, because the idea was aired just when a trend seemed to be developing in British broadcasting for reviving old sitcoms. The BBC, for example, had 'updated' *The Fall and Rise of Reginald Perrin* (which ended in 1979) as *Reggie Perrin* in 2009. The digital channel Dave had followed suit later the same year, bringing back *Red Dwarf* (after an absence of ten years) for three special episodes, before going on to commission a full series for 2012. The BBC, also in 2012, had reactivated *Absolutely Fabulous* for yet another outing. Even more recently, another digital channel, GOLD, had brought back *Yes, Prime Minister* (last seen in 1988) for a new series at the start of 2013, and plans had also been announced by ITV for a revival of *Birds of a Feather* (which had ended in 1998).

If *Open All Hours* was ever going to return, therefore, this seemed like the best time to try it. There were still good reasons, however, to think carefully before pushing ahead.

The most obvious problem, of course, was that Ronnie Barker, having passed away in 2005, was going to be, whether anyone liked it or not, the ghost that would haunt this sitcom. Even though the *Reggie Perrin* remake had proceeded with Martin Clunes taking the place of the deceased Leonard Rossiter, and *Yes, Prime Minister* had been resurrected without the brilliant trio of Paul Eddington, Nigel Hawthorne and Derek Fowlds, both the public and critical reaction to these changes had been, at best, ambivalent and, at worst, damning. The thought of anyone, no matter how talented, replacing the much-missed Ronnie Barker as Arkwright seemed similarly injudicious, and, in any case, neither David Jason nor Roy Clarke would have countenanced such a conceit. It also made no real sense to bring back an ancient Arkwright when the new show was going to focus on the now rather elderly Granville.

There were, nonetheless, other concerns within the BBC, particularly about that obsession of modern mainstream broadcasting: demographics. Would, for example, the corner shop sitcom, with its close-knit community of regular customers, seem just too antiquated and alien to the millions of young viewers who had grown up with massive supermarkets as well as the phenomenon of online shopping? If such potential viewers might find the *situation* old fashioned, might they also find the whimsical, wry and expletive-free style of *comedy* old fashioned, too? Then, of course, there were the older fans who had grown up with the original series: would *they* be disappointed, or even offended, by an updated *Open All Hours*?

The BBC's anxieties about younger viewers were soon assuaged by its market research. Thanks to fairly regular repeats on the nostalgia TV channels and still healthy sales of DVD box sets, as well as innumerable clips (and in many cases whole episodes) available via the internet, an encouraging number of young viewers had already discovered, and come to love, the show, and there seemed to be plenty who were open to the prospect of seeing it return. It was actually the more mature viewers, with the fondest memories of the original series, who looked to be more divided about it coming back older and altered, but even among this group there seemed a big enough proportion whose curiosity would compel them to watch the revival.

There was also obviously still a huge amount of affection for David Jason – or rather, since 2005, *Sir* David Jason – among the broad viewing audience, who were always keen to welcome him back to a peak-time slot on terrestrial television. His only recent foray back into comedy, BBC One's 2011 *The Royal Bodyguard*, had been deemed a disappointment, but, as with any hint of another re-booting of *Only Fools and Horses*, the suggestion of *Open All Hours* making a return sounded, to most of his loyal fans, a reassuringly swift and straightforward way to see him back at the top of his form.

It was eventually decided, therefore (thanks in part to Mark Freeland's persistence), to take a gamble and commission the comeback. A full 40 years after the pilot episode was aired, and 28 years after Arkwright last ended the show by standing outside and gazing up at the stars, *Open All Hours* was going to be back in business.

It seemed an ironic task for Roy Clarke as its writer, because he was now obliged to take a sitcom that had always knowingly ignored the passage of time and suddenly wind the clock on several decades. Arkwright was long gone, Granville and Nurse Gladys had grown old, and there were new customers to be mixed in with a few of the familiar faces. It was going to have to seem the same but very different.

There were discussions with Sir David Jason – 'We spent afternoons sitting around giggling about the show in the 70s,' Clarke later revealed, 'remembering some of the things that had happened and the storylines'[438] – in which ideas for possible changes were bounced around and debated. The real work, however, began, as it always used to, with him sitting down alone and staring at a blank sheet of paper.

Clarke responded pragmatically by reflecting on the natural line of succession. Arkwright had always been grooming Granville to one day stand in his shoes, so now would be that day: he would basically be the new Arkwright, only with his own peculiar little tics and tricks, still trapped in the corner shop.

Nurse Gladys, it was decided, had never quite made it to the altar with Arkwright, so she was left in the same place as before, perhaps a little sadder but still proudly self-reliant, keeping a discreet maternal eye on Granville from her vantage point across the road. While some of the old customers, like the actors who played them, were left respectfully in the past, one or two, such as Mavis (played by Maggie Ollerenshaw) and Mrs Featherstone (played by Stephanie Cole), were brought back to provide a sense of continuity amid the procession of new characters.

Most importantly of all, in terms of preserving the show's old comic dynamic, Granville required his own grudging protégé, so Clarke decided to give him a son, called Leroy, whose origins seemed almost as murky as his own. The result, supposedly, of a one-night stand in Blackpool 25 years before ('most people come back with a stick of rock'), Leroy would now be the one who was mothered by all the mature local women, while turning Granville green with envy by having considerably more success when flirting with the younger ones.

With this addition, the show could move on with its own comic triangle, with Granville, Leroy and Gladys interacting in much the same way as Arkwright, Granville and Gladys had done. The roots still went down much deeper than the shop floor; the ties between the key characters remained tight.

Finally, it was decided that, rather than try to ignore the absence of Ronnie Barker as Arkwright, the new show would embrace his memory and honour it on the screen. 'I knew that huge absence was going to be there in everyone's mind,' Roy Clarke later explained, 'and so I thought we might as well face it and *use* it.'[439]

All of this fell into place remarkably quickly for Clarke, who only took about a fortnight, and a few drafts, to come up with a coherent version of the complete script. He then sent it on promptly to Sir David Jason, who, as Clarke would note, was delighted with his efforts: 'David said to me that when he read the script for the first time it felt like it had never been away.'[440]

The production process could now start to progress, and so a team began to be formed. Sarah Hitchcock, among whose track record included a spell overseeing *Last of the Summer Wine*, was brought in as Associate Producer to run the day-to-day operations. The much-admired Sydney Lotterby, who was by this time well into his eighties, had long retired from active programme-making, and so his old duties were divided up between two younger talents.

Gareth Edwards was hired as the show's new producer. A 47-year-old who had previously won praise for his work on such shows as *Spaced* (1999), *That Mitchell and Webb Look* (2006–10) and Ronnie Corbett's *The One Ronnie* (2010), he was known to work well with casts and crews, and shape their shows with great sensitivity and shrewdness. He was, understandably, cautious about the potential hazards that might be lurking ahead – 'Making any comedy programme is risky. There's always the chance that we might make something that we think works and, you know, nobody else agrees'[441] – but was determined to see the project succeed.

Dewi Humphreys was then chosen as the director. A very experienced and versatile maker of sitcoms, his previous credits included ten episodes of *The Vicar of Dibley* (1994–8), one series of *Absolutely Fabulous* (2003), both series of *The Old Guys* (2009–10), John Sullivan's three-part prequel to *Only Fools and Horses* called *Rock & Chips* (2010–11), and 71 episodes of BBC One's mainstream comedy juggernaut *My Family* (2000–11). Well known to Sir David Jason, who liked what he had seen of his work, he was another eminently suitable recruit.

The casting, overseen by Jane Davies, commenced soon after. Following Sir David and Lynda Baron, the next two actors to be signed up were Stephanie Cole and Maggie Ollerenshaw, both of whom were surprised and delighted to get the call. 'I heard quite early on in the year,' Cole would recall, 'because, when something like that is mooted, one of the first things they do is ring around the agents of the main actors to check on availability. So I was thrilled to be told that this was being planned.'[442]

The only new recruit among the key members of the cast was James Baxter, a 23-year-old Sunderland-born actor best known to viewers, at that stage in his career, as 'Jake Doland', a character he played from 2007–9 in the long-running ITV soap *Emmerdale*. Only a little taller than David Jason, with brown hair, expressive eyebrows and a boyish demeanour reminiscent of Granville in his younger days, he looked a good choice to work under the new 'Guv'nor'.

A whole host of guest stars were then booked up to play the part of various new customers. Johnny Vegas, Mark Williams, Brigit Forsyth, Kulvinder Ghir, Sally Lindsay, Nina Wadia and (for a blink-and-you'll-miss-it cameo) one half of the Chuckle Brothers, Barry Elliott, were among the other actors invited.

It was decided, more or less immediately, to film the external scenes back up in Balby, at exactly the same locations as before, basing the main scenes outside Helen Ibbotson's Beautique hairdressing salon in Lister Avenue. It was fortunate for all concerned that the building was still there.

The property had actually been threatened with demolition in 2006 to make way for new developments, but was saved after the intervention of the Doncaster Against Demolition campaign (whose petition was signed by the likes of Sir David Jason, Sir Terry Wogan, Sir David Frost, Stephen Fry, Richard Briers, Bernard Cribbins, Tim Brooke-Taylor and Alan Yentob). It was then put up for sale by auction in 2008 (complete with a one-bedroom first-floor apartment, a store yard and an outside lavatory), but, after attracting a top bid of £132,500, its reserve price was not met and the shop remained in the Ibbotson family.

Now aged 82, Ibbotson had actually retired 15 years earlier, and the business was now run by her daughter, Lisa Taylor, but, after first hearing about plans for the new programme through the media, both of them were delighted when the BBC contacted them directly, at the start of October 2013, to arrange for the hire of the premises once again. 'A man from the BBC came to the shop last Thursday and took me outside,' Ibbotson said at the time. 'He told me it was all a bit top secret as they hadn't been given the go-ahead yet. He then rang me on Monday and said it's going ahead.'[443]

The set designing team, led by David Hitchcock, duly arrived early in the morning of Saturday 16 November, for two days of hard work converting the smart little hair salon back into Arkwright's cluttered groceries and provisions emporium. 'It's exactly as it was all those years ago,' gasped Hitchcock when he first set eyes on the actual façade of the old salon. 'This is such a rare thing to happen, because what premises has remained the same for nearly 30 years?'[444] With the chippies already busy sawing and drilling, and the lorries being unloaded, and with all of the familiar brands (Quaker Oats, Maxim Light Bulbs, Cook's Matches, Astonish Wood Floor Cleaner, Fairy Liquid) being placed in position (by 2013, there were far fewer concerns, thanks to the clearer guidelines, about the propriety of such things), slowly but surely over the next few hours the shop was gradually woken up from its 28-year hibernation. To add another local touch, displays of fresh fruit and veg were brought in direct from Doncaster market, and several copies of the *Doncaster Free Press* were put up prominently on view. By 8am on Monday, when filming was scheduled to start, everything was in place. Arkwright's was open again.

'It's really funny that the shop is now filled with modern stuff,' said Lisa Taylor as she took in how her salon had just been transformed. 'We were watching the old re-runs recently and there was all the old food and cleaning products on the shelf. Now it's got things like lottery tickets for sale – which certainly weren't about when it used to be filmed. The two old tin baths outside are now plastic ones too. It is very strange to think I was here last week hairdressing. The first time they came here to film I was a young girl and it has just been part of my growing up. By next Friday it will be back to normal again – you won't even be able to tell they were here.'[445]

Standing outside that shop once again, surveying all of the strange knick-knacks spread out like tendrils below and around the windows, Sir David Jason was genuinely taken aback by the sense of *déjà vu*:

That was stunning, to return to the same street. And the other streets around there are the same, the shop is the same, it's all the same place, after 28 years. And the people were so warm and receptive, and so keen to see it back. They stood patiently, watching us all – some of them stood there all day! And again it was that strange thing when you'd think to yourself, 'Gosh, is it *really* that many years ago since we were here?' And here we are now, doing it all over again! I know it maybe sounds a trite thing to say, and it's been said so many times before, but really: it feels like only yesterday.[446]

It was the same for all the other long-established members of the cast. Lynda Baron, for example, would note that, for a sitcom whose pre-publicity had once been so low key it could have been slid under a hotel door, the hype that was already hovering over this new production had made the prospect of a return to Balby seem slightly surreal ('When the special was first announced, you would've thought someone had invented the wheel with all the fuss, so it was quite a responsibility'[447]), but, once back *in situ*, the emotion was palpable: 'A couple came over and one of them said, "I used to watch you filming when I was a little girl. And here's my daughter come to watch you today." And that was quite moving.'[448] The more people there were watching, the more that others seemed to arrive: 'That street felt as though they owned us then, and they still feel as though they own us.'[449]

Maggie Ollerenshaw was similarly impressed:

They were looking at us and we were looking at them! I don't think either of us could quite believe that the other was there again after all that time. It really was quite bizarre. In most ways it all looked exactly the same. The only things that were different were that some people had got new doors on their houses, there were some 'TO LET' signs up, and, of course, there were a few satellite dishes. But otherwise it was exactly the same.'[450]

Stephanie Cole agreed:

The unit base was a little way from where we filmed, so we'd be 'carred up' to the actual location, and the moment that we hit the street it really was quite extraordinary. It not only looked just like it used to look but also the people there were just as friendly as they used to be. They were baking cakes and coming out with cups of tea and inviting us into their homes to sit down because it was a bit nippy. They were just as lovely and welcoming as they'd been all those years before. I thought it was amazing.[451]

She also reflected on the one man that everyone there now missed:

I think the most poignant thing of all – and I think it must have been particularly difficult for David – was that, as you looked around and took it all in, you really did expect Ronnie Barker to walk round the corner at any moment. It was hard to accept that he wasn't there and you weren't suddenly going to see him again. His spirit was very present all the time that we were there.[452]

Lynda Baron felt the same:

That did make the experience bitter sweet, because we were missing a lot of people, and of course especially Ronnie. And, even though we now had a marvellous new director, I also still missed Sydney Lotterby, who was the best ever producer/director at the BBC. But, on the other hand, to see all the people there who were so thrilled to see us was really, really lovely.[453]

There was little time, however, for the team to indulge in much nostalgia, because everyone was now playing a different, more 'evolved' version of their old character, and so they needed to resume it and revise it swiftly to suit the schedule. The three actors with the most to do, in this sense, were Sir David Jason, Maggie Ollerenshaw and Stephanie Cole. For Sir David, he needed to go straight on camera and seem immediately recognizable as Granville, but also intriguingly different. 'It *is* a bit difficult for me,' he said at the time, 'because this time I'm playing the "Ronnie B. part" and it's huge, there are a lot of words to remember in such a short time, so at the moment I'm still struggling.'[454]

It was a similar challenge for Maggie Ollerenshaw and Stephanie Cole. Ollerenshaw, for example, needed to settle back into a character whose younger self, she knew from personal experience, remained a vivid personality in the public imagination: 'Even after the last series had long gone it was still a nightmare going shopping! I always had to make sure that I knew exactly what I wanted, because otherwise I'd start to get all of those knowing looks that implied, "Oh, yes, there you are, Mavis, you can't decide on anything, you're always changing your mind!" It went on and on!'[455] There were now, however, one or two changes to assimilate for the new episode: 'I was married to someone in the original series, although you never saw him, and he's gone now so she's single again. That's one difference. And another is that I've been given a sister, who guards her from Granville, with whom there's always been a bit of sexual tension, so some comedy can come from that. She's still mainly the old Mavis, though – she still can't make up her mind!'[456]

Stephanie Cole had to contend with rather more significant changes. The last time she had played Mrs Featherstone, she was a frighteningly stern woman who had become obsessed with thoughts of getting her cold and clammy hands on Arkwright's warm and well-padded wallet. She now had to play her as an even odder sort of character, still grimly austere but also bizarrely coquettish, who has transferred her peculiar affections to the person whom she had previously dismissed as 'weird': Granville.

'She *was* different,' Cole later reflected:

But it was actually much easier for me to play her this time round, because, firstly, it was a much smaller part than David's, but also, and most importantly of all, I was now finally the right age to play my character. I was 30 years too young when I originally played it. So actually, although she had changed in some ways, it was much easier for me this time around to play her. And, of course, Roy is such a good writer, who writes for you as well as for the character you're playing, so there wasn't any necessity for any input from me. He knows exactly what he's doing.[457]

One of the most important tasks during this location work, both in front of and behind the cameras, was to build up a bond between Sir David Jason and James Baxter. With their characters locked so closely together, it was essential that they engaged with each other as actors.

It would not take long. James Baxter, as he would later freely admit, was thrilled to find himself sharing scenes with such a distinguished comic actor. 'I would go to bed watching *Only Fools and Horses*,' he said. 'I would go as far as to say that with comedy, he is the first actor I really fell in love with and admired.'[458] There really was a sense that, just as Sir David had done all those years ago when working alongside Ronnie Barker, Baxter was now relishing serving his apprenticeship with his own 'Guv'nor': 'We would sit after filming in the hotel bar. We have to make sure our chemistry is there. Once I got over that "pinch myself every 15 minutes" stage, it was just amazing. I'm just watching a master at what they do.'[459]

Sir David, in turn, found it easy to work with the younger actor:

He's slotting in beautifully. He takes direction extremely well, and I certainly wouldn't want to be trying to teach him to suck eggs or to tell him how to do it. He's his own man, and he's constructing his character, and he's doing it beautifully well. So our relationship is built on two actors working out their relationship as characters within this piece. But he'll have to watch it, though – I'm keeping my eye on him, don't you worry![460]

One of the most reassuring things about all of the days that were spent there in Balby was the sense of camaraderie among the cast, which seemed as strong as it was in the past. It was particularly enjoyable, as Sir David later noted, to be able to lock wits, both on and off camera, with the women who, along with him, had helped make the old shows so memorable:

They make life so much easier. Because we'd been there and worked so well together, and these again are very experienced actresses. And in order to do comedy well you have to have a sense of the ridiculous, and you have to have a sense of fun, and these ladies have it in spades. And they're consummate actresses. And so put all of those elements together and you've got a combination that you can't wait to get back to work with, because it's *not* like work, it's just like having a party.[461]

Stephanie Cole agreed:

It was lovely, because Lynda and Maggie Ollerenshaw and David and myself had done it many times before, and Roy Clarke was there which was great, and then we had the new members of the team, who were fresh and keen, so the atmosphere was terrific – lively, friendly and funny. And we didn't feel any pressure when we were preparing. I dare say David did, because he carried the show, but the rest of us didn't. We had a wonderful script, a really good director and producer, a lovely cast, so, while you're actually doing it, you just concentrate on getting it done as well as you can do it. Once you've done it, then you hope that it gets the audience it deserves and you hope the audience enjoys it, but before that you're all in this nice little bubble.[462]

Probably the only thing that was not eerily familiar during location filming (at least as far as the original stars were concerned) was Granville's legendary delivery bike. Although Sir David had to ride it up the street and round the corner, like he had done so many times before, he found it much harder to manage than he had done in the past. 'That bike was a pain in the butt in more ways than one,' he later explained, 'because the gears hadn't been sorted out properly and it was quite difficult to ride, but it was wonderful to see it again.'[463]

Once this and a couple of other stunts were negotiated safely, the filming was over. The design crew started removing the signage and stock, the crates were loaded back on to the lorries, and then the team returned to London. Everyone was delighted with how smoothly the process had gone.

The next stage was the studio recording, which was due to take place two weeks later on Tuesday 3 December, at the BBC's new base at MediaCityUK in Salford. The cast and crew thus arrived early in the morning for the usual rehearsals and run-throughs, and then, at 8pm, in front of a studio audience (among whom were two very special guests, Roy Clarke and Sydney Lotterby), the special was shot.

Whether it was mainly down to the sudden surge of hype, or the still-strong sense of nostalgia, or something as old fashioned and human as open-minded curiosity, is not entirely clear, but the interest that had been shown by the public, up to this point, was exceptionally intense. Once tickets (which, as is the norm, were free) had been advertised for the event, more than 28,000 people applied to be in the studio audience – despite there being just 360 seats available.[464]

Those who were fortunate enough to be there on the night could sense that this was a very special occasion. There was not only a camera crew to film the actual show. There was also a second camera crew to film the filming of the show for the purposes of a tie-in documentary.

Once the lights went down and the recording commenced, the key characters emerged, the laughter began, and the audience, as well as the actors, quickly relaxed as it became clear that the new show was working. The unfamiliar characters arrived, the familiar humour continued, and the old till still misbehaved. The reception grew warmer and louder as each minute passed.

At the end, when the lights went back up, the members of the cast came out again, stood together in a line, and bowed to the audience, who gave them a standing ovation. There was relief, and pride, in the reaction that the show, on the night, had elicited.

The actors, when asked in the days that followed, certainly felt very satisfied with how it had all gone. The long applause was their reward for all the planning, all the preparation and all the worry. The revival, it seemed, had passed its first test.

Sydney Lotterby, having watched it, was happy to give it his blessing. 'I enjoyed it,' he said of the recording. 'It was good to see again all of the people who were there, that I'd cast originally, back on the set. My mind, obviously, kept comparing it all to the shows that *I* did, and that was interesting, but I thought it went down very well in its own right.'[465]

Roy Clarke, as the man who had brought it all back, was understandably delighted. 'It's been a real trip down memory lane for me,' he said at the time, 'and I've had a ball.'[466]

STILL OPEN ALL HOURS

A couple of weeks later, Sir David Jason, reflecting on where they now were, was upbeat in his outlook for the episode, feeling that, judging by the reaction of the studio audience, they had got the tone just right for mainstream television:

It's British humour. There's a lot of innuendo, there's a lot of suggestiveness, there's a lot of stuff that's clouded and left for you to work it out, and so the audience has got to do a little bit of work, but they know what we're talking about. And it's so cleverly disguised, wrapped up in beautiful language, and that's the joy of it. That's what makes it funny. You *imply* certain things and you don't say it. You leave the audience to work it out for themselves. And everybody has got in their own mind a slightly different interpretation of how the innuendo is placed, and so they get their own little enjoyment from arriving at that.[467]

He was not expecting the special to match the spectacular results, in terms of viewing figures, that the original series had achieved – 'No-one ever will get those audiences again, because the world's so different with all the channels and the internet'[468] – but he professed himself quietly confident that, on this occasion, it would still do rather well. The revival was going to work.

He would not dare to think beyond the broadcast date but, buoyed by the experience of bringing the show back to life, he could not help sounding positive about its future. 'No-one would dare close the shop!' he insisted. 'We're leaving it in such a way that even if it's never seen again, it's still out there… It's like Narnia. It's always there somewhere.'[469]

CHAPTER FOURTEEN

Still Open All Hours

One day, Granville, all this will be yours,
lock-lock-lock-lock-lock stock and barrel.

The special festive episode, entitled *Still Open All Hours*, was scheduled for broadcast in Britain on the evening of 26 December 2013. This meant it faced a double challenge: not only would it have to do justice to its own great tradition, but it was also one of the BBC's key hopes in the annual battle for the biggest Christmas audiences.

The latter obligation, in particular, meant that the new edition of *Open All Hours* simply *had* to be a success. The mainstream channels do not take risks with their festive specials. Once chosen, they are subjected to the hard sell. The corner shop sitcom was thus going to be marketed as if it was a veritable comic superstore.

There were press releases. The BBC, for example, sent journalists a suitably upbeat set of quotes about the forthcoming revival, full of the rather robotic-sounding enthusiasm that executives appear to think will seem perfectly natural to ordinary viewers. Mark Freeland, for example, promised that the programme would 'bring broad grins to lots and lots of faces at Christmas', while the controller of BBC One, Charlotte Moore, agreed that the 'Christmas schedule suddenly feels complete with the addition of this classic British comedy'.[470]

There were photo opportunities and video exclusives. Members of the cast and crew could hardly go anywhere during this period without having their actions snapped and shot for various promotional purposes, and most of them were brought back to the studios to record interviews for the tie-in documentary, *Open All Hours: A Celebration*, that would be shown a day after the special itself.

There were press features, including several major celebrations of the show's illustrious past as one of Britain's best-loved sitcoms. Indeed, many of the same newspapers that had barely seemed to notice the sitcom when it was last on the screen now competed with each other to 'remember' how popular it had actually been.[471]

There were online stories, teasers and tweets. The popular TV-oriented website Digital Spy, for example, proved a willing publicist, trumpeting everything from a 'first-look picture' of the filming[472] to a set of positive soundbites from the key participants,[473] while the influential comedy website Chortle did much the same.[474] The *Daily Mail*'s website, however, outdid all of its competitors for sheer speculative enthusiasm by featuring (on 19 November) no fewer than 45 pictures of scenes being rehearsed and filmed on location in Doncaster, accompanied by a series of wild and (probably knowingly) misleading guesses as to what the images might mean (such as, wrongly, a supposedly tearful breakdown on set by Sir David Jason, and a possible scene mourning the death of Arkwright).[475]

There were also innumerable, relentlessly repetitive, television trailers, popping up long before the programme was scheduled to appear in order to alert everyone to its existence. 'Coming very soon!' the message said, even when it meant 'coming quite some time in the future'.

It was the way of the world in contemporary broadcasting. Thanks to a generation of terrestrial TV executives who both overestimate the threat of a multi-channel age, and underestimate the public's ability to separate the few precious grains of wheat from the masses of worthless chaff, every promising forthcoming programme risks outstaying its welcome long before it has even arrived. *Still Open All Hours* was now no exception to the rule.

There could not, of course, have been more of a contrast with the (lack of) promotion of the original four series. Whereas each one of those had practically been abandoned in a basket on viewers' darkened doorsteps, the imminent arrival of this new special seemed as though it was being heralded by everything from marching bands and cheerleaders to micro-managed marketeers banging on the windows and shouting through the letterboxes.

It was all hugely, richly, ironic. Anyone under the age of about 40, who was now exposed to all of this hyper-professional puffery, would surely have assumed that the original *Open All Hours* had always been warmly embraced by the broader media, and carried shoulder-high by all the metropolitan cognoscenti right up to the top of the ratings. The fact that it had actually achieved what it had achieved without any real or consistent assistance from anybody was a story that, strangely enough, got lost beneath all of the current hype and hullabaloo.

The irony was certainly not lost on the likes of Roy Clarke, Sir David Jason and Lynda Baron, who could still recall the many snubs that their sitcom had suffered. They were, nonetheless, delighted to see that it was now, belatedly, getting the kind of respect and attention that it had always deserved.

It was broadcast on Boxing Day at 7.45pm on BBC One, where it was expected to benefit from the momentum of an early evening schedule that traditionally outperformed all of its competitors during the festive season. Sure enough, inheriting an audience of 8.3 million from *EastEnders*,[476] *Still Open All Hours* had an eminently good chance, on the night, of seeing off such rival attractions as BBC Two's Christmas edition of *University Challenge*, ITV's showing of the already over-familiar 2010 movie *Harry Potter and the Deathly Hallows: Part 1*, Channel 4's re-screening of the even more over-familiar 1996 movie *Independence Day*, and Channel 5's imported Michael Bublé Christmas special.

The stage, therefore, was set. It was now up to the show itself.

The shop looked basically the same when the episode opened. There were still cartons of fruit and vegetables on display outside the windows, along with a familiar assortment of stepladders, plastic plant pots, pet food, spades, shovels, wicker baskets, baths, bowls, brushes and dusters. The prices, of course, had risen quite dramatically since the last time the shop had been seen, although there were a few 'BOGOF' stickers in prominent positions, and a 'ONE STOP SHOP' sign above the door to draw curious customers inside.

The delivery bike, this time, was nowhere to be seen, with a couple of tables of freshly farmed produce standing close to where it used to be perched on the pavement. The milk float, however, hummed past just like before as a new day of shopping slowly dawned.

The most striking difference now was the absence of Arkwright. As the solo cornet played the usual tune, only Granville – a shorter, balder, much older-looking Granville – stepped out on to the street in the famous old overalls, rubbing his hands together just like his uncle used to do and bracing himself for business. Within seconds he is trying, unsuccessfully, to charm a passer-by inside, pointing out to her that 'you don't get this personal touch at the supermarkets, do you?'

It soon becomes clear that much has happened since the last time that we saw him. His uncle has passed away, with his presence commemorated with a portrait hanging high up on the wall in the back room. Granville's own youthful idealism and restlessness, meanwhile, have also gone, to be replaced by world-weary cynicism and a sense of resignation regarding his roots.

The big, bright and boyish orbital eyes, which used to dart about in search of women and adventure, are now partly hooded by fleshy eyelids that have long since ceased to spring back up with surprise. Similarly, the once-mobile mouth, so often curved upwards in bright defiance of his uncle's dour demeanour, has now drooped into a default mode of stoical disappointment.

He has not yet acquired his uncle's trademark stutter, but he does have a habit of mimicking it on certain occasions by way of a kind of homage. 'You forget,' he says as he prepares to push some more unlikely products on to an unsuspecting public, 'that I was t-t-t-t-trained by the m-m-m-master!'

Having had his aptitude for shopkeeping mocked and maligned so often during middle age, he perhaps needs something to prove to him that he really is the boss now – so he has a son, Leroy, to boss about. Just as maddeningly impractical and day-dreamy as he used to be, Leroy wanders around the shop wearing cheap sunglasses and bumping into things ('You have to make these little sacrifices in the name of cool'), moaning about how rundown and rickety everything is ('when are you going to get these pipes fixed?') and wondering about his true parentage (LEROY: 'I often wonder if I'm really somebody else. I don't even *look* like you.' GRANVILLE: 'When I was your age even *I* didn't look like me').

Now that Granville is finally at the top of the pecking order, he spends plenty of time pecking away at Leroy, much as Arkwright used to do to him. The subject of the missing mother, once again, is a frequent source of caustic comments from the father to the supposed son: 'You ought to be able to find your father in the dark. Your mother did. The first time'; 'If you want casual, think of your mother – everybody else did!'; 'She left you out there on my doorstep for some nugget in the motor trade. He could offer her a nearly-new Jaguar. What chance did I have with "Buy One, Get One Free"?'

Although Leroy, much to Granville's envy and irritation, is frequently fussed over by everyone from Gladys to countless young girls, the old grocer is determined to keep him stuck safely inside, where he can school him in the ways of shopkeeping. Whether it is learning to survive the demonic cash register, or pushing unwanted products on to the public, Leroy, it is clear, is going to have to serve the traditional Arkwright apprenticeship. Even the old delivery bike, if Granville gets his way, will eventually be pushed into Leroy's path ('I've got to slow my lad down somehow!')

Apart from Leroy, however, Granville's focus is firmly on the daily duty to keep the till ringing. His primary concern, once that 'CLOSED' sign is turned over to 'OPEN', is to lure the locals inside.

The neighbourhood, clearly, has changed considerably, with a now much richer ethnic mix on show (which was not quite as reflective of reality as the London-based programme makers might have thought, bearing in mind that the population of Doncaster, at the time, was still estimated as being 93.21 per cent 'British and white', although it did capture a more general trend in the broader region[477]), as well as wider range of ages. It still seems like Arkwright Country, although the only Cyril who is now on view appears to be of Indian descent, and in place of that old Tyke tittle-tattle Mrs Blewett is an Asian *bakait* named Mrs Hussein.

Gladys Emmanuel is still there across the road, where her old white Morris Minor remains parked outside her house. Now retired from being a nurse, she is living on her own, having lost not only her mother but also her fiancé, Arkwright.

Still a regular visitor to the shop, her relationship with Granville is of the relaxed and candid kind that comes from sharing so much for so long in each other's life. With both of them a little sadder and wiser than before, they probably remind each other of what they have lost and what hopes they no longer have, so there is a melancholic quality to their meetings as they muddle through another aimless day:

GLADYS: You're an old tightwad, like your uncle!

GRANVILLE: *Old tightwad?* Coh! Could we settle for a 'prime of life, perfectly formed and in magnificent condition' kind of tightwad?

GLADYS: Eh, he trained you well!!

GRANVILLE: Don't be bitter. He *would* have married you, given time.

GLADYS: *Time?* An alternative view is that he died sooner than pay for the wedding!

GRANVILLE: All right, so you haven't got matrimony. How about some anchovy paste?

GLADYS: Yuck!

GRANVILLE: No, no, special offer!

GLADYS: You'll never get rid of that anchovy paste. They're staunch potted meat round here!

She is still like a mother to him, but now she treats the term more as a noun than a verb. Instead of fussing over him protectively and holding his head to her ample chest, she is more likely these days to slap him playfully on the cheek and push him back to work. She is all tough love and discreet devotion, and he, in turn, is all low-key affection and quiet respect:

GRANVILLE: I could do with a bit of mothering.

GLADYS: Ha, we all know what *you* could do with. Keep taking the pills!

[She sets off for the door with her shopping]

GRANVILLE: That's three pound fifty.

GLADYS: I'll see you Friday – save me a small white loaf!

Granville feels invisible these days. Having relied on the kindness of about 12 of the local women for help with bringing up baby Leroy,

226

STILL OPEN ALL HOURS

there is now a veritable procession of middle-aged mother figures all inquiring after their handsome-looking surrogate son ('How's the lad?'), while Granville, who used to inspire a similar kind of widespread maternal concern, rarely merits even a perfunctory 'How are you?'

The one woman who still clearly does have feelings for him is Wavy Mavis, whose newly single status, given the meekness of her nature, probably came about through widowhood being imposed rather than divorce being decided. Although still a slave to her own indecision, she is, nonetheless, sure of her enduring affection for Granville:

MAVIS: Good morning, Granville.
GRANVILLE: Good morning, Mavis.
MAVIS: I'm all right as far as 'Good morning', and then I never know what to say. That's me finished.
GRANVILLE: There's no problem. I'm gobby enough for both of us. Do you know that the small grocer makes an ideal pet?

[She just smiles non-committally]

GRANVILLE: I like what you're wearing.
MAVIS: Oh, it's just something I threw on. And off. And on again.
GRANVILLE: You look better since you got rid of that bum of a husband.
MAVIS: I must have liked him once. I can't remember why.
GRANVILLE: I could never understand why you weren't unfaithful to him. It wasn't as though I didn't *try.*
MAVIS: You were always nice. I used to come in the shop more than I really needed.
GRANVILLE: Ha, yeah, well, it was a hell of a romance, weren't it? The closest we ever got was when we had both our hands on the same tin of baked beans.

227

Mavis is to Granville what Nurse Gladys was to Arkwright: his one great object of desire. Unfortunately for Granville, his Nurse Gladys equivalent comes (in the style of one of his own dubious 'buy one, get one free' offers), with a corresponding equivalent to Nurse Gladys's disapproving mother: in this case, Mavis's older sister, Madge.

Madge is as intolerant of Granville as Gladys's mother used to be of Arkwright. The only difference is that Gladys's mother was hidden from view, whereas Madge has a tendency of barging in on a potentially romantic scene like a maverick member of the vice squad:

MADGE:	Don't be listening to him! He'll give you all sorts of old twaddle! It's what they do!
GRANVILLE:	Good morning to you, too, Madge. We can't get our twaddle in edgeways with you!
MADGE:	And where were you when I was reversing?
MAVIS:	Well, you know I daren't look.
MADGE:	Well, you look at *him!*
MAVIS:	*[Dreamily]* He doesn't race his engine!
GRANVILLE:	Hang on – could we have a little talk about that?
MADGE:	Don't be looking at him soft! Ask him how much is his belly pork!
GRANVILLE:	I'm not sure I follow that train of thought. Anyway, it's no dearer than up the road.
MADGE:	We'll have a quarter. *[Adopts posh accent]* And a quarter of *haaaslet.*
GRANVILLE:	*Haslet?* Thank you!

[He heads over to the bacon slicer]

MAVIS:	Ooh, I daren't look when he's using that bacon slicer!
MADGE:	Well, he's not charging enemy trenches!
GRANVILLE:	No – and he's not over-charging either! Except for certain *awkward* customers, who are *designed* for such purposes!
MAVIS:	*[Still with her eyes shut]* Has he finished?
MADGE:	He's still *gobbing!* He hasn't *started* yet!

If Madge is not enough of a threat to Granville's pursuit of happiness, he now also has to contend with 'The Black Widow', Mrs Featherstone, who is eyeing him like an unclaimed ISA:

MRS FEATHERSTONE: Oh, we could have made a dream team, your uncle and me. With his grasp of the mercenary and my gift for the thrifty. But he was blinded by a bigger bosom.

GRANVILLE: Yes, he always did expect a lot for his pound, didn't he?

MRS FEATHERSTONE: Of course, it helped that she could bandage his injured parts and keep an eye on his mild hernia. So I lost, I always feel, on a technicality. But *he* lost the opportunity to awaken my flame.

GRANVILLE: Well, I know he never knew where he left his matches...

MRS FEATHERSTONE: You'd be surprised what burns behind a respectable exterior.

GRANVILLE: Well, behind some exteriors, er, you can see how it is easily overlooked.

MRS FEATHERSTONE: I've trained two husbands to an early grave. Discipline is my watchword. But...for a genuine soul mate...of strict financial probity, on national holidays and certain personal festivities, there could be the occasional... frolic.

GRANVILLE: I never thought of you in a *frolic*, Mrs Featherstone!

MRS FEATHERSTONE: Under strict operational conditions. One must be realistic. I know how you men are.

GRANVILLE: Really? How are we, Mrs Featherstone?

MRS FEATHERSTONE: Call me 'Delphine'. *[She runs her fingers suggestively up his lapel]* I think we are ready to take us to the next level.

GRANVILLE: Oh! Look at that! Is *that* the time? Yes it is! I must go and see if I can get –

[She reaches out and pulls him back by his grocer's overcoat]

MRS FEATHERSTONE: I have *watched* you, lad. Growing in wisdom. To you I am always available on a consultancy basis. And there could be more, Granville. It is the age of the cougar. *Grrrr!*

The one thing that gives Granville a sense of security, the one thing upon which he can always rely, is his ability to sell absolutely anything that happens to be in his shop. 'You t-t-taught me some stuff, didn't you, eh?' he says, chuckling mischievously as he looks up fondly at Arkwright's portrait hanging on the wall. 'I'll never get into heaven. Probably be closed anyway. These big companies don't work the hours that we do, do they, eh?'

Arguably the highlight of the episode, due in part to the interplay of the actors and in part to the confident comedy writing, was the scene in which Granville, at his most artfully Arkwright-like, bids to dupe the most gullible of his current crop of customers, the aptly named 'Wet' Eric (very nicely played by Johnny Vegas), into snapping up some stock that had previously seemed unsellable:

GRANVILLE: Oh, is it a trough of low depression, or is it Eric? How's it going, Eric?
ERIC: What's this stuff you've got, then?
GRANVILLE: 'Stuff'? 'What's this *stuff*'? Eric, this place is full of *stuff*, isn't it? This is an Aladdin's *cave!* It's the *horn* of plenty! You're going to have to get a bit closer than 'stuff'! Now, is it my imagination, or are you a bit low in spirit?
ERIC: So would *you* be if you were married to her back home.
GRANVILLE: I thought you did better than might have been expected. She's not unattractive.
ERIC: I know. But what does she *do* with it? Nothing!

GRANVILLE: Are you telling me you've lost some of the music of your honeymoon days?

ERIC: Well, it's never exactly the full orchestra, but I'm down to solo trumpet.

GRANVILLE: We ought to form a duet. You know, people of our generation are in the deprivation zone of playtime.

ERIC: *Playtime???* If I didn't have an Xbox, I wouldn't get any!

GRANVILLE: There *are* ways, you know, to put the colour back in your cheeks.

ERIC: *[Shiftily]* Are we talking 'over eighteen, unlocking your full potency' here?

GRANVILLE: We are.

ERIC: That's *it!* That's the *stuff!*

GRANVILLE: But are you *ready* for it?

ERIC: Oh, I'm ready! I'm *ready!!* Can I ask…ready for *what*, exactly?

GRANVILLE: For the road back to playtime!

ERIC: Er, when you say 'back'…have you got anything for anyone who's never really been there in the first place?

[Granville pats Eric's arm paternally and leads him over to the tower of cans of anchovy paste]

GRANVILLE: Well, I have to warn you, this stuff, y'know, is a life-changer.

ERIC: I'm up for that!

GRANVILLE: Right, now listen: don't overdo it at first. You know: small amounts – *pace* yourself. This stuff has a double whammy. You get your general *health* stimulus, plus *[he whispers something sensational into Eric's ear].*

ERIC: *…FROM ANCHOVY PASTE?*

GRANVILLE: Oh, yes, it's the fish oils. Nature's secret. Because way back then, y'know, we were *all*

fish. *This* stuff will put a tiger in your tank. I'll
tell you what: it will transform your nights.
But I warn you – you've *got* to take it easy.
Small amounts, *pace* yourself, spread it *thinly.*

ERIC: Or else...what?

GRANVILLE: Or else your entire *life* will be playtime!

ERIC: ...I'll take two!!!

It all ends, predictably, in frail male British failure, because Eric, it
later transpires, has mistakenly applied the paste externally ('I've never
had an easy moment since I put it on!'), while Granville, in an ill-
conceived attempt to show Leroy why he should learn to love the
delivery bike, appears to have bruised his grocer's quirk. 'It's a duet,
i'nt it?' he groans as he and Eric limp back into the shop as Gladys and
Leroy stand and snigger.

The episode then seems to end, much like any of the old ones
ended, with the old shopkeeper venturing outside as the evening
advances, to start packing up the products on display and reflect on the
events of the day:

> Oh, it's been a funny old day… I've seen more of Wet Eric than is
> customary… I believe I'm near a breakthrough with that bacon
> slicer… I thought Mavis was looking good. But then I always
> think Mavis is looking good… That's a powerful rear light. Unless
> it's Wet Eric still glowing in the dark.

The monologue is interrupted, however, by the unexpected arrival of
Mrs Featherstone, excited after having received by mistake the romantic
note that Granville had intended for Mavis, and kissing him powerfully
before he has a chance to escape. 'But it isn't Christmas yet!' he gasps. 'It
feels like it to me!' she replies, before disappearing back into the darkness.

The episode, in keeping with the spirit of its much-loved
predecessors, did without anything that might have passed as a proper
plot, preferring instead to probe the key relationships and play with the
other characters. The quota of customers, on this particular occasion,
was exceptionally high, with no fewer than 13 of them making the

entrance seem more like a rapidly revolving door. It was quite difficult, as a consequence, for more than a few of them to appear genuinely three-dimensional rather than just random vessels for certain lines.

There was also a strong sense of *déjà vu* about some elements in the episode. Granville's devious scheme, for example, to convince Wet Eric that a neglected can of anchovy paste contains aphrodisiacal powers, echoed Arkwright's attempt (in series three, episode two) to persuade Cyril that a packet of previously unloved Jamaican ginger cake could actually be used as a marital aid, while Granville's tumble from the old delivery bicycle seemed to be a mere reprise of the time when Arkwright ended up suffering the same undignified fate (in series three, episode three).

Still Open All Hours, in this sense, did feel a little too eager to please, as if it were more like a free 'sample' DVD tucked inside a weekend newspaper than a truly substantial revival of a major sitcom. Burdened by the extra responsibility of being one of the BBC's designated 'blockbusters' of the Christmas period, the show seemed somewhat scared of doing what it had always done best – slowing the pace, sharpening the focus and generally revelling in the drollery to be had from the most humdrum moments of ordinary life – and strained instead to speed through all of the buffoonery.

The critics, not entirely unsurprisingly, were generally unconvinced by the revival. Having recently endured a succession of disappointing reboots and reprises of classic sitcoms, they were hardly in the most receptive of moods to welcome what they probably regarded as merely yet another symbol of television's neurotic disinclination to dare to try something that was actually new.

Ben Lawrence, writing in the *Daily Telegraph*, found the glut of guest stars to be an error of judgement ('the various dialogues were too brief for you to get a handle on anyone') and felt that the episode as a whole 'didn't work'[478]; Will Dean, in *The Independent*, hoped that the new episode would at least 'push younger viewers to the original [shows]', but confessed that there was much of the special that struck him as simply 'odd' (most notably the gap left by Ronnie Barker, which he felt made the show as imbalanced as 'Garfunkel without Simon' or 'Wise without Morecambe')[479]; while, right at the most negative end of the scale, the

Sunday People's Adam Postans simply requested 'let's never speak again of *Still Open All Hours*'[480] and the *Sunday Mirror's* Kevin O'Sullivan declared that it was 'Time to shut up shop'.[481] Several other critics, perhaps reprising the indifference their respective papers showed to the original series, simply decided to damn the programme with silence.

Once again, however, the public seemed to disagree. The viewing figures for the show were strikingly good: an estimated 12.23 million watched the show, adding almost 4 million to the audience that it had inherited from *EastEnders* – not only the biggest audience of the season for BBC One, but also the biggest audience of the season for any programme on British television, and the biggest audience for any comedy programme since 2007, and the third biggest in over a decade.[482]

'It was just wonderful,' Roy Clarke would say of the popular reaction. 'You never know. You really never know. But it couldn't have gone better and I'm very grateful for that.'[483]

The sitcom, once again, had succeeded. It might not have reached the high standards set by the original series, or retrieved all of its old charm, and it was never going to make up for the absence of Ronnie Barker as Arkwright, but, in the circumstances, it had met all of the challenges it had been set and, in some ways, had even exceeded expectations.

There was only one question left that had not yet been answered. That question was: 'Is that it for *Open All Hours?*'

CHAPTER FIFTEEN

The Story Goes On

We have to plan ahead, you know,
in the service industries.

There was a strange period of confusion following the success of the Christmas edition of *Still Open All Hours*. In answer to the question 'Is that it?' some sources said 'Yes' while others said 'No'.

The first couple of weeks after the show had been seen were full of strikingly positive headlines about the fact that it had topped the ratings. 'OPEN ALL HOURS IS BOXING DAY WINNER FOR BBC', announced *The Guardian*.[484] 'STILL OPEN ALL HOURS SNATCHES CHRISTMAS RATINGS HONOURS', reported *Metro*.[485] 'A BOXING DAY HIT', declared the *Daily Mirror*.[486] 'TV VIEWERS HAIL THE ONE-OFF RETURN OF CLASSIC SITCOM OPEN ALL HOURS AS "WARMLY NOSTALGIC" AND "A FITTING TRIBUTE TO RONNIE BARKER"', trumpeted a garrulous *Daily Mail*.[487] It was the talk of the television industry. Then, however, it all went quiet, and, after a week or so more of silence, the rumours started to circulate.

On 22 January 2014, the *Daily Mirror* featured a story claiming that *Open All Hours* was now closed for good, 'despite the Christmas special proving a ratings winner'. Noting that the show 'may have won a near 40% audience share on Boxing Day [it was actually 44%] but it was savaged by TV critics including the *Daily Mirror*'s Ian Hyland', the paper went on to say: 'A Beeb insider revealed: "Impressive ratings are only part of the recipe for success. The fact that the organisation have [sic] been slow off the mark to commission a new series and get contracts tied down is a telling sign."'[488]

This report was promptly repeated by numerous other news outlets both in print and online, although no official announcement had been made by the BBC. There then followed a plethora of 'what went wrong?' articles and discussions (with many of them grouping the programme alongside other vintage sitcoms recently judged to have 'failed' with their respective revivals), with most concluding that it was for the best that the show had now been consigned, once and for all, to history.

All of this, however, was contradicted on 30 January, when the BBC announced that *Still Open All Hours* would indeed be commissioned as a new six-part series. In a press release to mark the decision (which, it can now be revealed, had actually been taken on 7 January[489]), Shane Allen, the controller of BBC comedy commissioning, was quoted as saying: 'The resounding success of the Christmas revival showed the huge and enduring audience affection for this much-loved classic. Roy [Clarke] has done a terrific job of updating the characters whilst keeping what was warm-hearted and enjoyable about the world of the original series.' Mark Freeland, now billed as controller of fiction and entertainment, added: 'We were all delighted by the response that the Christmas Special received. It was so difficult to shut up shop after that. So we haven't. Granville's is well and truly open for business.'[490]

There were also comments from Sir David Jason and Roy Clarke. Sir David said: 'I am so delighted that we are doing a series of *Still Open All Hours* as the feedback from our Christmas Special has been so rewarding and encouraging. We want to have more fun giving the audience the kind of show they seemed to appreciate.' Clarke added: 'I'm delighted. It's like going back home.'[491]

There then followed a second spate of media reports, hurriedly moving the revival out of the 'flop' category and back into the one reserved for 'hits'. The emphasis now was on the spectacular ratings and the positive responses. It was rather like having to rely on *Dad's Army*'s notoriously doom-laden but shamelessly contrary Private Frazer to be one's sole showbiz correspondent: 'I never doubted ye for a minute!'

After all of the ebullient announcements, it was time for the production to commence. The team behind the scenes was expanded to oversee the series: Sarah Hitchcock was re-appointed as production executive; Gareth Edwards returned as executive producer; Alex Walsh-

Taylor (whose credits included Simon Day's seriously underrated 2003 sitcom *Grass* and Nick Frost's 2006 sci-fi comedy *Hyperdrive*) came in as producer; Andy Bennions (who had previously worked on *Miranda* in 2009 and *Twenty Twelve* in 2012) was added as production manager; and Dewi Humphreys was back again as director. The main cast, on the other hand, was unchanged: apart from Sir David himself, Lynda Baron, Stephanie Cole, Maggie Ollerenshaw, Brigit Forsyth and James Baxter were all re-enlisted to continue with their respective characters. With dates being discussed and diaries compared, the process thus began cranking into action.

Roy Clarke, meanwhile, settled down at home in Goole in the East Riding of his beloved Yorkshire and simply picked up from where he had left off at Christmas: Granville and Leroy would be back inside the shop, baffling each other with their conflicting attitudes and actions; Gladys would be back across the road, keeping a careful eye on both of them; Mavis would still be flirting nervously with Granville, while her sister, Madge, would be doing her best to keep them apart; and the usual wide range of ordinary eccentrics would be coming in and out of the door. 'Business as usual,' Clarke said with a smile.[492]

The expectations among the returning members of the cast were high. Stephanie Cole, for example, remarked: 'The feedback I got personally after [the Christmas special] went out was a delight. People were stopping me when I was out and about to say how much they loved it and laughed, and they were asking whether there would be any more shows. It was all very, very positive. So I wasn't surprised when we were told we were now doing a series. In fact I think the potential is there for it to go on beyond that.'[493]

Maggie Ollerenshaw was similarly optimistic: 'The demand is definitely there, so we're delighted to be back. I know it will be great fun to do, and I just hope that we make people laugh all over again, and that they really like it. And it would be particularly nice if they liked it *so* much we could have *another* six episodes!'[494]

Sir David Jason echoed such sentiments, expressing his own excitement at being reunited, once again, with so many familiar faces, and stressing how much he was looking forward to finding new things to do as the downtrodden but slyly defiant Granville. 'I can't wait!'[495]

As the team thus waited eagerly for the action to start, the supportive publicity – once so hard to find for this sitcom – now flowed freely and fully. 'There is a lot of interest in the new series', said Sarah Hitchcock, 'with questions coming in from Doncaster tourist office, local and national press and all kinds of places.'[496] Sir David, who was currently promoting the paperback edition of his autobiography, was questioned for clues about the plans for the programme whenever he was interviewed on radio or television during this period, and all of his fellow actors found themselves being asked much the same. 'The level of curiosity is amazing,' confirmed Stephanie Cole. 'But I'm afraid I can't tell them anything because I haven't seen the scripts yet myself.'[497]

Lynda Baron, who at the time was busy appearing on stage in Hugh Whitemore's critically acclaimed play *Stevie* (about the life of the poet Stevie Smith), had to field similar queries, but she, too, was beginning to get caught up in the sense of anticipation. 'I did have a word with Roy Clarke,' she later revealed. 'I said, "Oh, you know, seeing as my love interest is now gone, what on earth will I be doing?" But', she added with great affection, 'he didn't give anything away – he's such a secretive bugger!' She was thus left, like everyone else, to speculate: 'I just hope that Gladys will have an interesting job now, because I just don't believe that she will ever retire. She's much too busy a person, as well as quite a clever woman. So I'll be as fascinated as the audience will be to find out what the devil Gladys is up to!'[498]

One sign of the broader interest being aroused by the imminent revival came early on in the year, when a stage version of *Open All Hours*, which was based on the original shows (and adapted, with the permission of Roy Clarke, by Gary Simmons and his directing partner Jane Aston), was taken on a lengthy UK tour. A real labour of love that featured a painstakingly reconstructed set of Arkwright's store, complete with the familiar array of products ('We spent twelve months or more purchasing old tins and saving original food packaging,' said Simmons[499]), along with all of the well-known props ('The bike came from Clacton-on-Sea. It was in pieces and my father spent a long time restoring it. The notorious till came from Reading and the scales from just outside Manchester'[500]), it saw Simmons himself as Arkwright, Jon

Hall as Granville and Mary Singh as Nurse Gladys, and met with an enthusiastic reception.[501]

A second sign was a well-attended *Open All Hours* exhibition, which was hosted by the Portland Basin Museum at Ashton-under-Lyne in Lancashire. Running for nine consecutive months and featuring such relics from shopping days past as antique carrier bags, faded 'to do' lists, vintage food packaging, pre-decimal notes and coins and a suitably intimidating-looking ancient till, the installation showcased an age when most people's experience of seeking out their essential comestibles involved 'walking up and down the high street visiting the butcher, the baker and the greengrocer'.[502] It also, of course, attracted many fans of the television show that had inspired it.

Yet another sign came at the start of the summer, when the nostalgia TV channel GOLD began showing all of the old episodes of the original series of *Open All Hours* again (fairly unusually, screened in their proper sequence). In contrast to the typical low-key and routine approach to such re-runs, prominent advertisements were taken out in the national newspapers and magazines to herald the forthcoming schedules and underline their topical significance.

There were also repeats of the recent *Still Open All Hours* special (and the tie-in documentary) on various channels abroad. Australia and New Zealand, home to two of the sitcom's biggest and most avid international audiences, were particularly eager to remind their viewers not only of the show's past successes but also of its future promise.

The cultural climate, therefore, was encouragingly benign. The doubts were still around, but plenty of people were willing the new series to succeed.

Location filming, which began in September, took place, as usual, in Balby, much to the pleasure and excitement of those fans who lived in the area. As had happened with the shooting of the special in the previous year, hordes of people gathered outside the newly converted corner shop in Lister Avenue to witness the unfolding of yet another chapter in the story of *Open All Hours*.

It was very different to the old days, when only those who were physically there could take in what was being created in front of their eyes. Now people could film sequences on their phones and post them straight on to the internet, and tweet their images and impressions from one minute to the next. It worked in the other direction, too: those among the team with their own Twitter accounts, such as Gareth Edwards and James Baxter, were able to do the same. The immediacy, and intensity, of all the coverage would mean that fans all over the country (and, indeed, all over the world) could follow the production's progress all the way from the rehearsals to the studio.

Studio recordings, this time, would take place from 10 October in London at Teddington Studios. Some of the cast would have preferred to have taken this very northern show back up to Manchester, as with the previous year's special, and staged all of the episodes in front of a northern audience, but London, on this occasion, was deemed, logistically, a more practical location for recording an entire series. 'Speaking as a northerner myself,' Maggie Ollerenshaw said, 'I did feel that was a bit of a shame, but I guess it couldn't be helped.'[503]

There were numerous guest actors who were now ready to join the team, led by Johnny Vegas, whose cleverly judged cameo appearance as 'Wet Eric' had been one of the undisputed highlights of the Christmas special. The new customers Roy Clarke had conjured up were apportioned among the performers, including such familiar figures as Tim Healy (as a recurring character called 'Gastric') and Paula Wilcox (as 'Melody').

Once the rehearsals commenced, the sense of momentum picked up and the creative ideas started to flow. Props were prepared and played with, scenes were explored in a variety of ways, lines were tried out and timed, and on-screen relationships were further fleshed out and developed. With all of the sounds and sights, it now really felt as though the series was actually happening.

The mood among the team as a whole was exceptionally bright as the work went on. Nobody wanted it to stop. Indeed, long before the series reached the screen, the hopes were growing that another one would follow it. There were other customers still queuing up to come through that corner shop door. There were more stories waiting to be told.

'The aim is just to keep going with it,' Roy Clarke declared. 'I'm Yorkshire – that's what we do!'[504]

EPILOGUE

Don't just crit there siticizing!

They thought it was all over. Actually, time and again, they thought it was all over. It still isn't.

Some fans will prefer just to think about the original four series. Others will be happy to embrace the new ones, too. All of them, however, will surely agree on one thing: the story of *Open All Hours* has been, in terms of television history, a truly remarkable one full of fortitude, faith and fun.

The corner shop sitcom kept on proving the sceptics wrong. Shelved after the pilot in favour of something that was deemed a better bet; shelved again after its first series, again in favour of something that was deemed a better bet; brought back somewhat reluctantly after five more years only to be left to fend for itself; shelved yet again, this time for three more years, when other projects were felt to have a greater claim on the time of the cast and crew; then ignored for awards after it returned to command record audiences; then consigned carelessly to the past until it was unexpectedly revived 28 years later for a one-off special, only for it to perform so strongly that a new series was soon commissioned.

That is quite a track record. The ultimate sitcom underdog, it just never gave up. It kept on earning the right, again and again, to come back and re-claim its audience.

This, then, is not a story of bitter frustration. It is a story of glorious triumph.

The main reason why this sitcom succeeded, against all the odds, is because it was actually very, very good. This ought to be so blindingly obvious that it seems a mere truism straight out of the Sybil Fawlty School of 'The Bleedin' Obvious' – and to most members of the public it most certainly is. In an age of broadcasting, however, when many executives seem to have convinced themselves that the only way that a programme can excel is through a remorseless campaign of overbearing hype (rather than through something so untrustworthy as actual talent), the story of *Open All Hours* offers a sobering and salutary lesson to the commissioning editors and channel controllers of today.

Contrary to what appears to be a common assumption in the TV industry of today, viewers are not a passive mass of dim-witted vessels. They are actually quite active, alert and discerning.

Open All Hours did not succeed because of any clever marketing campaign, inspired scheduling or great outpouring of critical support. It succeeded because it was good and because people recognized – without repeated prodding from the PR departments – that it was good. That, again, might seem depressingly simplistic to those who appear intent on making the business of television seem depressingly complex, but, more often than not, that is how entertainment can and should work.

Open All Hours worked so well because it had a great writer, a great cast and a great director. Yes, it probably would have done even better than it did if it had received the occasional promotional push, smarter scheduling and a fairer share of critical appreciation, but even when it was left on its own, thanks to the rare ability of those involved, it still won the admiration and affection of well over 18 million people.

That is what talent can achieve. That is why it deserves to be trusted far more often.

The team responsible for *Open All Hours* always knew the true value of what they were creating. They were always far too dignified and polite to say so, but, after the success of each new series, they were perfectly entitled to say to all the doubters: 'We told you so.'

'It's always been a very pleasant memory for me,' Roy Clarke remarked when asked to reflect on the show. 'It seemed to work from word one and we never looked back.'[505]

That was indeed how it happened. The cast and crew kept returning to it, just like the audiences, because they genuinely enjoyed the show so much.

The brilliant Ronnie Barker, always spoilt for choice for possible projects, made the show happen, and then, even though he was offered relatively little encouragement to do so, he went back to it whenever he had the chance. *Open All Hours*, he would say, was the sitcom that he 'enjoyed doing the most' – even more so than *Porridge* – because of all the fun that he had in the making of it, and because he felt the viewers could see that on the screen.[506]

Sir David Jason was the same: no matter how much success he enjoyed elsewhere as he soared from supporting roles right up high into stardom, he never lost any of his affection for the show in which he was, ostensibly at least, still the 'little feed'. His partnership with Ronnie Barker produced comedy performances that are among the very best in the history of British sitcoms, and continue to inspire and delight to this day.

Lynda Baron, whose clever and artful contributions made Nurse Gladys into an iconic comedy figure in her own right, was also full of appreciation for the enduring appeal of the show as a whole. 'We absolutely loved doing it, of course, but you're not fully aware of just how popular a show like that is with the public when you're actually making it, because you're so busy doing it and then you move straight on to the next job, but over the years it's become clearer to me how much people love it. I think they really like the *idea* of it. David Jason always says it's like a weird little country somewhere, and I think he's right. It's this funny little corner of England that will forever be *Open All Hours*. People *want* it to be there, and want to believe that that street is what we make of it.'[507]

There were no fights or factions behind the scenes. There were no ugly clashes of ego. There were just good people making a good show. That might not have made for much tabloid-friendly publicity, but it certainly did make for plenty of warm and witty entertainment, and that is much, much more important.

When so many television shows now feature someone demanding loudly that viewers 'give it up' and roar their approval, the grown-up humility of *Open All Hours* seems all the more refreshing. It earned every last bit of the applause that it received, because it always treated its viewers with the utmost care and respect.

Sir David Jason, when asked in 2013 about his hopes when he returned to the show, focused on what he, Ronnie Barker and Roy Clarke had always focused on – the audience: 'If I can just give them half an hour to put their feet up and escape into our world, to bring a smile to them and their family, then that's the way I want to be remembered.'[508]

That is the attitude that made *Open All Hours* come to please so many people. That is why it continues to be remembered with such fondness, and why we will always be grateful to those who brought it to the screen.

EPISODE GUIDE

Regular Credits

Created by Roy Clarke; written by Roy Clarke; theme music by Joseph Ascher, arranged by Max Harris; produced and directed by Sydney Lotterby.

Regular Cast

Ronnie Barker (Albert E. Arkwright); David Jason (Granville E. Arkwright); Lynda Baron (Nurse Gladys Emmanuel).

Pilot (1973, BBC2)

Open All Hours (25 March 1973)
It is another very ordinary day at Arkwright's. The owner is eager to start selling, while his nephew is desperate to start living.
Featuring: Yootha Joyce (Mrs Scully), Sheila Brennan (Nurse Gladys Emmanuel), David Valla (Bread Man), Elissa Derwent (Girl from Petrol Station), Keith Chegwin (Keithy) and Adam Barker (Tiny Boy).

Series One (1976, BBC2)

Full of Mysterious Promise (20 February 1976)
Arkwright is trying to sell a shipment of old tins without labels, Nurse Gladys is looking forward to a small brown loaf and two large tea cakes, and Granville is intrigued by what the woman might be getting up to inside number 87.
Featuring: John Lawrence (Mr Bristow), Gillian McClements (Gloria), Kathy Staff (Mrs Blewett), Peter Wallis (Winston), Kenneth Farringdon (TV Doctor), Vivienne Johnson (TV Wife), Michael Sharvell-Martin (TV Husband).

A Mattress on Wheels (27 February 1976)
Arkwright has always been content to deliver any grocery orders by bike rather than van. Granville, however, points out that, with a van, there would be plenty of room in the back for Gladys…
Featuring: Juliet Cooke (Eva), Jean Heywood (Vera Burns), George Innes (Used Car Salesman), Barbara Keogh (Mrs Ellis), Harry Markham (Freddie), Liz Baytes (Customer).

A Nice Cosy Little Disease (5 March 1976)
Feeling worn out by the wear and tear of self-employment, Arkwright craves to rest his tired head on Nurse Gladys's 'regal bosom'. Realizing that it will take more than run-of-the-mill fatigue to reach that fragrant destination, he decides to simulate a more eye-catching kind of ailment.
Featuring: Juliet Aykroyd (Linda Mulgrave), Tony Aitken (Norman), Graham Armitage (Man from Matlock Mutual Protection Society), Clare Kelly (Mrs Braddock), Barbara Keogh (Mrs Ellis).

Beware of the Dog (12 March 1976)
A spate of burglaries has prompted Arkwright to crank up security in and around his shop. Granville, meanwhile, is trying to work out if too much elderberry wine enabled him to have carnal action without any carnal knowledge.
Featuring: Kevin Moreton (Boy), Shirley Steedman (Maureen).

Well Catered Funeral (19 March 1976)
The passing of Parsloe, Arkwright's old school chum, prompts Granville to ponder human mortality, and Arkwright the cost of the catering.
Featuring: Reginald Barratt (Mr Wilkinson), John Challis (Bread Man), Kathy Staff (Mrs Blewett), Liz Dawn (Woman Outside Shop).

Apples and Self Service (26 March 1976)
A shipment of slow-selling apples drives Arkwright to experiment with some unconventional marketing strategies.
Featuring: Edna Doré (Woman Wanting Firelighters), Madge Hindle (Mrs Jardine), John McKelvey (Hard of Hearing Man), Michael Redfern (Southerner), Roy Denton (Customer 1), John Cazabon (Customer 2).

Series Two (1981, BBC1)

Laundry Blues (1 March 1981)
Arkwright needs to placate two angry people: Nurse Gladys Emmanuel, who is demanding that he buy a modern washing machine, and the VAT man, who wants him to attend to his accounts.
Featuring: Maggie Ollerenshaw (Mavis), Matthew Scurfield (Man from Bus Stop), Renu Setna (VAT Man), Nick Stringer (Neville), Deep Roy (Man in Washing Machine).

The Reluctant Traveller (8 March 1981)
Granville has the chance of some romance with the local milk woman, but, before he can play, he needs to get Arkwright to stay away.
Featuring: Barbara Flynn (The Milk Woman), Maggie Ollerenshaw (Mavis), Kathy Staff (Mrs Blewett).

Fig Biscuits and Inspirational Toilet Rolls (15 March 1981)
The fig biscuits are not shifting in Arkwright's shop, and the 'inspirational' toilet rolls are piling up as well. Some smart sales techniques are required.
Featuring: Howard Crossley (Man in Car), Mike Kelly (Delivery Man), Maggie Ollerenshaw (Mavis), Kathy Staff (Mrs Blewett), Gordon Salkilld (Workman), Richard Reid, Terry Durran, John Holland, Tony Pryor, Reg Woods and Alan Talbot (Smokers).

The New Suit (22 March 1981)
Nurse Gladys has decided that Arkwright will need a new suit if he is to accompany her in public. He, however, is unconvinced that he needs a change – let alone the expense.
Featuring: Michael Bilton (Hypnotist), Frances Cox (Mrs Parsloe), Frances Goodall (Woman on Bench), Emrys James (Eli Bickerdyke), Kathy Staff (Mrs Blewett).

Arkwright's Mobile Store (29 March 1981)
Arkwright is in top selling form, even persuading non-smokers to buy cigarettes, but Gladys is looking for signs of greater ambition. His response is to buy a clapped-out old ice-cream van.

Featuring: Maggie Ollerenshaw (Mavis), Brian Peck (Customer), Kathy Staff (Mrs Blewett), Paula Tilbrook (Mrs Tattersall).

Shedding at the Wedding (5 April 1981)
There is a wedding to attend, but Arkwright's new suit reeks of mothballs.
Featuring: Roger Elliott (Mr Bristow), Stuart Fell (Motorcyclist), Patsy Smart (Mrs Fielding), Kathy Staff (Mrs Blewett).

St Albert's Day (19 April 1981)
Arkwright suspects a foreign-looking customer of shoplifting. Needing to check what might be in his pockets, Arkwright invents a new half-holiday, St Albert's Day, complete with a frisking ritual.
Featuring: Frances Cox (Mrs Parsloe), Oscar Quitak (Statchyk), Teddy Turner (Gordon Stackpool).

Series Three (1982, BBC1)

An Errand Boy by the Ear (21 March 1982)
Arkwright is rattled: Granville is struggling to pull his weight, and a posh woman has turned up who declares that the shop is 'quaint'.
Featuring: Bridget Ashburn (Mrs Turner), Stephanie Cole (Mrs Featherstone), Madge Hindle (Posh Customer), Maggie Ollerenshaw (Mavis), Sue Race (Mrs Ellis), Nick Stringer (Helpful Man), Carl Mervyn (Customer).

The Ginger Men (28 March 1982)
The ginger cake has been over-stocked, so some creative marketing is urgently required.
Featuring: Stephanie Cole (Mrs Featherstone), Helen Cotterill (Julie), Barbara Flynn (Milk Woman), Bert Gaunt (Bert the Bread Man), Tom Mennard (Cyril), Alan Starkey (Thorndyke), Margaret Braden (Customer).

Duet for Solo Bicycle (4 April 1982)
As if it isn't hard enough for Granville to impress women, his delivery bike has now started to squeak.

STILL OPEN ALL HOURS

Featuring: Stephanie Cole (Mrs Featherstone), Barbara Flynn (Milk Woman), Sally Miles (Mrs Whittington), Donald Morley (Man Looking for Directions), Maggie Ollerenshaw (Mavis), Liz Whiting (Wendy).

How to Ignite Your Errand Boy (11 April 1982)
Arkwright is looking at developing some homemade, and therefore cheap, products in the shed out the back. His first idea, unfortunately for Granville, concerns firelighters.
Featuring: Stephanie Cole (Mrs Featherstone), Frances Cox (Mrs Parsloe), Howard Crossley (Milk Round Supervisor), Barbara Flynn (Milk Woman), Frank Marlborough (Dogman), Norman Robbins (Delivery Man), Tom Mennard (Cyril), David Thackwray (Boy).

The Man from Down Under (18 April 1982)
Chalky White, one of Nurse Gladys Emmanuel's old admirers, has returned from Australia for a visit. Arkwright, fiercely protective of his fiancée, is determined to see him off.
Featuring: Stephanie Cole (Mrs Featherstone), Janet Davies (Mrs Blake), Barbara Flynn (Milk Woman), Johnny Leeze (Man Whose Tyres Were Let Down), Maggie Ollerenshaw (Mavis), Teddy Turner (Gordon Stackpool).

The Cool Cocoa Tin Lid (25 April 1982)
The sight of a young man sporting headphones, sunglasses, an open shirt and jeans convinces Granville that he, too, could be 'cool'. The problem is that he has to make do with a cocoa tin lid for a manly medallion.
Featuring: John Bleasdale (Dennis), Helen Cotterill (Julie), Barbara Flynn (Milk Woman), Tony London (Youth), Mollie Maureen (Old Woman).

Christmas Special (1982, BBC1)

Mini-episode, part of *The Funny Side of Christmas* (27 December 1982)
It is Christmas morning, and Arkwright and Granville are due to go across the road to have their festive lunch with Gladys. One of them, however, is not at all happy about the fact that this is supposed to be a holiday from shopping.

Series Four (1985, BBC1)

Soulmate Wanted (1 September 1985)
Granville is so desperate for romance he has started advertising for someone special. Arkwright, upon hearing about this, cannot resist trying to manage the situation.
Featuring: Stephanie Cole (Mrs Featherstone), Gilly Coman (Girl Who Answers Advert), Christine Ozanne (Customer), Norman Robbins (Mr Halliwell), Jean Warren (Michelle).

Horse-Trading (8 September 1985)
Arkwright re-discovers ten old wooden clothes horses among his dusty stock. Luckily for him, a local Yorkshire-Asian shopkeeper seems interested in taking them off his hands.
Featuring: Charlotte Barker (Customer), Barbara Flynn (Milk Woman), John Rutland (Black Lead Polish Customer), Nadim Sawalha (Albert Gupta), Alan Starkey (Thorndyke).

The Housekeeper Caper (15 September 1985)
Arkwright's impatience with his fiancée leads him to devise a plan to push her to the altar: he advertises for a live-in housekeeper in the hope that it will make Nurse Gladys so jealous that she will rush straight into marriage. Rather than fast-track him a wife, however, the plan threatens to force the 'Black Widow' upon him.
Featuring: Joe Belcher (Shopfitter), Stephanie Cole (Mrs Featherstone), Frances Cox (Mrs Parsloe), Barbara Flynn (Milk Woman), Patricia Kane (Little Old Lady), Sandra Voe (Mrs Bickerdyke).

The Errand Boy Executive (22 September 1985)
Granville has just met Stephanie, a young woman from the local boutique, and impressed her by claiming that he is an 'executive'. When she visits the shop, however, Arkwright has to decide whether or not he should play along with the deception.
Featuring: Stephanie Cole (Mrs Featherstone), Howell Evans (Victor, Vac Sales Rep), Julie Shipley (Stephanie), Sandra Voe (Mrs Bickerdyke).

Happy Birthday Arkwright (29 September 1985)
It is Arkwright's birthday, and Granville is set to celebrate by cutting two whole pence off carrots. As if that is not enough to spoil the shopkeeper's day, it is also rumoured that a man from *The Good Shop Guide* is due to visit the area.
Featuring: Stephanie Cole (Mrs Featherstone), Barbara Flynn (Milk Woman), Howard Lew Lewis (Byron), Tom Mennard (Cyril), John Owens (Windscreen Smear Customer).

The Mystical Boudoir of Nurse Gladys Emmanuel (6 October 1985)
There are two things that need to be done: Arkwright wants to finally get into Nurse Gladys's bedroom, and Granville wants finally to get a new till. There is, it seems, a deal to be struck.
Featuring: Barbara Ashcroft (Mrs Turnbull), Bobby Bragg (Customer), Stephanie Cole (Mrs Featherstone), Frances Cox (Mrs Parsloe), Barbara Flynn (Milk Woman), Eric Richard (Cash Register Salesman).

40th Anniversary Christmas Special (2013, BBC One)

Still Open All Hours (26 December 2013)
Having always been told that 'One day, all of this will be yours', Granville has indeed finally inherited Arkwright's shop, which he now runs with his own son, Leroy. He currently has two tasks to complete: speeding up the sale of anchovy paste, and slowing down the extra-curricular exploits of his errand boy.
Featuring: David Jason (Granville), Lynda Baron (Gladys Emmanuel), James Baxter (Leroy), Catherine Breeze (Mrs Hemstock), Stephanie Cole (Mrs Featherstone), Emily Fleeshman (Hayley), Maggie Ollerenshaw (Mavis), Brigit Forsyth (Madge), Johnny Vegas (Wet Eric), Mark Williams (Planters Tea Salesman), Kulvinder Ghir (Cyril), Sally Lindsay (Mrs Agnew), Nina Wadia (Mrs Hussein), Barry Elliott (Mr Marshall), Misha Timmins (Cindy), Sally Womersley (Mrs Travis), Nadine Mulkerrin (Ashley), Kathryn Hunt (Vera).
Produced by Gareth Edwards and directed by Dewi Humphreys.

ACKNOWLEDGEMENTS

It is a sign of the under-appreciation of *Open All Hours* that (unlike any other BBC show that I've researched over the past 20 years) it does not even have its own programme file preserved in the BBC's archives. After piecing together the relevant details from various other sources, I hope that this book will serve as the chronicle that the show has always deserved.

I must thank Lorna Russell at BBC Books, for asking me to write it, and Charlotte Macdonald and Lizzy Gaisford for their tireless efforts to help see it through to completion. It was a genuine pleasure to work with them. The copy-editor, Sarah Chatwin, was exceptionally impressive; I hope many other authors benefit from such fine and tactful professionalism.

Roy Clarke could not have been more helpful and supportive, even though he was busy writing a new series of the show at the time. He is one of the best men in British comedy, as well as one of its best writers.

Sydney Lotterby was a fine and gentlemanly guide to the planning behind the scenes. His insights were invaluable.

James Gilbert, another British broadcasting great, was, as always, generous with his time and kind with his advice. He clarified some key points.

Lynda Baron provided many fascinating recollections and shrewd insights. Her help was genuinely invaluable.

I am very grateful to Stephanie Cole, Maggie Ollerenshaw, Sheila Brennan and Bobby Bragg for sharing their memories of working on the show. Their kindness was greatly appreciated. Among the members of the latest production team, I am particularly indebted to Sarah Hitchcock for sparing the time to discuss the new series.

My thanks also go to everyone at the BBC Written Archives Centre, who once again could not have been more helpful and welcoming. I am particularly grateful to Jeff Waldman, who answered many queries and was always a reassuringly sound source of advice.

I must also record my thanks to the staff of the following institutions: the National Archives; the British Library, Newspaper Library and Sound Archive; the V&A Department of Theatre and Performance; and the University of Cambridge Library (especially Neil Hudson).

Some rare and invaluable recordings were supplied by 'The Doc' at www.oldtimetv.net. I am, not for the first time, very grateful for the assistance. Thanks also go to Holly Davidson, John Grant, Richard Spendlove and Richard Webber.

My agent, Mic Cheetham, ensured that this project went ahead at a rapid pace. I very much appreciate her support.

Finally, my heartfelt thanks go to Vera McCann and Silvana Dean. I would not have achieved anything without them.

Graham McCann
Cambridge 2014

BIBLIOGRAPHY

Open All Hours

Barker, Ronnie, *It's Hello – from Him!* (London: New English Library, 1988).

Bell, Jack, 'Serving Up the Laughs', *Daily Mirror*, 20 February 1976, p.17.

Coady, Matthew, 'Suffering in a Good Cause', *Daily Mirror*, 26 March 1973, p.18.

Fiddick, Peter, 'Open All Hours', *The Guardian*, 28 February 1976, p.8.

Gosling, Ray, 'Shop Talk', *Radio Times*, 28 February–6 March 1981, pp.6–7.

Jason, Sir David, *David Jason: My Life* (London: Century, 2013).

Martin, Brendan, 'Treats in Store', *Radio Times*, 31 August–6 September 1985, p.15.

Nutkins, Kirsty, 'A Treat in Store', *Daily Express* (Saturday Magazine), 21 December 2013, pp.8–9.

O'Connor, John, 'Open All Hours', *New York Times*, 1 September 1987, p.AR4.

Roche, Elisa, 'G-g-g-goodness, Granville is back', *Daily Express*, 19 November 2013, p.3.

Rose, Gillian, 'Clarke's winning formula is his seaside "disguise"', *The Stage*, 16 October 1986, p.19.

Sparks, Christine, *Open All Hours* (London: BBC, 1976).

Towler, James, 'Seven of One', *The Stage*, 29 March 1973, p.12.

General

Auden, W.H., *Collected Poems* (London: Faber and Faber, 1991).

Barker, Ronnie, *It's Hello – from Him!* (London: Hodder & Stoughton, 1988).

— *Dancing in the Moonlight* (London: Coronet, 1994).

— *All I Ever Wrote: The Complete Works* (London: Essential, 1999).

— *Fork Handles: The Bery Vest of Ronnie Barker* (London: Ebury Press, 2013).

Berman, Ronald, 'Sitcoms', *Journal of Aesthetic Education*, Vol. 21, No. 1 (Spring, 1987), pp.5–19.

Bradbury, David and McGrath, Joe, *Now That's Funny!* (London: Methuen, 1998).

Corbett, Ronnie, *High Hopes* (London: Ebury Press, 2000).

— *And It's Goodnight from Him . . .: The Autobiography of the Two Ronnies* (London: Penguin, 2007).

Cotton, Bill, *The BBC as an Entertainer* (London: BBC, 1977).

— *Double Bill* (London: Fourth Estate, 2000).

Frost, David, *An Autobiography* (London: HarperCollins, 1993).

Gambaccini, Paul and Taylor, Rod, *Television's Greatest Hits* (London: Network Books, 1993).

Grade, Michael, *It Seemed Like a Good Idea at the Time* (London: Macmillan, 1999).

James, Clive, *Clive James on Television* (London: Picador, 1991).

Jeffries, Stuart, *Mrs Slocombe's Pussy* (London: Flamingo, 2000).

Lewisohn, Mark, *Radio Times Guide to TV Comedy* (London: BBC, 1998).

McCabe, Bob, *The Authorized Biography of Ronnie Barker* (London: BBC Books, 2004).

McCann, Graham, 'Why the best sitcoms must be a class act', *London Evening Standard*, 21 May 1997, p.9.

— 'An offer we *can* refuse', *London Evening Standard*, 2 December 1998, p.68.

— *Morecambe & Wise* (London: Fourth Estate, 1998).

— 'Sit back and wait for the comedy', *Financial Times*, 24 November 1999, p.22.

— *Dad's Army: The Story of a Classic Television Show* (London: Fourth Estate, 2001).

— 'How to define the indefinable', *Financial Times*, 25 March 2003, p.22.

— 'Steptoe and Son', in Merullo, Annabel and Wenborn, Neil (eds.), *British Comedy Greats* (London: Cassell Illustrated, 2003), pp.179–82.

— *Spike and Co* (London: Hodder & Stoughton, 2006).

— *Fawlty Towers* (London: Hodder & Stoughton, 2007).

— (ed.), *A Poke in the Eye (With a Sharp Stick)* (London: Canongate, 2012).

— 'On Behalf of the Working Classes', in Young, Gordon (ed.), *The Comedy Carpet Blackpool: The Making of a World Class Monument to Comedy* (London: Booth-Clibborn Editions, 2013), pp.14–18.

— *A Very Courageous Decision: The Inside Story of Yes Minister* (London: Aurum Press, 2014).

Mellor, G.J., *The Northern Music Hall* (Newcastle upon Tyne: Frank Graham, 1970).

— *They Made Us Laugh* (Littleborough: George Kelsell, 1982).

Melvyn, Glenn, *The Love Match* (London: Samuel French, 1957).

Miall, Leonard, *Inside the BBC* (London: Weidenfeld & Nicolson, 1994).

Muir, Frank, *Comedy in Television* (London: BBC, 1966).

Nathan, David, *The Laughtermakers* (London: Peter Owen, 1971).

Pertwee, Bill, *By Royal Command* (Newton Abbott: David & Charles, 1981).

Priestley, J.B., *An English Journey* (London: Mandarin, 1994).

Scott, Peter Graham, *British Television: An Insider's History* (Jefferson, North Carolina: McFarland & Co, 1999).

Staff, Kathy, *My Story: Wrinkles and All* (London: Hodder & Stoughton, 1998).

Stone, Richard, *You Should Have Been In Last Night* (Sussex: The Book Guild, 2000).

Vine, Andrew, *Last of the Summer Wine: The Story of the World's Longest Running Comedy Series* (London: Aurum Press, 2010).

Webber, Richard, *Remembering Ronnie Barker* (London: Arrow, 2011).

INDEX

NOTES

Epigraph quotations:

Adam Smith, *An Inquiry into the Nature and Causes of the Wealth of Nations*, ed. Edwin M. Cannan, Vol. Two, Book IV, Chapter VII, Part III (Chicago: Chicago University Press, 1976), p.129.

Arkwright in Roy Clarke, 'Well Catered Funeral', *Open All Hours*, series one, episode five, first broadcast 19 March 1976, BBC2.

Prologue

1   Source of viewing figures: Broadcasters' Audience Research Board (BARB); see Chapter 12. For details of the 2004 BBC poll, see Chapter 13.

2   John Lennon, 'Beautiful Boy (Darling Boy)', on the *Double Fantasy* album (Geffen Records, published by Lennon Music, 1980).

3   Woody Allen, *Everything You Always Wanted to Know About Sex* (*But Were Afraid to Ask)*, Twentieth Century-Fox, 1972.

4   Source: Institute for Retail Studies and Mintel.

5   The consumer watchdog *Which?* conducted the poll in 2010 to find Britain's favourite shopkeeper. Arkwright topped the list, followed by Ronnie Corbett for his portrayal of the hardware shopkeeper in *The Two Ronnies'* 'Four Candles' sketch, then Apu Nahasapeemapetilon from *The Simpsons* in third place, *Coronation Street's* Norris Cole in fourth, and, in joint fifth place, Mrs Slocombe and Mr Humphries from *Are You Being Served?* (See the *Sunday People*, 16 May 2010, p.8.)

6   Source: BARB; see Chapter 12.

7   Source: BARB; see Chapter 14.

Chapter 1

8   This contractual arrangement was confirmed to me by James Gilbert, interview with the author, 16 July 2014.

9   Ronnie Barker, *It's Hello – from Him!* (London: New English Library, 1988), p.146.

10 James Gilbert, interview with the author, 16 July 2014.

11 This was confirmed by James Gilbert, interview with the author, 16 July 2014. Hugh Leonard also had another script idea rejected.

12 *My Old Man*, by Gerald Frow and starring Clive Dunn, ran for two series on ITV (Yorkshire Television) between 1974 and 1975.

13 Roy Clarke, interview with the author, 19 June 2014.

14 Meecham & Son was a general stores in Crewkerne, Somerset, that had been founded in 1928 and run by the Meecham family until it closed for the final time in 1998 (see the *Daily Express*, 27 November 1998, p.22).

15 Barker, *It's Hello – from Him!* p.145.

16 Duncan Wood, internal memo, 29 July 1971, Roy Clarke Artist's File 1970–74, BBC Written Archives Centre (WAC).
17 W. H. Auden, Letter to Geoffrey Grigson, 17 January 1950, in Edward Mendelson (ed.), *Collected Poems* (London: Faber and Faber, 1991).
18 W. H. Auden, Letter to Lord Byron (1936), in Edward Mendelson (ed.), *Collected Poems* (London: Faber and Faber, 1991), p.89.
19 W. H. Auden, 'Lead's the Best' (1928), in Katherine Bucknell (ed.), *W. H. Auden: Juvenilia, Poems 1922–28* (London: Faber and Faber, 1994), p.128.
20 J. B. Priestley, *An English Journey* (London: Mandarin, 1994), p.254.
21 Sandy Powell, ventriloquist act, various versions extant on record and film.
22 Roy Clarke, quoted in the *Radio Times*, 28 February–6 March 1981, p.7.
23 Nancy Banks-Smith, *The Guardian*, 12 February 1983, p.6.
24 Ray Galton and Alan Simpson, 'Divided We Stand', *Steptoe & Son*, series seven, episode six, first broadcast 27 March 1972, BBC1.
25 Roy Clarke, interview with the author, 19 June 2014.
26 There are many references to the supposed influence of L. E. Riddiford on Roy Clarke's writing of Arkwright. See, for example, 'Plan for new Open All Hours series', in the online edition of *The Star* (South Yorkshire), 19 November 2013, http://www.thestar.co.uk/what-s-on/out-about/plan-for-new-open-all-hours-series-1-6259023.
27 Roy Clarke, interview with the author, 19 June 2014.
28 Ibid.
29 Barker, *It's Hello – from Him!*, p.145.
30 'The Box Sketch', written by Jimmy James.
31 James Casey and Frank Casey, 'Good for Money', *The Clitheroe Kid*, series fourteen, episode three, first broadcast 31 May 1970, BBC Radio 2.
32 Pauline Devaney and Edwin Apps, 'Only Three Can Play', *All Gas and Gaiters*, series one, episode six, first broadcast 7 March 1967, BBC1.
33 James Casey and Frank Casey, 'Robbin' Jim and his Merry Men', *The Clitheroe Kid*, series eleven, episode three, first broadcast 15 October 1967, BBC Radio 2.
34 *Ramsbottom Rides Again* (1956), screenplay by John Baxter and Basil Thomas, with additional comedy sequences by Arthur Askey and Glenn Melvyn.
35 Barker, *It's Hello – from Him!*, p.67.
36 Ibid.
37 Ibid., p.145.
38 Roy Clarke, interview with the author, 19 June 2014.
39 Quoted from the original script for the pilot episode (BBC WAC).
40 Transcribed from the broadcast version of the pilot episode.
41 Roy Clarke, interview with the author, 19 June 2014.

Chapter 2
42 David Jason, *David Jason: My Life* (London: Century, 2013), p.186.
43 Ibid., p.227.
44 Barker, *It's Hello – from Him!*, p.146.
45 Ronnie Barker, quoted by Bob McCabe, *The Authorized Biography of Ronnie Barker* (London: BBC Books, 2004), p.185.
46 Ronnie Barker, quoted by David Jason, *David Jason: My Life*, p.234.

47 David Jason, quoted in the *Radio Times*, 31 August–6 September 1985, p.15.
48 Jason, *David Jason: My Life*, p.234.
49 Ibid.
50 Sheila Brennan, interview with the author, 10 June 2014.
51 Sydney Lotterby, speaking in the documentary *Open All Hours: A Celebration*.
52 Sheila Brennan, interview with the author, 10 June 2014.
53 Camera script, pilot episode (BBC WAC).
54 Ibid.
55 Source: BBC Editorial Guidelines.
56 Source: BBC WAC.
57 On 8 March 1973, the Provisional Irish Republican Army (IRA) conducted its first operation in England since the start of 'The Troubles' ('Na Trioblóidí'), planting four car bombs in London: a fertilizer bomb in a car outside the post office in Broadway and also at the BBC's armed forces radio studio in Dean Stanley Street (both of which were defused successfully), and one near the Old Bailey and another at the Ministry of Agriculture off Whitehall (both of which exploded, killing one man and injuring a further 238). See *The Times*, 9 March 1973, p.1.
58 Sheila Brennan, interview with the author, 10 June 2014.
59 Ronnie Barker, quoted by Richard Webber, *Remembering Ronnie Barker* (London: Arrow, 2011), p.204.
60 Sheila Brennan, interview with the author, 10 June 2014.
61 Ibid.
62 Ronnie Barker, quoted by McCabe, *The Authorized Biography of Ronnie Barker*, p.199.
63 Roy Clarke, interview with the author, 19 June 2014.
64 Camera scripts (BBC WAC).
65 Sheila Brennan, interview with the author, 10 June 2014.
66 Ibid.

Chapter 3
67 The Lofthouse Colliery mining disaster, near Wakefield in West Yorkshire, occurred on 21 March 1973, when a torrent of floodwater burst through the coal face, endangering the lives of the 30 men who were working 300 feet down at the time. Most managed to escape, but 7 remained trapped in an air pocket. The subsequent week-long attempt to rescue them dominated the national news, but ended in tragedy when only one body was recovered. See *The Guardian*, 27 March 1973, p.1.
68 See, for example, *The Guardian*, 24 March 1973, p.3, and *The Times*, 24 March 1973, p.8.
69 *Daily Express*, 24 March 1973, p.11.
70 Jackie Pallo (1926–2006) was a professional wrestler who became such a familiar figure on British television during the era when wrestling was a regular fixture on the small screen (1960s–70s) that he took to styling himself Jackie 'Mr TV' Pallo.
71 According to the BBC's own figures, the show was watched by '4.9% of the BBC2 audience'. The notional total TV audience at the time was 50,500,000, but the 'BBC2 audience' meant, literally, the number of people within that total who were currently able to receive BBC2. In 1973, this number was calculated at 41,350,000. The whole audience for this particular edition of *Seven of One*, therefore, was 4.9%

of the latter figure: 2,026,150. (My thanks to Jeff Walden at the BBC WAC for clarifying this issue for me.)

72   See Roger Silvey, 'The Measurement of Audiences', BBC Lunch-Time Lecture, 12 January 1966.

73   Audience Research Report (dated 8 May 1973), on *Seven of One*, 'Open All Hours', 25 March 1973 (BBC WAC).

74   Source: BBC WAC.

75   James Gilbert, interview with the author, 16 July 2014.

76   Ibid.

77   James Gilbert, interview with the author, 16 July 2014.

78   *The Times*, 6 September 1974, p.13.

79   *The Times*, 10 May 1975, p.16.

80   See, for example, *The Times*, 5 January 1973, p.10. Stanley Reynolds, in his review, praised Roy Clarke for his gift 'for capturing human grotesquerie in an objective comic style' and for placing it in a context which he found 'unnervingly socially true'.

81   Alan Coren, *The Times*, 4 November 1976, p.11.

82   Roy Clarke Artist's File 1970–74, BBC WAC. On 18 October 1973, Bill Cotton agreed with Jimmy Gilbert that the BBC should offer Clarke a 'non-exclusive contract', initially for two years, as soon as possible. This was subsequently agreed, and Clarke's first commission under this arrangement was a second series of *Last of the Summer Wine*.

83   Roy Clarke Artist's File 1970–74, BBC WAC. Noting that Roy Clarke had 'agreed to accept' the offer, Duncan Wood commissioned the pilot on 10 May 1973, with a deadline for Clarke to submit his script by 1 June 1973. There was no title for the proposed episode, which was merely referred to internally as 'Project No. 011430190'). There is no record in the relevant files as to why the project failed to reach the screen, although Morecambe and Wise's producer/director of the time, John Ammonds, told me more generally (in conversations during research for my book, *Morecambe & Wise* [London: Fourth Estate, 1988]) that there were several occasions during this period when ideas for other kinds of shows were mooted before swiftly being dropped as either too much of a gamble or simply impractical in terms of their schedule. As for Roy Clarke's memories of the project, there are none. He told me (interview 19 June 2014): 'I don't even recall being asked! And I loved Morecambe and Wise, so I wouldn't have thought I'd forget something like that. But, no, I can't remember a thing about it. I can see now from the records that it happened, but it's a blank I'm afraid.'

84   Barker, *It's Hello – From Him*, p.136.

85   Richard Briers, for example, once remarked to me (interview with the author, 8 November 2007) how he felt most absorbed and engaged when playing characters that he disliked: 'Take Tom Good [in *The Good Life*] – he was such an awful, selfish, stubborn man! No concern for his poor young wife or anyone else, he just decides on this new life for himself and expects her to just fit in with his plans even though it brings with it all that hardship. Getting up at five in the morning to do the goats! Then there's Martin Bryce [in *Ever Decreasing Circles*] – a really irritating, ratty little man! An absolute nightmare! And the one I played in *The Other One* – Ralph Tanner. What a monster! A liar, a fantasist, a bit of a bully – horrible! But that made

them so much fun to play, and, once you've found their vulnerabilities – they *have* to have vulnerabilities to soften them – it helped make them funny. I hope I'm nothing like them, but I found them fascinating to play.'

86 Roy Clarke Artist's File 1975–79 (BBC WAC). Jimmy Gilbert first discussed the new show as 'The Shop' in a memo dated 21 January 1975. He noted the change of name in a memo dated 7 October 1975. Sydney Lotterby confirmed the change of title in a memo dated 12 January 1976.
87 Roy Clarke Artist's File 1975–79 (BBC WAC).
88 Ronnie Barker TV Artist's File 1971–80 (BBC WAC).
89 David Jason Artist's File, BBC WAC.
90 Ronnie Barker, quoted by Jason, *David Jason: My Life*, p.247.

Chapter 4
91 Sheila Brennan, interview with the author, 10 June 2014.
92 Roy Clarke, interview with the author, 19 June 2014.
93 James Gilbert, interview with the author, 16 July 2014.
94 Sydney Lotterby, interview with the author, 8 July 2014.
95 Sheila Brennan, interview with the author, 10 June 2014.
96 James Gilbert, interview with the author, 16 July 2014.
97 Sheila Brennan, interview with the author, 10 June 2014.
98 *Daily Express*, 20 February 1976, p.12.
99 *Daily Express*, 12 July 1965, p.12.
100 *Daily Express*, 20 February 1976, p.12.
101 Ibid.
102 *Daily Express*, 14 October 1965, p.1.
103 Dennis Ramsden, quoted by Webber, *Remembering Ronnie Barker*, p.211.
104 Lynda Baron Artist's File 1971–80, BBC WAC.
105 Lynda Baron, interview with the author, 22 August 2014.
106 Ibid.
107 Helen Ibbotson, quoted in the online edition of *The Star* (South Yorkshire), 9 October 2013, http://www.thestar.co.uk/news/breaking-new-version-of-open-all-hours-will-be-filmed-in-doncaster-1-6129435.
108 Sydney Lotterby, interview with the author, 8 July 2014.
109 Ibid.
110 *The Times*, 20 February 1976, p.27.
111 *Daily Mirror*, 20 February 1976, p.17.
112 *Radio Times*, 14–20 February 1976, p.3.
113 'A Mattress on Wheels', series one, episode two.
114 'Apples and Self Service', series one, episode six.
115 'A Mattress on Wheels', series one, episode two.
116 'Beware of the Dog', series one, episode four.
117 Ibid.
118 Ibid.
119 'A Nice Cosy Little Disease', series one, episode three.
120 Ibid.
121 'A Nice Cosy Little Disease', series one, episode three.
122 Peter Fiddick, *The Guardian*, 28 February 1976, p.8.

123 Roy Clarke, interview with the author, 19 June 2014.
124 Hazel Holt, *The Stage*, 1 April 1976, p.25.
125 Nancy Banks-Smith, *The Guardian*, 6 March 1976, p.8.
126 Source: BBC WAC.
127 Audience Research Report (dated 16 March 1976), on *Open All Hours*, 20 February 1976 (BBC WAC). For background information on the BBC's study of audiences during that era, see Roger Silvey, 'The Measurement of Audiences', BBC Lunch-Time Lecture, 12 January 1966.
128 See, for example, the Audience Research Report (dated 5 May 1954), on *Running Wild* (BBC WAC), quoted in my *Morecambe & Wise*, p.110.
129 Audience Research Report (dated 16 March 1976) on *Open All Hours*, 20 February 1976 (BBC WAC).
130 Ibid.
131 Audience Research Report (dated 14 April 1976) on *Open All Hours*, 26 March 1976 (BBC WAC).
132 Ibid.
133 Ibid.
134 Ibid.
135 Ibid.
136 Roy Clarke, interview with the author, 19 June 2014.

Chapter 5
137 See Barker, *It's Hello – from Him!*, p.132.
138 See my *Only Fools and Horses* (London: Canongate, 2011), pp.60–6.
139 Roy Clarke, interview with the author, 19 June 2014.
140 James Gilbert, interview with the author, 16 July 2014.
141 Christine Sparks, *Open All Hours* (London: BBC, 1976). The book drew closely on Roy Clarke's original scripts from 1976 to re-tell the various stories in the form of a novella.
142 *The Albany Herald*, 16 January 1982, p.13.
143 Ed Vincent, 'Robin's Return', *Open All Night*, episode 2, first broadcast 5 December 1981, ABC.
144 Source: Joint Industry Committee for Television Audience Research (JICTAR).
145 Roy Clarke Artist's File 1980–84, BBC WAC.
146 Paul Eddington, for example, was being paid a mere £750 per episode for the first series of *Yes Minister* (source: BBC WAC: *Yes Minister* File T70/34/1, Progs 1–7 [First Series]).
147 BBC WAC: *passim.*
148 Ronnie Barker, quoted by Jason, *David Jason: My Life*, p.244.
149 Ibid., p.228.
150 Roy Clarke Artist's File 1980–84, BBC WAC. All seven scripts were accepted on 6 January 1981, but then the seventh was rejected at the start of the following month and a new script was soon written and accepted. Clarke wrote the revisions carefully so no further external shooting was required.
151 The first series had used 34 Lister Avenue as Gladys's residence (see Chapter 4), but, at some point during the five-year gap between that being broadcast and the second series being filmed, the owners made changes to the exterior. Sydney Lotterby, on

his return to Balby, did not feel that the new decor was the right look for the scenes in the sitcom, so he changed the location to next door at number 32, where it would remain for the rest of the run.

152 Lynda Baron, interview with the author, 22 August 2014.
153 Ibid.
154 Barker, *It's Hello – from Him!*, pp.145–6.
155 Barker, quoted by McCabe, *The Authorized Biography of Ronnie Barker*, pp.146–7.
156 Ibid., p.99.
157 Jason, *David Jason: My Life*, pp.289–90.
158 Ibid., pp.289–90.
159 Kathy Staff, *My Story – Wrinkles and All* (London: Hodder & Stoughton, 1997), p.98.
160 Jason, *David Jason: My Life*, p.242.
161 Quoted from the original script for 'St Albert's Day', series two, episode seven (BBC WAC).
162 Transcribed from the broadcast version of 'St Albert's Day', series two, episode seven.
163 Sydney Lotterby, interview with the author, 8 July 2014.
164 Roy Clarke, interview with the author, 19 June 2014.
165 Jason, *David Jason: My Life*, p.242.
166 Ibid.
167 Sydney Lotterby, interview with the author, 8 July 2014.
168 Ibid.

Chapter 6

169 See *The Times*, 28 February 1981, p.9 and 12 March 1981, p.29.
170 *The Observer*, 1 March 1981, p.48.
171 'Fig Biscuits and Inspirational Toilet Rolls', series two, episode three.
172 Ibid.
173 'Laundry Blues', series two, episode one.
174 'Arkwright's Mobile Store', series two, episode five.
175 'The Reluctant Traveller', series two, episode two.
176 'The New Suit', series two, episode four.
177 'Fig Biscuits and Inspirational Toilet Rolls', series two, episode three.
178 'Laundry Blues', series two, episode one.
179 'Arkwright's Mobile Store', series two, episode five.
180 'Laundry Blues', series two, episode one.
181 Ibid.
182 'Shedding at the Wedding', series two, episode six.
183 'Fig Biscuits and Inspirational Toilet Rolls', series two, episode three.
184 'Shedding at the Wedding', series two, episode six.
185 Ibid.
186 Ibid.
187 'Laundry Blues', series two, episode one.
188 'Fig Biscuits and Inspirational Toilet Rolls', series two, episode three.
189 Ibid.
190 'Laundry Blues', series two, episode one.

191 'Shedding at the Wedding', series two, episode six.
192 Ibid.
193 'Laundry Blues', series two, episode one.
194 'Fig Biscuits and Inspirational Toilet Rolls', series two, episode three.
195 Source: JICTAR.
196 Source: JICTAR.

Chapter 7
197 Roy Clarke, interview with the author, 19 June 2014.
198 Pilot edition, first broadcast, as an episode of *Seven of One*, 25 March 1973, BBC2.
199 Ibid.
200 'The Reluctant Traveller', series two, episode two.
201 Pilot edition, first broadcast, as an episode of *Seven of One*, 25 March 1973, BBC2.
202 'Fig Biscuits and Inspirational Toilet Rolls', series two, episode three.
203 Camera script, pilot episode (BBC WAC).
204 Pilot edition, first broadcast, as an episode of *Seven of One*, 25 March 1973, BBC2.
205 'A Nice Cosy Little Disease', series one, episode three.
206 'Shedding at the Wedding', series two, episode six.
207 'Laundry Blues', series two, episode one.
208 Ibid.
209 Pilot edition, first broadcast, as an episode of *Seven of One*, 25 March 1973, BBC2.
210 'Well Catered Funeral', series one, episode five.
211 Ibid.
212 Pilot edition, first broadcast, as an episode of Seven of One, 25 March 1973, BBC2.
213 Ibid.
214 'The New Suit', series two, episode four.
215 'A Mattress on Wheels', series one, episode two.
216 Ibid.
217 Ibid.
218 Ibid.
219 'Fig Biscuits and Inspirational Toilet Rolls', series two, episode three.
220 Pilot edition, first broadcast, as an episode of *Seven of One*, 25 March 1973, BBC2.
221 'The New Suit', series two, episode four.
222 'A Mattress on Wheels', series one, episode two.
223 'The New Suit', series two, episode four.
224 Ibid.
225 'Laundry Blues', series two, episode one.
226 Ibid.
227 Ibid.
228 'Full of Mysterious Promise', series one, episode one.
229 'The Reluctant Traveller', series two, episode two.
230 Pilot edition, first broadcast, as an episode of *Seven of One*, 25 March 1973, BBC2.
231 Roy Clarke, interview with the author, 19 June 2014.
232 'Full of Mysterious Promise', series one, episode one.

Chapter 8
233 'Fig Biscuits and Inspirational Toilet Rolls', series two, episode three.

234 Ibid.
235 'Arkwright's Mobile Store', series two, episode five.
236 'Fig Biscuits and Inspirational Toilet Rolls', series two, episode three.
237 'Arkwright's Mobile Store', series two, episode five.
238 'Laundry Blues', series two, episode one.
239 'Apples and Self Service', series one, episode six.
240 'Laundry Blues', series two, episode one.
241 'St Albert's Day', series two, episode seven.
242 Pilot edition, first broadcast, as an episode of *Seven of One*, 25 March 1973, BBC2.
243 Ibid.
244 Ibid.
245 Ibid.
246 Ibid.
247 'Laundry Blues', series two, episode one.
248 Ibid.
249 Ibid.
250 Pilot edition, first broadcast, as an episode of *Seven of One*, 25 March 1973, BBC2.
251 'A Nice Cosy Little Disease', series one, episode three.
252 Pilot edition, first broadcast, as an episode of *Seven of One*, 25 March 1973, BBC2.
253 'The Reluctant Traveller', series two, episode two.
254 'A Mattress on Wheels', series one, episode two.
255 'The Reluctant Traveller', series two, episode two.
256 'A Mattress on Wheels', series one, episode two.
257 'Fig Biscuits and Inspirational Toilet Rolls', series two, episode three.
258 Ibid.
259 'Full of Mysterious Promise', series one, episode one.
260 'A Nice Cosy Little Disease', series one, episode three.
261 'The Reluctant Traveller', series two, episode two.
262 'A Mattress on Wheels', series one, episode two.
263 'Fig Biscuits and Inspirational Toilet Rolls', series two, episode three.
264 'The Reluctant Traveller', series two, episode two.
265 'Full of Mysterious Promise', series one, episode one.
266 'A Mattress on Wheels', series one, episode two.
267 Ibid.
268 Ibid.
269 Ibid.
270 'The Reluctant Traveller', series two, episode two.
271 'Beware of the Dog', series one, episode four.
272 'Fig Biscuits and Inspirational Toilet Rolls', series two, episode three.
273 'Laundry Blues', series two, episode one.
274 'A Mattress on Wheels', series one, episode two.
275 'The New Suit', series two, episode four.
276 'Arkwright's Mobile Store', series two, episode five.
277 'Laundry Blues', series two, episode one.
278 'Full of Mysterious Promise', series one, episode one.
279 'Fig Biscuits and Inspirational Toilet Rolls', series two, episode three.
280 'St Albert's Day', series two, episode seven.

281 'Laundry Blues', series two, episode one.
282 'St Albert's Day', series two, episode seven.
283 'A Mattress on Wheels', series one, episode two.
284 Pilot edition, first broadcast, as an episode of *Seven of One*, 25 March 1973, BBC2.
285 'Apples and Self Service', series one, episode six.
286 'Full of Mysterious Promise', series one, episode one.
287 Ibid.
288 Pilot edition, first broadcast, as an episode of *Seven of One*, 25 March 1973, BBC2.
289 Ibid.
290 'A Nice Cosy Little Disease', series one, episode three.
291 Ibid.
292 Ibid.
293 Ibid.
294 'The Reluctant Traveller', series two, episode two.
295 'A Mattress on Wheels', series two, episode two.
296 'Laundry Blues', series two, episode one.
297 'Beware of the Dog', series one, episode four.
298 'Laundry Blues', series two, episode one.
299 Cornershop, 'Brimful of Asha' (1997), written by Tjinder Singh, published by Universal Music Publishing Group.
300 'A Mattress on Wheels', series two, episode two.
301 'Laundry Blues', series two, episode one.
302 'Full of Mysterious Promise', series one, episode one.
303 'Arkwright's Mobile Store', series two, episode five.

Chapter 9
304 Norman Evans, 'Over the Garden Wall', quoted in Graham McCann, 'On Behalf of the Working Classes', in Gordon Young (ed.), *The Comedy Carpet Blackpool: The Making of a World Class Monument to Comedy* (London: Booth-Clibborn Editions, 2013).
305 'Full of Mysterious Promise', series one, episode one.
306 'Shedding at the Wedding', series two, episode six.
307 'Full of Mysterious Promise', series one, episode one.
308 'Fig Biscuits and Inspirational Toilet Rolls', series two, episode three.
309 'The Reluctant Traveller', series two, episode two.
310 'Arkwright's Mobile Store', series two, episode five.
311 'Fig Biscuits and Inspirational Toilet Rolls', series two, episode three.
312 'The New Suit', series two, episode four.
313 'St Albert's Day', series two, episode seven.
314 Ibid.
315 'The Reluctant Traveller', series two, episode two.
316 'Arkwright's Mobile Store', series two, episode five.
317 'Laundry Blues', series two, episode one.
318 'Fig Biscuits and Inspirational Toilet Rolls', series two, episode three.
319 Ibid.

Chapter 10

320 On 16 July 1981, a memo was circulated within the BBC's light entertainment department revealing that there was some doubt as to whether Roy Clarke should be asked to write a new series called *The Magnificent Evans*, or write a third series of *Open All Hours*. Various opinions were subsequently aired, but on 17 September 1981 John Howard Davies confirmed his decision to postpone *The Magnificent Evans* indefinitely (it would not be made until 1984) and commission a third series of *Open All Hours*. The script deadline was 8 January 1982, with Clarke receiving £3000 per episode. (Source: Roy Clarke Artist's File1980–84, BBC WAC.)

321 'An Errand Boy by the Ear', series three, episode one.

322 'Duet for Solo Bicycle', series three, episode three.

323 Ibid.

324 'The Cool Cocoa Tin Lid', series three, episode six.

325 'The Ginger Men', series three, episode two.

326 Ibid.

327 'Duet for Solo Bicycle', series three, episode three.

328 'The Man from Down Under', series three, episode five.

329 See Staff, *My Story: Wrinkles and All*, pp.97–8. Roy Clarke had already sketched out some material for Mrs Blewett in the new set of scripts, so he now had to rewrite this for the new character of Mrs Featherstone, to be played by Stephanie Cole. Cole remembers how she came to be involved: 'In those days, in the old BBC rehearsal rooms at Acton, we'd all be working on our shows in the same place. And so, after the first series of *Tenko* had been shown, Ronnie Barker had recognized me and said hello to me in the lift. And then a short time after that my agent rang and said that Kathy Staff couldn't do the next series of *Open All Hours* and Ronnie wanted me to play a new character in her place. And I was delighted because it meant that I'd still be in this heavy drama but now I'd also be doing a wonderful comedy series at the same time. I was rehearsing in the morning with Ronnie and David and Syd Lotterby, and in the afternoon I was rehearsing *Tenko*. So it was a strange time in some ways but also very enjoyable' (interview with the author, 17 June 2014).

330 'How to Ignite Your Errand Boy', series three, episode four.

331 'The Ginger Men', series three, episode two.

332 'The Man from Down Under', series three, episode five.

333 'How to Ignite Your Errand Boy', series three, episode four.

334 'Duet for Solo Bicycle', series three, episode three.

335 'The Ginger Men', series three, episode two.

336 'An Errand Boy by the Ear', series three, episode one.

337 'The Man from Down Under', series three, episode five.

338 'Duet for Solo Bicycle', series three, episode three.

339 'How to Ignite Your Errand Boy', series three, episode four.

340 'An Errand Boy by the Ear', series three, episode one.

341 'The Cool Cocoa Tin Lid', series three, episode six.

342 'An Errand Boy by the Ear', series three, episode one.

343 'Duet for Solo Bicycle', series three, episode three.

344 Ibid.

345 'The Cool Cocoa Tin Lid', series three, episode six.

346 Ibid.
347 'Duet for Solo Bicycle', series three, episode three.
348 Ibid.
349 'How to Ignite Your Errand Boy', series three, episode four.
350 'Duet for Solo Bicycle', series three, episode three.
351 'An Errand Boy by the Ear', series three, episode one.
352 'The Ginger Men', series three, episode two.
353 Source: BBC WAC/BARB.

Chapter 11
354 Source: BBC WAC/BARB.
355 Jason, *David Jason: My Life*, p.291.
356 Ronnie Barker, quoted by McCabe, *The Authorized Biography of Ronnie Barker*, p.147.
357 Jason, *David Jason: My Life*, p.291.
358 David Jason, quoted by McCabe, *The Authorized Biography of Ronnie Barker*, p.197.
359 Barker, *It's Hello – from Him!*, p.136.
360 Letter to Stephen Edwards by Sheila Lemon, 16 July 1981, Roy Clarke Artist's File (BBC WAC).
361 BBC WAC.
362 Roy Clarke Artist's File 1980–84 (BBC WAC). The service mentioned in the contracts is RCTV, which stood for Rockefeller Center TV (not to be confused with the extant Venezuelan cable network Radio Caracas Televisión Internacional). RCTV – with the support of RCA – had recently negotiated an arrangement with the BBC which gave it first choice of all shows produced by the Corporation in return for an annual payment of $5 million.
363 Source: BBC WAC/BARB.
364 Roy Clarke Artist's File 1980–84 (BBC WAC).
365 Ibid.
366 See my *A Very Courageous Decision: The Inside Story of Yes Minister* (London: Aurum, 2014), Chapter 8.
367 Memo from Tom Rivers to John Howard Davies, 10 May 1984, Roy Clarke Artist's File 1980–84 (BBC WAC).
368 Memo from Michael Grade to various executives, 6 November 1984, Roy Clarke Artist's File 1980–84 (BBC WAC).
369 Roy Clarke Artist's File 1980–84 (BBC WAC): these comments were scribbled on Tom Rivers' copy of Michael Grade's memo (6 November 1984) by someone called 'Stephen' (almost certainly Stephen Edwards, head of copyright at the BBC and thus Tom Rivers' immediate superior).
370 Contract, Roy Clarke Artist's File 1980–84 (BBC WAC).
371 Roy Clarke, interview with the author, 19 June 2014.
372 Contracts (BBC WAC).
373 Sydney Lotterby, interview with the author, 8 July 2014.
374 Lynda Baron, interview with the author, 22 August 2014.
375 Stephanie Cole, interview with the author, 17 June 2014.
376 Bobby Bragg, interview with the author, 19 May 2014.
377 Ibid.

378 Stephanie Cole, interview with the author, 17 June 2014.
379 Bobby Bragg, interview with the author, 19 May 2014.
380 Ibid.
381 Ibid.
382 Ibid.

Chapter 12
383 Lynda Baron, quoted by Brendan Martin, 'Treats in Store', *Radio Times*, 31 August–6 September 1985, p.15.
384 Ray Galton and Alan Simpson, 'The Bird', *Steptoe & Son*, series one, episode one, first broadcast, 14 June 1962, BBC TV.
385 'Soulmate Wanted', series four, episode one.
386 Ibid.
387 'The Errand Boy Executive', series four, episode four.
388 'Soulmate Wanted', series four, episode one.
389 Ibid.
390 'The Errand Boy Executive', series four, episode four.
391 'Soulmate Wanted', series four, episode one.
392 'The Housekeeper Caper', series four, episode three.
393 'The Mystical Boudoir of Nurse Gladys Emmanuel', series four, episode six.
394 'The Housekeeper Caper', series four, episode three.
395 'The Mystical Boudoir of Nurse Gladys Emmanuel', series four, episode six.
396 Ibid.
397 Ibid.
398 Ibid.
399 Ibid.
400 'Horse-Trading', series four, episode two.
401 'Happy Birthday Arkwright', series four, episode five.
402 'The Housekeeper Caper', series four, episode three.
403 Ibid.
404 'Soulmate Wanted', series four, episode one.
405 Ibid.
406 Ibid.
407 'The Housekeeper Caper', series four, episode three.
408 Ibid.
409 Ibid.
410 'Soulmate Wanted', series four, episode one.
411 'The Housekeeper Caper', series four, episode three.
412 Ibid.
413 'Horse-Trading', series four, episode two.
414 'The Housekeeper Caper', series four, episode three.
415 'Soulmate Wanted', series four, episode one.
416 'Horse-Trading', series four, episode two.
417 'The Errand Boy Executive', series four, episode four.
418 Ibid.
419 'Happy Birthday Arkwright', series four, episode five.
420 'The Housekeeper Caper', series four, episode three.

421 Source: BARB.
422 Source: BARB.

Chapter 13
423 Letter from Tom Rivers, assistant head of copyright, to Shelia Lemon, Roy Clarke's agent, 1 November 1984, Roy Clarke Artist's File 1980–84 (BBC WAC).
424 Roy Clarke, interview with the author, 19 June 2014.
425 Reported in *The Sunday Times*, 20 October 1985, p.21.
426 Roy Clarke, interview with the author, 19 June 2014.
427 Ronnie Barker, quoted by McCabe, *The Authorized Biography of Ronnie Barker*, p.208.
428 A repeat in August 1997, for example, won an audience of 9.09 million – the sixth biggest audience of the week (source: BARB).
429 The BBC's Top Ten British Sitcoms were: 1. *Only Fools and Horses*; 2. *Blackadder*; 3. *The Vicar of Dibley*; 4. *Dad's Army*; 5. *Fawlty Towers*; 6. *Yes Minister*; 7. *Porridge*; 8. *Open All Hours*; 9. *The Good Life*; 10. *One Foot in the Grave*.
430 Source: http://www.islaclinics.com/ISLA-News.html.
431 Helen Ibbotson, quoted in the *Halifax Courier*, 11 May 2006, p.3.
432 Roy Clarke, interview with the author, 19 June 2014.
433 Ibid.
434 Sir David Jason, interviewed off-air by the BBC, 19 December 2013 (used with permission).
435 Roy Clarke, interview with the author, 19 June 2014.
436 Ibid.
437 Sir David Jason, quoted in the online edition of *The Star* (South Yorkshire), 25 December 2013, http://www.thestar.co.uk/news/interview-david-jason-and-lynda-baron-chat-about-open-all-hours-special-1-6326632.
438 Roy Clarke, interview with the author, 19 June 2014.
439 Ibid.
440 Ibid.
441 Gareth Edwards, speaking in *Open All Hours: A Celebration*, first broadcast on 27 December 2013 on BBC1.
442 Stephanie Cole, interview with the author, 17 June 2014.
443 Helen Ibbotson, quoted in the online edition of the *Yorkshire Post*, 10 October 2013, http://www.yorkshirepost.co.uk/news/main-topics/general-news/arkwright-s-corner-shop-is-now-a-h-h-hairdresser-s-1-6130053.
444 David Hitchcock, speaking in *Open All Hours: A Celebration*, first broadcast 27 December 2013, BBC1.
445 Lisa Taylor, quoted in the *Yorkshire Post*, 19 November 2013, p.5.
446 Sir David Jason, interviewed off-air by the BBC, 19 December 2013.
447 Lynda Baron, quoted in the online edition of the *Doncaster Free Press*, 18 December 2013, http://www.doncasterfreepress.co.uk/news/interview-david-jason-and-lynda-baron-on-open-all-hours-return-1-6323227.
448 Lynda Baron, interview with the author, 22 August 2014.
449 Ibid.
450 Maggie Ollerenshaw, interview with the author, 16 June 2014.
451 Stephanie Cole, interview with the author, 17 June 2014.

452 Ibid.
453 Lynda Baron, interview with the author, 22 August 2014.
454 Sir David Jason, interviewed off-air by the BBC, 19 December 2013.
455 Maggie Ollerenshaw, interview with the author, 16 June 2014.
456 Ibid.
457 Stephanie Cole, interview with the author, 17 June 2014.
458 James Baxter, quoted by Monica Turnbull in the *Sunderland Echo*, 27 November 2013, p.8.
459 Ibid.
460 Sir David Jason, interviewed off-air by the BBC, 19 December 2013.
461 Ibid.
462 Stephanie Cole, interview with the author, 17 June 2014.
463 Sir David Jason, quoted in the online edition of the *Doncaster Free Press*, 18 December 2013.
464 Source: BBC WAC.
465 Sydney Lotterby, interview with the author, 8 July 2014.
466 Roy Clarke, speaking in *Open All Hours: A Celebration*, first broadcast 27 December 2013, BBC1.
467 Sir David Jason, interviewed off-air by the BBC, 19 December 2013.
468 Ibid.
469 Sir David Jason, quoted by Kirsty Nutkins, 'A Treat in Store', *Daily Express* (Saturday Magazine), 21 December 2013, pp.8–9.

Chapter 14
470 BBC Press Release, 7 October 2013.
471 See, for example, 'Why We Love *Open All Hours*', *Daily Mail*, 9 October 2013, p.9.
472 http://www.digitalspy.co.uk/tv/news/a533859/david-jason-stars-in-still-open-all-hours-first-look-picture.html#~oDwuUbVDEiQ3lL
473 http://www.digitalspy.co.uk/tv/news/a521620/sir-david-jason-to-star-in-open-all-hours-christmas-special.html#~oDww1Tm6BarDF7
474 http://www.chortle.co.uk/news/2013/10/07/18812/open_all_hours_is_back
475 http://www.dailymail.co.uk/tvshowbiz/article-2509959/Sir-David-Jason-wipes-away-tear-reprises-role-Granville-whilst-filming-Open-All-Hours-Christmas-special.html
476 Source: BARB.
477 Source: Office for National Statistics, Ethnic Breakdown, 2011.
478 Ben Lawrence, *Daily Telegraph*, 27 December 2013, p.42.
479 Will Dean, *The Independent*, 27 December 2013, p.31.
480 Adam Postans, *Sunday People*, 29 December 2013, p.33.
481 Kevin O'Sullivan, *Sunday Mirror*, 29 December 2013, p.29.
482 Source: BARB. On the night, it was estimated that an average of 9.4 million people watched the show, but the subsequent 'consolidated' total amounted to 12.23 million. Consolidated data incorporates playback of time-shifted content within seven days of the original broadcast. By 'consolidated', the industry means that 'timeshift viewing' (people watching after the actual transmission time via various forms of digital 'catch-up' services), has been added to the data from the 'live viewing' to produce consolidated viewing data, which is then made available eight

days after the original transmission date. Consolidated data is now described as 'the BARB Gold Standard' used by the industry.

483 Roy Clarke, interview with the author, 19 June 2014.

Chapter 15

484 *The Guardian*, 28 December 2013, p.9.

485 *Metro*, online edition, 27 December 2013, http://metro.co.uk/2013/12/27/still-open-all-hours-snatches-christmas-ratings-honours-from-mrs-browns-boys-4243259/.

486 *Daily Mirror*, 28 December 2013, p.3.

487 *Daily Mail*, online edition, 26 December 2013, http://www.dailymail.co.uk/tvshowbiz/article-2529610/Still-Open-All-Hours-hailed-warmly-nostalgic-fitting-tribute-Ronnie-Barker.html.

488 *Daily Mirror*, 22 January 2014, p.3.

489 The date of the commission was confirmed to me by the production executive, Sarah Hitchcock (interview with the author, 21 August 2014).

490 BBC press release, 30 January 2014.

491 Ibid.

492 Roy Clarke, interview with the author, 19 June 2014.

493 Stephanie Cole, interview with the author, 17 June 2004.

494 Maggie Ollerenshaw, interview with the author, 16 June 2014.

495 Sir David Jason, interviewed on *Lorraine*, broadcast on ITV1, 4 June 2014.

496 Sarah Hitchcock, interview with the author, 21 August 2014.

497 Stephanie Cole, interview with the author, 17 June 2014.

498 Lynda Baron, interview with the author, 22 August 2014.

499 Gary Simmons, *Open All Hours* (stage play), press release, 2014.

500 Ibid.

501 See, for example, the review in the online edition of *Shrewsbury Today*, 26 July 2014: http://www.shrewsburytoday.co.uk/review-open-all-hours-at-theatre-severn/.

502 Leaflet, Portland Basin Museum, 2014.

503 Maggie Ollerenshaw, interview with the author, 16 June 2014.

504 Roy Clarke, interview with the author, 19 June 2014.

Epilogue

505 Roy Clarke, interview with the author, 19 June 2014.

506 Ronnie Barker, quoted by McCabe, *The Authorized Biography*, p.197.

507 Lynda Baron, interview with the author, 22 August 2014.

508 Sir David Jason, interviewed off-air by the BBC, 19 December 2013.